MW00445951

Petrarch's Remedies for Fortune Fair and Foul:
A Modern English Translation of
De remediis utriusque Fortune,
with a Commentary

in five volumes

Publication of this work was assisted
by a grant from the Publications Program of the
National Endowment for the Humanities, an independent
federal agency; and by a grant from the Andrews Foundation.

PETRARCH'S
Remedies for
Fortune Fair and Foul

VOLUME 5

PETRARCH'S
Remedies for
Fortune Fair and Foul

A Modern English Translation of
De remediis utriusque Fortune,
with a
Commentary

BY
CONRAD H. RAWSKI

Volume 5

REFERENCES

Bibliography, Indexes, Tables and Maps

INDIANA UNIVERSITY PRESS
Bloomington & Indianapolis

© 1991 by Conrad H. Rawski

All rights reserved

No part of this book may be reproduced or utilized in any form or by any means, electronic or mechanical, including photocopying and recording, or by any information storage and retrieval system, without permission in writing from the publisher. The Association of American University Presses' Resolution on Permissions constitutes the only exception to this prohibition.

Manufactured in the United States of America

Library of Congress Cataloging-in-Publication Data

Petrarca, Francesco, 1304–1374.
    [De remediis utriusque fortunae. English]
    Petrarch's Remedies for fortune fair and foul : a modern English translation of De remediis utriusque fortune, with a commentary / by Conrad H. Rawski.
      p.   cm.
    Includes bibliographical references.
    Contents: v. 1. Book I—Remedies for prosperity, translation—v. 2. Book I—Remedies for prosperity, commentary—v. 3. Book II—Remedies for adversity, translation—v. 4. Book II—Remedies for adversity, commentary—v. 5. References—bibliography, indexes, tables and maps.
     ISBN 0-253-34844-7 (v. 1)
     I. Rawski, Conrad H.   II. Title.
PQ4496.E29D413 1991
189'.4—dc20
                                      88-46015

ISBN 0-253-34844-7 (v. 1 : alk. pa.)
ISBN 0-253-34845-5 (v. 2 : alk. pa.)
ISBN 0-253-34846-3 (v. 3 : alk. pa.)
ISBN 0-253-34847-1 (v. 4 : alk. pa.)
ISBN 0-253-34848-X (v. 5 : alk. pa.)
ISBN 0-253-34849-8 (set)

1 2   3   4   5   95 94 93 92 91

CONTENTS

INDEXES

TABLES AND MAPS

Bibliography

Publications Referred To in the Commentary

I. WORKS BY PETRARCH

Cited by abbreviated title only. For further detail on these works, cf. III, Other Publications, below: Fowler (1916); Fucilla (1982); Jasenas (1974); and *Petrarch: Catalogue* (1974).

1. ❖ COLLECTED WORKS

1501   *Librorum Francisci Petrarchae Impressorum Annotatio* . . . Venice, Simon de Luere for Andrea Torresani, 1501. Second collective edition of the Latin works.

1581   *Francisci Petrarchae Florentini—Opera quae extant omnia* . . . Basel, Sebastian Henricpetri, 1581. The second edition of the complete works.

Prose (1955)   Francesco Petrarca: *Prose*. Ed. G. Martellotti et al. Milan, Ricciardi, 1955.

Rime (1951)   Francesco Petrarca: *Rime, Trionfi e Poesie latine*. Ed. F. Neri et al. Milan, Ricciardi, 1951.

2. ❖ SINGLE WORKS

Africa   *L'Africa*. Ed. N. Festa. Edizione nazionale. Vol. i. Florence, Sansoni, 1926.

Buc. carm.   *Il Bucolicum carmen e i suoi commenti inediti*. Ed. Antonio Avena. Padua, Società cooperativa tipografica, 1906. Avena's text is available in Bergin (1974). See Martellotti (1968), below, III.

Collatio   "La Collatio inter Scipionem Alexandrum Hanibalem et Pyrrum." Ed. Guido Martellotti. In *Classical, Mediaeval, and Renaissance Studies in Honor of B. L. Ullman*. Vol. ii, pp. 145–168. Rome, Edizioni de Storia e Letteratura, 1964. Repr. in Martellotti (1983), chap. 30. Note also G. Crevatin, "Scipione e la fortuna di Petrarca nell'umanesimo." *Rinascimento*, Ser. ii, vol. xvii (1977), pp. 3–30.

De ocio *De ocio religiosorum.* Text of 1581. Also *Studi e testi.* Ed. Rotondi and Martellotti. Città del Vaticano, 1958.

DR *De remediis utriusque Fortune.* Texts of 1501 and 1581. Also ibid. Ed. Niccolò Lucaro. Cremona, Bernard de Misintis & Caesar Parmensis, 1492.

De vir. ill. *De viris illustribus.* Ed. G. Martellotti. Edizione nazionale. Vol. i. Florence, Sansoni, 1964—
Ibid. Ed. Luigi Razzolini. With Italian trans. Donato Albanzani. 2 vols. Bologna, Romagnoli, 1874, 1879.

De vita sol. *De vita solitaria.* In *Prose* (1955). Ed. G. Martellotti. Pp. 286–591.

EPISTOLAE

Fam. *Familiares. Le familiari.* Vols. i–iii, ed. V. Rossi; Vol. iv, ed. V. Rossi and U. Bosco. Edizione nazionale. Vols. x–xiii. Florence, Sansoni, 1933–1942.

Met. *Metricae.* In Francesco Petrarca, *Poesie minori.* Vols. ii, iii. Ed. D. Rossetti. 3 vols. Milan, Società tipogr. de' classici italiani, 1829–1834.

Sen. *Seniles.* Texts of 1501 and 1581. *Sen.* i, 1, ii, 1, iii, 9, iv, 3, vi, 2, x, 2, xi, 2, xvii, 2, xviii, 1. In *Prose* (1955), pp. 1028–1159 and 2–19. (Griseldis = *Sen.* xvii, 3; *Posteritati* = *Sen.* xviii, 1.) On other *Seniles* published separately, *see* Wilkins (1959), pp. ix–x.

SN *Sine nomine.* P. Piur. *Petrarcas "Buch ohne Namen" und die paepstliche Kurie.* Halle, Niemeyer, 1925.

Var. *Variae.* In *Petrarcae Epistolae de rebus familiaribus et variae.* Ed. G. Fracassetti. Vol. iii. Florence, Le Monnier, 1863. *Var.* 12 in Piur (1933), pp. 243–244.

Misc. E. H. Wilkins and G. Billanovich. "The Miscellaneous Letters of Petrarch." *Speculum* 37 (1962), pp. 226–243.

LAP For the letters addressed to Petrarch, *see* Wilkins (1960), pp. 121–128; and Wilkins (1959), p. 129. For the letters from Francesco Nelli, *see* Cochin (1892) and (1901).

Epitaph for His Grandson In Rossi (1930). Vol. ii, p. 73.

INVECTIVAE

Contra eum In E. Cocchia, "Magistri Iohannis de Hysdinio Invectiva contra Fr. Petrarcham et Fr. Petrarchae Contra cuiusdam Galli calumnias apologia." Società Reale di Napoli, R. Accademia di Archeologia,

Lettere e Belle Arti. *Atti*, N.S., vii, (1920), pp. 93–202. Parts in *Prose* (1955).

Contra med.   *Invective contra medicum.* Ed. P. G. Ricci. Rome, Ediz. di Storia e Letteratura, 1950.

Invettive contro un medico. Ed. M. Schiavone. Milan, Marzorati, 1972.

Contra quendam   *Invectiva contra quendam magni status hominem sed nullius scientie aut virtutis.* Ed. P. G. Ricci. Florence, Le Monnier, 1949. A large part in *Prose* (1955).

De sui ipsius   *De sui ipsius et multorum ignorantia.* Ed. L. M. Capelli. Paris, H. Champion, 1906. Parts in *Prose* (1955).

Itin. syr.   *Itinerarium syriacum. Itinerarium breve de Janua usque ad Ierusalem et Terram Sanctam.* Ed. G. Lumbroso. In R. Accademia dei Lincei, *Rendiconti.* Classe di scienze morali, Ser. IV, iv (1888), 390–403. Also in idem, *Memorie italiane del buon tempo antico.* Turin, E. Loescher, 1889. Pp. 16–49.

Orations   In A. Hortis, *Scritti inediti di Francesco Petrarca.* Trieste, Tipografia del Lloyd austro-ungarico, 1874. Note Godi (1970). The Paris oration (1361) is published in A. Barbeu de Rocher, "Ambassade de Pétrarque auprès du roi Jean le Bon." In Académie des Inscriptions et Belles-Lettres de l'Institut Impérial de France, *Mémoires présentés par divers savants,* Sér. II, iii (1854), pp. 172–228. Also in Godi (1965).

Ps. poen.   *Penitential Psalms. Les psaumes pénitentiaux publiés d'après le manuscrit de la Bibliothèque de Lucerne.* Ed. H. Cochin. Paris, L. Rouart, 1929.

Rer. mem. libri   *Rerum memorandarum libri iv.* Ed. G. Billanovich. Edizione nazionale. Vol. xiv. Florence, Sansoni, 1945.

Rime   *Le rime.* In *Rime* (1951). Ed. F. Neri. Pp. 3–477.

Secretum   *Secretum.* In *Prose* (1955). Ed. E. Carrara. Pp. 22–215.

De secreto curarum conflictu. Dialogi tres . . . Regii Lepidi, Franciscus Mazalis, 1501 (the second edition of the *Secretum*).

Testament   *Petrarch's Testament.* Ed. and trans. T. E. Mommsen. Ithaca, N.Y., Cornell University Press, 1957.

Trionfi   *Trionfi.* In *Rime* (1951). Ed. F. Neri. Pp. 481–578.

3. ❖ ENGLISH TRANSLATIONS

Translations of minor portions of a work are not included.

Anthologies   Robinson, J. H., and H. W. Rolfe. *Petrarch*: The First Modern Scholar and Man of Letters. New York, G. P. Putnam's Sons, 1914.

Thompson, D. *Petrarch*: A Humanist among Princes. New York, Harper & Row, 1971.

Wilkins, E. H. *Petrarch at Vaucluse*: Letters in Verse and Prose. Chicago, University of Chicago Press, 1958. (1958b)

Africa   Bergin, T. G., and A. S. Wilson. *Petrarch's* Africa. New Haven, Yale University Press, 1977.

Bucolicum carmen   Bergin, T. G. *Petrarch's* Bucolicum carmen. New Haven, Yale University Press, 1974.

De remediis utriusque Fortune   Twyne, Thomas. *Phisicke against Fortune, as well prosperous, as adverse* . . . London, Richard Watkyns, 1579. STC 19809. Also available in facsimile, ed. B. Kohl, Delmar, N.Y., Scholars' Facsimiles & Reprints (vol. 359), 1980. See Diekstra (1966); and Rawski (1967) and (1971).

De vita solitaria   Zeitlin, J. *The Life of Solitude by Francis Petrarch*. Urbana, University of Illinois Press, 1924.

EPISTOLAE

Familiares   Bernardo, A. S. *Francesco Petrarca*: Rerum familiarum libri i–viii. Albany, State University of New York Press, 1975.

Bernardo, A. S. *Francesco Petrarca*: Letters on Familiar Matters. Rerum familiarum libri ix–xvi, xvii–xxiv. Baltimore, Johns Hopkins University Press, 1982, 1985.

Bishop, M. *Letters from Petrarch*. Bloomington, Indiana University Press, 1966.

Cosenza, M. E. *Petrarch's Letters to Classical Authors*. Chicago, University of Chicago Press, 1910.

Seniles   Bishop, M. *Letters from Petrarch*. Bloomington, Indiana University Press, 1966.

Sine nomine   Zacour, N. P. *Petrarch's Book without a Name*. Toronto, Pontifical Institute of Mediaeval Studies, 1973.

INVECTIVAE

De sui ipsius et multorum ignorantia   Nachod, H. "Francesco Petrarca." In E. Cassirer, *The Renaissance Philosophy of Man*. Chicago, University of Chicago Press, 1948. Contains translations of *Fam.* iv, 1; *De sui ipsius* (with minor omissions); *Fam.* i, 7; and parts of *Sen.* i, 6, and v, 2.

Orations   Wilkins, E. H. "Petrarch's Coronation Oration." In Wilkins (1955), pp. 300–313.

Rime   Armi, A. M. *Petrarch*: Sonnets & Songs. New York, Pantheon, 1946.

Durling, R. M. *Petrarch's Lyric Poems*. Cambridge, Harvard University Press, 1976.

Secretum   Draper, W. H. *Petrarch's Secret; or, The Soul's Conflict with Pas-sion* . . . London, Chatto and Windus, 1911.

Testament   Mommsen (1957).

Trionfi   Wilkins, E. H. *The Triumphs of Petrarch*. Chicago, University of Chicago Press, 1962.

II. WORKS BY ANCIENT AND MEDIEVAL AUTHORS

Editions and Translations

CIL—Corpus inscriptionum latinorum; *CSEL*—Corpus scriptorum ecclesiasticorum latinorum; *CSM*—Corpus scriptorum de musica; *IMU—Italia medioevale e umanistica*; LCL—Loeb Classical Library; *PG*—Migne, *Patrologia Graeca*; *PL*—Migne, *Patrologia Latina*; *SVF*—Stoicorum veterum fragmenta.

Abelard, Peter

Opera omnia. PL 178.

Sic et non. Ed. B. B. Boyer and R. McKeon. Chicago, University of Chicago Press, 1976.

Der Ackermann aus Boehmen. See Johannes von Tepl.

Ad Herenn. Ad C. Herennium. With an English trans. by H. Kaplan. LCL.

Agricola, Georg

De re metallica libri xii. Basel, Froben, 1556. Trans. and comm. H. C. Hoover and Lou H. Hoover. *Mining Magazine* (London), 1912; New York, Dover, 1950.

Alain de Lille

Anticlaud.	*Anticlaudianus. PL* 210, cc. 481–576.
	Sheridan, J. J. *Alan of Lille*: Anticlaudianus, or The Good and Perfect Man. Toronto, Pontifical Institute of Mediaeval Studies, 1973.
Ars praedic.	*De arte praedicatoria. PL* 210, cc. 109–198.
De planctu nat.	*Liber de planctu naturae. PL* 210, cc. 431–482.
De virt.	*De virtutibus et de vitiis et de donis Spiritus Sancti.* Ed. O. Lottin. *Medieval Studies* xii (1950), pp. 20–56.
Dist. dict. theol.	*Liber in distinctionibus dictionum theologicalium. PL* 210, cc. 687–1012.
Eluc. in Cant. Cant.	*Elucidatio in Cantica Canticorum. PL* 210, cc. 51–110.

Regulae | Regulae theologicae. PL 210, cc. 617–684.
Sermo de contemptu mundi. See Wallach (1966), below, III.

Sent. | Liber sententiarum. PL 210, cc. 229–264.
(For further editions of Alain's works, see Evans [1983], pp. 14–19.)

Albertus Magnus

Libellus de alchimia. Ed. V. Hines, S.C.N. Berkeley, University of California Press, 1958.

Alcuin

Disp. de rhet. | Disputatio de rhetorica et de virtutibus . . . The Rhetoric of Alcuin and Charlemagne. Trans. and ed. Wilbur S. Howell. Princeton, Princeton University Press, 1941.

Ambrose

De Abraham. PL 14, cc. 419–500.

De exc. frat. Satyri | De excessu fratris sui Satyri ii. PL 16, c. 1398.

De Nabuthe Jesraelita. CSEL xxxii, 480–481. PL 14, cc. 731–756.

De officiis ministrorum. | PL 16, cc. 25–184.

De virg. | De virginitate. PL 16, cc. 265–302.
Hexaem. | Hexaemeron. PL 14, cc. 123–274.
In Luc. | Expositio Evangelii sec Lucam. PL 15, cc. 1527–1850. CSEL iv.

Amm. Marc.

Ammianus Marcellinus. With an English trans. by J. C. Rolfe. 3 vols. LCL.

Anonymus 4

Der Musiktraktat des Anonymus 4. Ed. F. Reckow. 2 vols. Wiesbaden, F. Steiner, 1967. Archiv für Musikwissenschaft. Beihefte, 4 and 5.

Anselm of Canterbury

Cur Deus homo. PL 158, cc. 359–432. Trans. in S. N. Deane, St. Anselm: Basic Writings. LaSalle, Ill., Open Court, 1966. Pp. 173–288.

De gramm. | The De Grammatico of St. Anselm: The Theory of Paronymy. Ed. D. P. Henry. Notre Dame, Ind., University of Notre Dame Press, 1964.

Monolog. | Monologion. PL 158, cc. 141–224. S. N. Deane, ibid. Pp. 35–144.
Proslog. | Proslogion. PL 158, cc. 223–242. S. N. Deane, ibid. Pp. 1–34.

Appian's Roman History. With an English trans. by Horace White. 4 vols. LCL.

Apuleius

    Apologia. Ed. and trans. H. E. Butler. Oxford, Oxford University Press, 1909.

    Florida. Ibid.

Metam.   *Metamorphoseon. The Golden Ass*. With an English trans. by W. Adlington. Rev. S. Gaselee. LCL.

    De deo Socratis. Opera. Ed. Petrus Colvius. Leiden, Raphelengius, 1588. (Note Morhof [1747], vol. i, p. 906.)

De Platone   *De Platone et eius dogmate. Opera* (1588). Ed. Petrus Colvius.

Aristotle

Cat.   *Categoriae vel Praedicamenta*. Ed. L. Minio-Paluello. Paris, Desclée, de Brouwer, 1961. *Aristoteles latinus*. Vol. i, 1–5.

    Categories, On Interpretation, Prior Analytics. With an English trans. by H. P. Cooke and H. Tredennick. LCL.

    De anima. Opera (1590). Vol. i, pp. 379–406. *On the Soul, Parva Naturalia, On Breath*. With an English trans. by W. S. Hett. LCL.

    De coelo. Opera (1590). Vol. i, pp. 266–304. *On the Heavens*. With an English trans. by W. K. C. Guthrie. LCL.

De gen.   *De generatione animalium*. Ed. H. J. Drossaart-Lulofs. Paris,
anim.   Desclée, de Brouwer, 1966. *Aristoteles latinus*. Vol. xvii, 2.

    Generation of Animals. With an English trans. by A. L. Peck. LCL.

De part. an.   *De partibus animalium et earum causis. Opera* (1590). Vol. i, pp. 592–640. *Parts of Animals*. With an English trans. by A. L. Peck. LCL.

De somniis   *De somniis*. With an English trans. by W. S. Hett. LCL.

    Economics. See Oeconomica.

Eth. Nic.   *Ethica Nicomachea*. Ed. R. A. Gauthier, Leiden-Paris, Brill; Desclée, de Brouwer, 1972–1974. *Aristoteles latinus*. Vol. xxvi, 1–3.

    Nicomachean Ethics. With an English trans. by H. Rackham. LCL.

Hist. anim.   *Historia animalium*. With an English trans. by A. L. Peck. 2 vols. LCL.

Magna mor.   *Magna moralia*. With an English trans. by C. C. Armstrong. LCL.

Metaph.   *Metaphysica*. Ed. G. Vuillemin-Diem. Paris-Leiden, Desclée, de Brouwer, 1970–1976. *Aristoteles latinus*. Vol. xxv, 1–1a, 2. *Metaphysics*. With an English trans. by H. Tredennick. LCL.

Meteor.   *Meteorologicorum libri iv. Opera* (1590). Vol. i, pp. 325–369. *Meteorologica*. With an English trans. by H. D. P. Lee. LCL.

Oeconomica   *Aristotelis quae feruntur Oeconomica*. Ed. F. Susemihl. Leipzig, Teubner, 1887.

Phys.   *Physica* (Translatio Vaticana). Ed. A. Mansion. Paris, Desclée, de Brouwer, 1957. *Aristoteles latinus*. Vol. vii, 2. *Physics*. With an English trans. by P. Wicksteed and F. M. Cornford. LCL.

Poet.	*De arte poetica*. Ed. L. Minio-Paluello. Paris, Desclée, de Brouwer, 1968. *Aristoteles latinus*. Vol. xxxiii, 1–2. *Poetics*. With an English trans. by W. H. Fyfe. LCL. English trans. I. Bywater in *Rhetoric*, below.
Pol.	*Politica* (Translatio imperfecta). Ed. P. Michaud-Quantin. Paris, Desclée, De Brouwer, 1961. *Aristoteles latinus*. Vol. xxix, 1. *Politics*. With an English trans. by H. Rackham. LCL.
Post. anal.	*Posterior Analytics*. With an English trans. by H. Tredennick. LCL.
Rhet.	*Rhetorica*. Ed. L. Minio-Paluello. Leiden, Brill, 1978. *Aristoteles latinus*. Vol. xxxi. *Rhetoric and Poetics*. Trans. W. R. Roberts & I. Bywater. Ed. F. Solmsen. New York, Random House, 1954. Modern Library.
	Topica. Ed. L. Minio-Paluello. Paris, Desclée, de Brouwer, 1969. *Aristoteles latinus*. Vol. v, 1–3. *Topics*. With an English trans. by E. S. Forster. LCL.
	Operum Aristotelis . . . nova editio (Casaubon) . . . Lyons, Guillelmus Laemarius, 1590. Cited as *Opera* (1590).
	The Complete Works of Aristotle: The Revised Oxford Translation. Ed. J. Barnes. 2 vols. Princeton, Princeton University Press, 1984. Bollingen Series, 71.2.

Arrian

Arrian. With an English trans. by E. Iliffe Robson and P. Brunt. LCL.

Athanasius-Evagrius

Vita Antonii. PL 73, cc. 125–170.

Augustine

Conf.	*Confessionum libri xiii*. PL 32, cc. 659–969. Ed. L. Verheijen. Corpus christianorum, ser. lat., 27. Turnhout, Brepols, 1981. Trans. J. G. Pilkington in W. J. Oates, *Basic Writings of Saint Augustine*. 2 vols. New York, Random House, 1948. Vol. i, pp. 3–265.
Contra acad.	*Contra academicos*. PL 32, cc. 905–958. Ed. W. M. Green and K.-D. Daur. Corpus christianorum, ser. lat., 29. Turnhout, Brepols, 1970. *Against the Academics*. Trans. J. J. O'Meara. Westminster, Md., Newman Press, 1950. Ancient Writers, 12.
Contra Adamantum	*Contra Adamantum Manichaei discipulum*. PL 42, cc. 129–172; CSEL 25, 1, pp. 115–190.
Contra Faustum	*Contra Faustum Manichaeum*. PL 42, cc. 207–518. *A Select Library of the Nicene and Post-Nicene Fathers . . .* Trans. R. Stothert. Ser. 1, 4. Ed. P. Schaff. Buffalo, Christian Literature Co., 1887.
	De beata vita. PL 32, cc. 959–976. Corpus christianorum, ser. lat., 29, as above, *Contra acad*. Trans. R. A. Brown. Washington, D.C.,

Catholic University of America Press, 1944. Patristic Studies, 72.
Contra Secundinum Manichaeum. *PL* 42, cc. 577–602. *CSEL* 25,
2, pp. 905–947.
De beata vita. *PL* 32, cc. 959–976. *CSEL* 63, pp. 89–116. Latin
text, with an English trans. by F. E. Tourscher. Philadelphia, Peter
Reilly, 1937.

De civ. Dei   *De civitate Dei*. With an English trans. by G. E. McCracken, W. M.
Green, D. Wiesen, P. Levine, and E. M. Sanford. 7 vols. LCL.

De div.   *De diversis quaestionibus lxxxiii*. *PL* 40, cc. 11–100. Ed. P. Beck-
quaest.   aert. Œuvres de Saint Augustin. Sér. 1, 10. Paris, Desclée, de
Brouwer, 1952. *Eighty-three Different Questions*. Trans. D. Mosher.
Washington, D.C., Catholic University of America Press, 1982.
Fathers of the Church, 70.

De doct.   *De doctrina Christiana*. *PL* 34, cc. 15–122. *CSEL* 80. *On Christian
Doctrine*. Trans. D. W. Robertson. Indianapolis, Bobbs-Merrill,
1958. Trans. F. J. Shaw in *Augustine*. Chicago, Encyclopedia
Britannica, 1952. Great Books of the Western World.

De Gen. ad   *De Genesi ad litteram*. *PL* 34, cc. 245–486. Ed. P. Agaësse and A.
litt.   Solignac. Œuvres de Saint Augustin. Sér. 7, 48–49. Paris, Desclée,
de Brouwer, 1972.

De Gen.   *De Genesi contra Manichaeos*. *PL* 34, cc. 173–220.
contra
Manich.

De lib. arb.   *De libero arbitrio*. *PL* 32, cc. 1221–1310. *CSEL* 74. Corpus chris-
tianorum, ser. lat., 29, as above, *Contra acad*. *On Free Will*. In
Augustine: Earlier Writings. Trans. J. H. S. Burleigh. Philadelphia,
Westminster Press, 1953. Library of Christian Classics, 6. Pp.
102–217.
De magistro. *PL* 32, cc. 1193–1220. Corpus christianorum, ser.
lat., 29, as above, *Contra acad*. *Concerning the Teacher*. Trans. G.
C. Leckie in Oates (1948). Vol. i, pp. 361–395.
De musica. *PL* 32, cc. 1081–1194. Ed. G. Finaert and F. J. Thon-
nard. Œuvres de Saint Augustin. Sér. 1, 7. Paris, Desclée, de
Brouwer, 1947. *On Music*. Trans. C. Taliaferro in Fathers of the
Church. *Writings of Saint Augustine*. Vol. ii. New York, Cima,
1947. Pp. 153–379.

De op. mon.   *De opere monachorum*. *PL* 40, cc. 547–582. *CSEL* 41, pp. 531–
595. English trans. in *Treatises on Various Subjects*. Ed. R. J. Deferrari. New York, 1952. Fathers of the Church, 16.

De ord.   *De ordine*. *PL* 32, cc. 977–1020. Corpus christianorum, ser. lat.,
29, as above, *Contra acad*. Trans. R. P. Russell in Fathers of the
Church, *Writings of Saint Augustine*, vol. v. New York, Cima,
1948.

De quant. an.   *De quantitate animae*. *PL* 32, cc. 1035–1080. Ed. P. de Labriolle.

Œuvres de Saint Augustin. Sér. 1, 5. Paris, Desclée, de Brouwer, 1948.

De trin.   *De trinitate. PL* 42, cc. 819–1098. Ed. W. J. Mountain and F. Glorie. Corpus christianorum, ser. lat., 50, 1–2. Turnhout, Brepols, 1968. *The Trinity.* Trans. S. McKenna in Fathers of the Church. Washington, D.C., Catholic University of America Press, 1963.

De vera rel.   *De vera religione. PL* 34, cc. 121–172. *Of True Religion* in Burleigh (1953), pp. 218–283.

Enarr. in Ps.   *Enarrationes in Psalmos. PL* 36, cc. 67–1028, Ps. 1–79; 37, cc. 1033–1966, Ps. 80–150. Ed. D. E. Dekkers and I. Fraipont. Corpus christianorum, ser. lat., 38–40. Turnhout, Brepols, 1956. *St. Augustine on the Psalms.* Trans. S. Hebgin and F. Corrigan. Westminster, Md., Newman Press, 1960. Ancient Christian Writers, 29.

Ench.   *Enchiridion ad Laurentium, seu De fide, spe et caritate. PL* 40, cc. 231–291. Ed. R. Vander Plaetse and C. Beukers. Corpus christianorum, ser. lat., 46. Turnhout, Brepols, 1969. *Faith, Hope and Charity.* Trans. L. A. Armand. Westminster, Md., Newman Press, 1947. Ancient Christian Writers, 3.

Epistulae. PL 33. CSEL 24, 44, 57, 58. *St. Augustine: Letters.* Trans. W. Parsons in Fathers of the Church, 12, 18, 20, 30, 32.

In evang.   *In Johannis evang. tractatus CXXIV. PL* 35, cc. 1379–1976. *Homi-*
Ioan.   *lies on the Gospel of John.* Trans. J. Gibb and J. Innes. New York, Christian Literature Co., 1888. Select Library of the Nicene and Post-Nicene Fathers of the Church, Ser. 1, 7.

Quaest.   *Ad Simplicianum, De diversis quaestionibus. PL* 40, cc. 101–148.
Simpl.   *To Simplician—On Various Questions, Book i* in *Augustine*: Earlier Writings. Trans. J. H. S. Burleigh. Philadelphia, Westminster Press, 1953. Library of Christian Classics, 6. Pp. 370–406.

Retract.   *Retractationes. PL* 32, pp. 583–656. CSEL 36 (1), pp. 7–204.
Serm.   *Sermones. PL* 38, cc. 23–1484.
Solil.   *Soliloquiorum libri duo. PL* 32, cc. 869–904. *The Soliloquies of Saint Augustine.* Trans. T. Gilligan in Fathers of the Church. As *De Ord.*, above. Also Burleigh (1953), pp. 17–63.

Aulus Gellius
Noct. Att.   *Noctes Atticae.* With an English trans. by J. C. Rolfe. 3 vols. LCL.

Aurelius Victor
Caes.   *Liber de Caesaribus.*
De vir. ill.   *Incerti autoris Liber de Viris illustribus urbis Romae.* All ed. F. Pichlmayr. Leipzig, G. Teubner, 1911. *See also* (Pseudo-) Pliny the Younger.
Epit.   *Incerti autoris Epitome de Caesaribus.*

Ausonius

Lud. sept.   *Ludus septem sapientium.* In *Ausonius.* With an English trans. by
sap.   H. G. E. White. Vol. i, pp. 311–329. LCL.

Bartholomaeus Anglicus

De prop. rer.   *De proprietatibus rerum* (1601). Facsimile repr. Frankfurt, Minerva, 1964. *On the Properties of Things.* Trans. John Trevisa. 2
vols. Oxford, Clarendon Press, 1975.

Bernardus Silvestris

Cosmogr.   The *Cosmographia of Bernardus Silvestris.* Trans. with intro. and
notes W. Wetherbee. New York, Columbia University Press, 1973.
See also Comm. Aen.

Bersuire. *See* Pierre Bersuire.

Bible (Books cited using the abbreviations of the Vulgata Clementina.)
    Biblia Sacra juxta Vulgatam Clementinam . . . Rome, Desclée et
Soc., 1938.
Biblia Sacra. Basel, Johann Froben, 1495.
The Holy Bible, Translated from the Latin Vulgate. Old Testament,
Douay, 1609; New Testament, Rheims, 1582. Rev. R. Challoner.
Baltimore, John Murphy, 1899.

Boccaccio, Giovanni

    Corbaccio. See Il Corbaccio.
Decameron   *Decameron*: Edizione diplomatico-interpretativa dell' autografo
Hamilton 90, a cura di Charles S. Singleton. Baltimore, Johns
Hopkins University Press, 1974. *Il Decameron.* Ed. C. S. Single-
ton. 2 vols. Bari, Scrittori d'Italia, 1955. *Decameron*: The John
Payne Translation. Rev. and annot. C. S. Singleton. 3 vols. Berkeley, University of California Press, 1982.
De casib.   *De casibus illustrium virorum* (1520). Facsimile repr. With an
intro. by L. B. Hall. Gainesville, Fla., Scholar's Facsimiles & Reprints, 1962. L. B. Hall, *Giovanni Boccaccio*: The Fates of Illustri-
ous Men. Abr. New York, F. Ungar, 1965.
De clar.   *De claris mulieribus.* Ed. V. Zaccaria. Milan, Mondadori, 1967.
mul.   *Concerning Famous Women.* Trans. G. A. Guarino. New Bruns-
wick, N.J., Rutgers University Press, 1963.
Geneal.   *Genealogie deorum gentilium libri.* Ed. V. Romano. 2 vols. Bari,
deor.   Laterza, 1951. *Boccaccio in Defence of Poetry*: Genealogiae deorum
gentilium liber xiv. Ed. J. Reedy. Toronto, Pontifical Institute of
Mediaeval Studies, 1978. C. G. Osgood, *Boccaccio on Poetry, Being the Preface and the Fourteenth and Fifteenth Book of Boccaccio's*
Genealogia deorum gentilium . . . Princeton, Princeton University Press, 1930.
Il Corbaccio. Ed. T. Nurmela. Suomalaisen Tiedakatemian Toimituk-

sia: Annales scientiarum Fennicas. Ser. B, 146. Helsinki, 1968.

Il Corbaccio. Trans. and ed. A. K. Cassell. Urbana, University of Illinois Press, 1975.

L'Amorosa visione. Ed V. Branca. Milan, Mondadori, 1974. Tutte le opere, 5.

Opere latine minori. Ed. A. F. Massèra. Bari, Laterza, 1928.

Teseida   *Teseida delle nozze di Emilia*. Ed. A. Limentani. Milan, Mondadori, 1964.

The Book of Theseus. Trans. B. M. McCoy. New York, Medieval Text Association, 1974.

Boethius, Anicius Manlius Severinus

Cons. phil.   *Consolatio philosophiae*. With an English trans. by "I. T." Rev'd. H. F. Stewart. LCL, Boethius, pp. 128–411. *Philosophiae consolatio*. Ed. R. Del Re. Rome, Ediz. dell'Ateneo, 1968. *The Consolation of Philosophy*: Boethius. Trans. R. Green. Indianapolis, Bobbs-Merrill, 1962.

Contra Eut.   *Contra Eutychen et Nestorium*. LCL, Boethius, "The Theological Tractates." With an English trans. by H. F. Stewart and E. K. Rand.

De inst.   *De institutione arithmetica*. Ed. G. Friedlein. Leipzig, B. G.
arith.   Teubner, 1867. M. Masi. *Boethian Number Theory*: A Translation of *De institutione arithmetica*. Amsterdam, Rodopi, 1983.

De inst.   *De institutione musica*. Ed. G. Friedlein. Leipzig, B. G. Teubner,
mus.   1867. Note also O. Paul. *Boetius und die griechische Harmonik*: Des Ancius Manlius Severinus Boetius fuenf Buecher ueber die Musik . . . Leipzig, F. E. C. Leuckart, 1872.

Quomodo   *Quomodo substantiae in eo quod sint bonae sint cum non sint sub-*
subst.   *stantialia bona*. LCL, Boethius. Pp. 38–51.

Boner, Ulrich. *See* **Ulrich Boner.**

Breviarium Romanum ex decreto Sacrosancti Concilii Tridentini restitutum . . . 4 vols. Regensburg, F. Pustet (1911). For 14th c. *Breviaria*, note the list in *Die Musik in Geschichte und Gegenwart* ii, Kassel, Baerenreiter-Verlag, 1952, c. 317.

Brunetto Latini

Tresor   *Li livres dou Tresor*. Ed. F. J. Carmody. Berkeley, University of California Press, 1948.

Calcidius. *See* **Chalcidius.**

(Pseudo-) Callisthenes. *See* Wolohojian (1969), below, III.

Carmina Burana. (Ed. J. A. Schmeller.) Stuttgart, Litterarischer Verein, 1847. New ed. A. Hilka and O. Schumann. Vol. i, 1 (1930); i, 2 (1941); ii, 1 (1930). Heidelberg, C. Winter, 1930—

Cassiodorus

Inst.   *Cassiodori Senatoris Institutiones.* Ed. R. A. B. Mynors. Oxford, Clarendon Press, 1937. L. W. Jones, *An Introduction to Divine and Human Readings by Cassiodorus Senator.* New York, Columbia University Press, 1946. Records of Civilization: Sources and Studies, 40.

Cato

De re rust.   *De re rustica.* With an English trans. by W. D. Hooper. LCL.

Catullus

Catullus. With an English trans. by F. W. Cornish. LCL. *C. Valerius Catullus.* Ed. Joh. Anton Vulpius. Padua, J. Cominus, 1739.

Celsus, Aulus Cornelius

De med.   *De medicina.* With an English trans. by W. G. Spencer. 3 vols. LCL.

Censorinus

De die natali liber. Ed. F. Hultsch. Leipzig, B. G. Teubner, 1867.

Chalcidius

Comm. Tim.   *Timaeus. A Calcidio translatus commentarioque instructus.* Ed. J. H. Waszink. London, Warburg Institute; Leiden, E. J. Brill, 1962. *Plato latinus,* 4.

Chaucer, Geoffrey

The Complete Works of Geoffrey Chaucer. Ed. F. N. Robinson. Boston, Houghton Mifflin, 1933. —The important new version, *The Riverside Chaucer,* ed. L. D. Benson (Boston, Houghton Mifflin, 1987), appeared too late to be used in the Commentary.

Chrysostom, John. *See* John Chrysostom.

Cicero

Acad.   *Academica.* LCL, Cicero. Vol. xix. With an English trans. by H. Rackham.

Ad Att.   *Letters to Atticus.* LCL, Cicero. Vols. xxii–xxiv. With an English trans. by E. O. Winstedt.

Ad Quintum   *Cicero's Letters to His Brother Quintus.* LCL, Cicero. Vol. xxviii. With an English trans. by W. G. Williams.

Brutus. LCL, Cicero. Vol. v. With an English trans. by G. L. Hendrickson.

Brutus   *The Letters to Brutus.* LCL, Cicero. Vol. xxviii. With an English
Letters   trans. by M. Cary.

De amic.   *Laelius de amicitia.* LCL, Cicero. Vol. xx. With an English trans. by W. A. Falconer.

De div.   *De divinatione.* Ibid.

De domo sua. LCL, Cicero. Vol. xi. With an English trans. by N.

H. Watts.

De fato. LCL, Cicero. Vol. iv. With an English trans. by H. Rackham.

De fin.   *De finibus bonorum et malorum*. LCL, Cicero. Vol. xvii. With an English trans. by H. Rackham.

De inv.   *De inventione*. LCL, Cicero. Vol. ii. With an English trans. by H. M. Hubbell.

De leg.   *De legibus*. LCL, Cicero. Vol. xvi. With an English trans. by C. W. Keyes.

De nat.   *De natura deorum*. LCL, Cicero. As *Acad.*, above.
  deor.

De off.   *De officiis*. LCL, Cicero. Vol. xxi. With an English trans. by W. Miller.

De orat.   *De oratore*. LCL, Cicero. Vols. iii, iv. With an English trans. by E. W. Sutton and H. Rackham.

De part. or.   *De partitione oratoria*. LCL, Cicero. Vol. iv. With an English trans. by H. Rackham. *See De orat.*

De re publ.   *De re publica*. As *De leg.*, above.

De sen.   *Cato Maior de senectute*. As *De amic.*, above.

Ep. fam.   *Cicero's Letters to His Friends*. LCL, Cicero. Vol. xxv–xxviii. With an English trans. by W. G. Williams.

In Catil.   *In Catilinam i–iv*. LCL, Cicero. Vol. x. With an English trans. by L. E. Lord.

In Verr.   *In Verrem*. LCL, Cicero. Vols. vii, viii. With an English trans. by L. H. G. Greenwood.

Opt. gen. or.   *De optimo genere oratorum*. As *De inv.*, above.

Orator. LCL, Cicero. Vol. v. With an English trans. by H. M. Hubbell.

Parad. Stoic.   *Paradoxa Stoicorum*. As *De orat.*, above.

Part. orat.   *See De part. or.*

Philip.   *Philippics i–xiv*. LCL, Cicero. Vol. xv. With an English trans. by W. C. A. Ker.

Piso   *In Pisonem*. LCL, Cicero. Vol. xiv. With an English trans. by N. H. Watts.

Pro Archia. Ibid. Vol. xi. With an English trans. by N. H. Watts.

Pro Deiot.   *Pro rege Deiotaro*. Ibid. Vol. xiv.

Pro Marcello. Ibid.

Pro T. Annio Milone. Ibid.

Pro L. Murena. As *De inv.*, above.

Pro Roscio Comoedo. LCL, Cicero. Vol. vi. With an English trans. by J. H. Freese.

Rabir. perd.   *Pro Rabirio perduellionis reo*. LCL, Cicero. Vol. ix. With an English trans. by H. Grose Hodge.

Top.   *Topica*. As *De inv.*, above.

Tusc. disp.   *Tusculan Disputations.* LCL, Cicero. Vol. xviii. With an English trans. by J. E. King.

Claudian
De bello   *De bello Gildonico.* LCL, Claudian. Vol. i. With an English trans.
  Gild.   by M. Platnauer.
De bello   *De bello Gothico.* LCL, Claudian. Ibid. Vol. ii, pp. 125–173.
  Goth.
De cons Stil.   *De consolatu Stilichonis i–iii.* Ibid. Vol. i, pp. 364–393; vol. ii, pp. 2–69.
In Rufin.   *In Rufinum i–ii.* Ibid. Vol. i, pp. 24–97.
Panegyr.   *Panegyricus de tertio consolatu Honorii Augusti.* Ibid., pp. 268–285.
                   Phoenix. Ibid. Vol. ii, pp. 222–231.

Cod. Iust.
                   Codex Iustinianus. Ed. P. Krueger. Berlin, Weidmann, 1915.

Columella
Res rust.   *De re rustica i–ix.* With an English trans. by H. B. Ash, E. S. Forster, and E. Heffner. 2 vols. LCL.
Comm. Aen.   *Commentum super sex libros Eneidos Virgilii.* J. W. Jones and E. F. Jones. *The Commentary on the First Six Books of the* Aeneid *of* Vergil *Commonly Attributed to Bernardus Silvestris.* Lincoln, University of Nebraska Press, 1977. Trans. E. G. Schreiber and T. E. Maresca. Lincoln, University of Nebraska Press, 1979.

Cornelius Nepos
De exc. duc.   *De excellentibus ducibus exterarum gentium.* With an English trans. by J. C. Rolfe. LCL. Includes *De lat. hist.*
CS   *Scriptorum de Musica Medii Aevi Novam seriem a Gerbertina alteram* . . . Ed. E. de Coussemaker. 4 vols. Paris, A. Durand, 1864–1876. Repr. Milan, Bollettino Bibliografico Musicale, 1931. *See* also Coussemaker (1852), below, III.

(Cotton, John)
                   Johannes Afflighemensis. *De Musica cum Tonario.* Ed. J. Smits van Waesberghe. Rome, American Institute of Musicology, 1950. *CSM* 1.

Curtius Rufus
                   Quintus Curtius. With an English trans. by J. C. Rolfe. 2 vols. LCL.

Dante Alighieri
Conv.   *Convivio.* Ed. E. G. Parodi and F. Pellegrini. In *Le Opere di Dante*: Testo critico della Società Dantesca Italiana. 2d ed. Florence, Bemporad, 1960. Pp. 143–293. P. H. Wicksteed, *The Convivio of Dante Alighieri.* London, Temple Classics, 1903.

De vulg. el.   *De vulgari eloquentia.* Ed. P. Rajna. In *Le Opere di Dante*, as above, pp. 295–327.

Div. Comm.   *La Divina Commedia.* Ed. G. Vandelli. In *Le Opere di Dante*, as above, pp. 443–798. *Dante Alighieri*: The Divine Comedy. Trans. with comm. C. S. Singleton. 6 vols. Princeton, Princeton University Press, 1970–1975, Bollingen Series, 80. J. Ciardi, *The Divine Comedy*: Dante Alighieri (verse translation). New York, W. W. Norton, 1977.

Ep.   Letter to Can Grande. In *Epistole.* Ed. E. Pistelli. In *Le Opere di Dante,* as above, pp. 383–415. Trans. P. H. Wicksteed in *A Translation of the Latin Works of Dante Alighieri.* London, Temple Classics, 1940. Pp. 293–368.

Mon.   *Monarchia.* Ed. E. Rostagno. In *Le Opere di Dante*, as above. Pp. 329–381. Trans. P. H. Wicksteed, as above, pp. 125–280.

Quest. de   *Questio de aqua et terra.* Ed. E. Pistelli. *Le Opere di Dante,* as
aqua   above, pp. 467–480.

    Vita nuova. Ed. M. Barbi. In *Le Opere di Dante*, as above. Pp. 1–49. Trans. M. Musa. Bloomington, Indiana University Press, 1962.

    De imitatione Christi. (Ascribed to Thomas à Kempis.) Rome, Desclée & Co., 1948. *The Imitation of Christ.* Trans. L. Sherley-Price. Harmondsworth, Penguin, 1952.

Dicta Catonis   *Minor Latin Poets.* LCL. With an English trans. by J. W. Duff and A. M. Duff. Pp. 585–639.

Dig.   Part of the *Corpus iuris civilis Iustiniani* (which today has four parts: the Institutions, pub. November 21, A.D. 533; the Digests, pub. December 16, A.D. 533; the Codex, pub. November 16, A.D. 534; and the *Novellae*, most of them from the years A.D. 535–565). The *Digesta* pub. by Th. Mommsen and P. Krueger in *Corpus iuris civilis.* Berlin, Weidmann, 1920.

    Eneas. Texte critique. Ed. J. J. Salverda de Grave. Halle, Niemeyer, 1891. Bibliotheca Normannica, 4. Trans. J. A. Yunck. New York, Columbia University Press, 1974. Records of Civilization: Sources and Studies, 93.

Diodorus Siculus
    Bibliotheke. With an English trans. by C. H. Oldfather et al. 12 vols. LCL.

Diogenes Laertius
    Lives of Eminent Philosophers. With an English trans. by R. D. Hicks. 2 vols. LCL.

Eneas: A Twelfth-Century French Romance. Ed. and trans. J. A. Yunck. New York, Columbia University Press, 1974. Records of Civilization, Sources and Studies, 93.

Ennius

Fragments in *Remains of Old Latin*. LCL. Ed. and trans. E. H. Warmington. Vol. i.

Epicurus

Epicurus, the Extant Remains. Text, trans., and notes C. Bailey. Oxford, Oxford University Press, 1926. *The Stoic and Epicurean Philosophers*: Epicurus, Epictetus, Lucretius, Marcus Aurelius. Ed. W. J. Oates. New York, Random House, 1940.

Euripides

LCL, Euripides. With an English trans. by A. S. Way. 4 vols.

Eusebius
Hist. eccl.   *Ecclesiastical History*. With an English trans. by K. Lake and J. E. L. Oulton. 2 vols. LCL. *The History of the Church from Christ to Constantine*. Trans. G. A. Williamson, New York, New York University Press, 1966.

Fazio degli Umberti
Il Dit-   In *Il dittamondo e le rime*. Ed. G. Corsi. 2 vols. Bari, Laterza, 1952.
   tamondo

Fiori e vita de filosafi ed altri savi ed imperadori. Ed. C. Segre. In *La Prosa del Duecento*. Ed. C. Segre and M. Marti. Milan, R. Ricciardi, 1959. La letteratura Italiana. Storia e Testi, 3.

Firmicus Maternus
Math.   *Iulii Firmici Materni Matheseos libri viii*. Ed. W. Kroll et al. 2 vols. Leipzig, Teubner, 1897–1913.

Florus, L. Annaeus
Epit.   *Epitome of Roman History*. With an English trans. by E. S. Forster. LCL. As Cornelius Nepos, above.

Francesco Nelli. *See* Cochin, below, III.

Frederick II
Liber Aug.   *Liber Augustalis*. In J. L. Huillard-Bréholles, *Historia diplomatica Friderici II*. 6 vols. in 12. Paris, H. Plon, 1852–1861. Vol. i, pp. 1–178. J. M. Powell, *The* Liber Augustalis *or Constitutions of Melfi Promulgated by the Emperor Frederick II for the Kingdom of Sicily in 1231*. Syracuse, Syracuse University Press, 1971.

Frontinus

De aquis.   *De aquis urbis Romae i–ii.* LCL, Frontinus. With an English trans.
by C. E. Bennett.

Strat.   *Stratagems i–iv.* As above.

Fulgentius, Fabius Planciades
Opera. Ed. R. Helm. Leipzig, B. G. Teubner, 1898.
See also Liebeschuetz, below, III.

Geoffrey of Vinsauf
Poetria nova. In Leyser (1721), pp. 861–978. Also in E. Faral, *Les
arts poétiques du XIIe et du XIIIe siècle.* Paris, E. Champion (1924),
1958. M. F. Nims, Poetria nova *of Geoffrey of Vinsauf.* Toronto,
Pontifical Institute of Mediaeval Studies, 1967.

Gesta Rom. Gesta Romanorum. Ed. H. Oesterley. Berlin, Weidmann, 1872.

Giovanni da San Miniato. *See* Stolfi (1867), below, III.

Glossa ordinaria. (Ascribed to Walafrid Strabo.) *PL* 113–114.

Gower, John. *See* John Gower.

Greek   *The Complete Greek Drama.* Ed. W. J. Oates and Eugene O'Neill,
  Drama   Jr. 2 vols. New York, Random House, 1938.

Gregory I

Moral.   *Moralia in Job. PL* 75, cc. 509–1162; 76, cc. 9–782. *Morals on the
Book of Job by S. Gregory the Great* . . . Trans. with notes and
indices J. Bliss. 3 vols. in 4. Oxford, J. H. Parker, 1844–1850.
Library of Fathers, 18, 21, 23, 31.

GS. Scriptores ecclesiastici de Musica Sacra potissimum. Ed. M. Gerbert (1784). 3
vols. Milan, Bolletino Bibliographico Musicale, 1931.

Guido of Arezzo
Micrologus. Ed. J. Smits van Waesberghe. Rome, American Institute of Musicology, 1955. *CSM,* 4.

Guigo of Chastel

Meditationes   *Meditationes Guigonis, prioris Cartusiae.* Ed. A. Wilmart. OSB,
Études de Philosophie médiévale, 22 (1936), Also, incomplete, in
PL 153. *Meditations of Guigo, prior of the Charterhouse.* Trans. J. J.
Jolin. Milwaukee, Marquette University Press, 1951. Medieval
Philosophical Texts in Translation, 6.

Guillaume de Lorris and Jean de Meun. *See Roman de la Rose.*

Guillaume de Machaut
Le Jugement dou Roy de Behaigne. In *Oeuvres de Guillaume de
Machaut.* Ed. E. Hoepffner. Vol. i. Paris, Firmin Didot, 1908. Pp.

57–135. *Le Jugement du roy de Behaigne* and *Remede de Fortune*. Ed. J. I. Wimsatt and W. W. Kibler. Athens, University of Georgia Press, 1988.

Guy de Chauliac

Chirurgia | *Le grande chirurgie de Guy de Chauliac*. Ed. E. Nicaise. Paris, F.
magna | Alcan, 1890. *The Chirurgie of Guy de Chauliac*. Ed. M. S. Ogden. Oxford, Oxford University Press, 1971. EETS 265.

Halm (1863)

Rhetores latini minores. Ed. C. Halm. Leipzig, Teubner, 1863.

Henry of Settimello

De div. Fort. | *De diversitate Fortunae et Philosophiae consolatione i–iv*. In Leyser (1721). As *Geoffrey of Vinsauf*, above. Pp. 453–497.

Heraclitus

On the Universe. LCL, Hippocrates, below. Vol. iv, pp. 451–509.

Hermes Trismegistus

Asclepius. In A. D. Nock and A.-J. Festugière, *Corpus Hermeticum*. 4 vols. Paris, Collection Budé, 1945, 1954. Vol. ii. W. Scott, *Hermetica*: The Ancient Greek and Latin Writings Which Contain Religious or Philosophic Teachings Ascribed to Hermes Trismegistus. With English trans. and notes. 4 vols. Oxford, Clarendon Press, 1924–1936.

Herodotus

LCL, Herodotus. With an English trans. by A. D. Godley. 4 vols. Trans. G. Rawlinson in *Greek Historians*. Ed. F. R. B. Godolphin. 2 vols. New York, Random House, 1942. Vol. i, pp. 3–563. Latin text and comm. in *Herodoti Halicarnassei Historiarum libri ix*. Ed. Gottfried Jungermann. Geneva, Oliva Pauli Stephani, 1618.

Hesiod and the Homeric Hymns. With an English trans. by H. G. Evelyn White. LCL.

Hippocrates
Aph. | *Aphorisms*. LCL, Hippocrates. With an English trans. by W. H. S. Jones. Vol. iv, pp. 98–221.

Breaths | Ibid. Vol. ii, pp. 219, 253.

Hist. Aug. | *Historia Augusta. The Scriptores Historiae Augustae*. With an English trans. by D. Magie. 3 vols. LCL.

Homer

Iliad. With an English trans. by A. T. Murray. 2 vols. LCL.
Odyssey. With an English trans. by A. T. Murray. 2 vols. LCL.
R. Lattimore. *The Iliad of Homer*. Chicago, University of Chicago

Press, 1951.
R. Lattimore. *The Odyssey of Homer*. New York, Harper & Row,
1967.

Horace

Ars poet.	*De arte poetica.* In Horace, *Satires, Epistles and Ars poetica*. With an English trans. by H. R. Fairclough. LCL. Pp. 442–489.
Carm.	*Carmina.* In Horace, *Odes and Epodes*. With an English trans. by C. E. Bennett. LCL. Pp. 2–347.
Carm. saec.	*Carmen saeculare.* Ibid. Pp. 349–357.
Ep.	*Epistles.* LCL, Horace. As *Ars poet.*, above. Pp. 248–441.
Epod.	*Epodes.* LCL, Horace. As *Carm.*, above. Pp. 359–421.
Sat.	*Satires.* LCL, Horace. As *Ars poet.*, above. Pp. 2–245.

Hrabanus Maurus

De univ.	*De universo.* PL 111, cc. 9–614.
Exp. in prov. Sal.	*Expositio in Proverbia Salomonis.* PL 111, cc. 679–792.

Hugh of St. Victor

	De anima. PL 176, cc. 165–190.
De van.	*De vanitate mundi et rerum transeuntium usu.* Ibid., cc. 703–740.
Didasc.	*Didascalicon: De studio legendi.* Ed. C. H. Buttimer. Washington, D.C., Catholic University of America Press, 1939. Studies in Medieval and Renaissance Latin, 10. J. Taylor, *The* Didascalicon *of Hugh of St. Victor*. New York, Columbia University Press, 1961. Records of Civilization: Sources and Studies, 64.

Hyginus

Fab.	*Hygini Fabulae.* Ed. H. J. Rose. Leiden, Sijthoff, 1934.

Innocent III (Lotario dei Segni)

De miseria cond. hum.	*De miseria conditionis humane.* Ed. and trans. R. E. Lewis. Athens, University of Georgia Press, 1978.

Isidore of Seville

De nat. rer.	*De natura rerum.* PL 83, c. 983.
Diff.	*Differentiae.* PL 83, c. 10.
Etym.	*Isidori Hispalensis episcopi Etymologiarum sive Originum libri xx.* Ed. W. M. Lindsay. 2 vols. Oxford, Clarendon Press, 1911 (1962).
Lib. num.	*Liber numerorum qui in sanctis scripturis occurrunt.* PL 83, cc. 179–200.
Quaest. in Test. Vetus	*Quaestiones in Testamentum Vetus: In Genesin.* Ibid., c. 207.

Synon.   *Synonyma.* Ibid., cc. 825–856.

Jacobus de Voragine
Leg. aur.   *Legenda aurea, vulgo Historia Lombardica dicta.* Ed. J. G. Th.
                Graesse. Breslau, Koebner, 1890. G. Ryan and H. Ripperger.
                The Golden Legend of Jacobus de Voragine. 2 vols. New York,
                Longmans, Green, 1941.

Jacques de Liège
Spec. mus.   *Speculum musicae.* Ed. R. Bragard. Rome, American Institute of
                Musicology, 1955—

Jean de Hesdin
In Petr.   *Galli cuiusdam anonymi in Franciscum Petrarcham invectiva.* In
                Petrarch, *Opera* (1581). Pp. 1060–1068.

Jean Froissart
                Chroniques. Ed. A. Pauphilet and E. Pognon. Paris, Gallimard,
                1952. Bibliothèque de la Pléiade, 48. Pp. 373–948. *Chronicles, in
                Lord Berners' Translation.* Ed. Gillian and William Anderson.
                Carbondale, Southern Illinois University Press (1963). Centaur
                Classics.

Jehan de Joinville
                Histoire de Saint Louis. In *Historiens et chroniquers du Moyen Âge.*
                Ed. A. Pauphilet and E. Pognon. Paris, Gallimard, 1952. Bib-
                liothèque de la Pléiade, 48. Pp. 203–372.

Jerome
Adv. Iovin.   *Adversus Iovinianum.* PL 23, cc. 211–338.
Adv. Rufin.   *Apology against Rufinus i–iii.* PL 23, cc. 397–492. English trans. J.
                N. Hritzu. Washington, D.C., Catholic University of America
                Press, 1965. Fathers of the Church, 53.
Contra   *Dialogus contra Pelagianos.* PL 23, cc. 495–590. Also as Hritzu,
  Pelag.   above.
Ep.   *S. Eusebii Hieronymi epistulae.* Ed. I. Hilberg. CSEL 54–56.
                Selected Letters of St. Jerome. With an English trans. by F. A.
                Wright. LCL.
Hex. Hiob   *Hexaplar liber Hiob.* PL 29, c. 98.
In Ezech.   Commentary on Ezechiel. PL 25, cc. 15–490.
In Iovin.   *See Adversus Iovinianum.*
In Is.   Commentary on Isaias. PL 24, cc. 17–678.
In Matth.   Commentary on Saint Matthew. PL 26, cc. 15–218.
                Vita Pauli. PL 23, cc. 17–28.

Joachim of Fiore. *See* West (1983), below, III.

Johannes Afflighemensis. *See* (Cotton, John).

Johannes von Tepl
Ackerm.   *Der Ackermann aus Boehmen.* Ed. M. O'C. Walshe. London, Duckworth, 1951. *Der Ackermann aus Boehmen.* Ed. A. Bernt and K. Burdach. Berlin, Weidmann, 1917. Vom Mittelalter zur Reformation, 3, 1.

John Chrysostom
Quod nemo   *Quod nemo laeditur nisi a seipso. PG* 52, 459–480. Trans. in *A Select Library of the Nicene and Post-Nicene Fathers of the Church.* Ed. P. Schaff. New York, Christian Literature Co., 1886–1890. Vol. ix.

John de Hanville
     Architrenius. In Wright (1872). Vol. i, pp. 240–392.

John Gower
     Complete Works. Ed. G. C. Macaulay. 4 vols. Oxford, Clarendon Press, 1899–1902.
     The Major Latin Works of John Gower . . . Trans. E. W. Stockton, Seattle, University of Washington Press, 1962.

John of Salisbury
De sept.   *De septem septenis. PL* 199, cc. 945–964.
Enth.   *Entheticus.* Ibid., cc. 966–1004.
Metalog.   *Metalogicus.* Ibid., cc. 823–946. *Metalogicon.* Ed. C. C. I. Webb. Oxford, Clarendon Press, 1929. *The Metalogicon.* Trans. D. D. McGarry. Berkeley, University of California Press, 1955.
Policrat.   *Policraticus. PL* 199, cc. 370–822. *Policraticus.* Ed. C. C. I. Webb. 2 vols. Oxford, Clarendon Press, 1909. *The Statesman's Book of John of Salisbury, Being the Fourth, Fifth, and Sixth Books and Selections from the Seventh and Eighth Books of the Policraticus.* Trans. J. Dickinson. New York, A. A. Knopf (1927), 1962. J. B. Pike, *Frivolities of Courtiers and Footprints of Philosophers, Being a Translation of the First, Second and Third Books and Selections from the Seventh and Eighth Books of the Policraticus* . . . Minneapolis, University of Minnesota Press, 1938.

John the Scot. *See* Scotus Erigena.

Josephus Flavius
     LCL, Josephus. With English trans. by H. St. J. Thackeray, R. Marcus, A. Wikgren, and L. H. Feldman. 10 vols.

Julius Caesar
Afr.   *The African War.* With an English trans. by A. G. Way. In *Alexandrian, Spanish and African Wars.* LCL. Pp. 146–299.

Civ.   *The Civil Wars.* With an English trans. by A. G. Peskett. LCL.
Gall.   *The Gallic War i–viii.* With an English trans. by H. J. Edwards.
             LCL.

Julius Valerius. *See* Mueller (1846), below, III.

Justin
Epit. Trogi   *M. Iuniani Iustini Epitoma Historiarum Philippicarum Pompei
                 Trogi.* Ed. O. Seel. Leipzig, B. G. Teubner, 1935.

Juvenal
             [*Satyrae.*] Cum Antonii Mancinelli viri eruditissimi explanatione.
             Lyon, Nicholas Wolf for Stephen Gaynard, 1498. (Includes also
             the commentary of Badius Ascensius.) With an English trans. by
             G. G. Ramsay. LCL, *Juvenal and Persius.*

Kilwardby, Robert. *See* Robert Kilwardby.

Lactantius, Lucius Caecilius Firmianus
De ira   *Liber de ira Dei. PL* 7, cc. 77–148. Trans. M. F. McDonald in
                Lactantius: Minor Works. Washington, D.C., Catholic University
                of America Press, 1965. Fathers of the Church, 54.
De opif. Dei *De opificio Dei, vel formatione hominis. PL* 7, cc. 9–78. Trans. M.
                F. McDonald. As *De ira*, above.
Div. inst.   *Divinarum institutionem libri vii.* Ed. S. Brandt and N. Laubmann.
                CSEL 19. *The Divine Institutes.* Trans. M. F. McDonald. Washing-
                ton, D.C., Catholic University of America Press, 1964. Fathers of
                the Church, 49.
De mort.   *Liber de Mortibus persecutorum. PL* 7, cc. 189–276. Trans. M. F.
  pers.   McDonald. As *De ira*, above.
Phoenix   *PL* 7, cc. 275–284. Trans. M. F. McDonald. As *De ira*, above.

Langland, William. *See Piers the Plowman.*

Livy
             LCL, *Livy.* With English trans. by B. O. Foster, F. G. Moore, E. T.
             Sage, A. C. Schlesinger, and R. M. Greer (General Index). 14 vols.

Lucan
             Lucan. With an English trans. by J. D. Duff. LCL.

Lucretius Carus
             Lucretius. With an English trans. by W. H. D. Rouse. Rev. M. F.
             Smith. LCL. *See also* Oates (1940), under Epicurus.

Machaut. *See* Guillaume de Machaut.

Macrobius
Comm.   *Ambrosii Theodosii Macrobii Commentarii in somnium Scipionis.*
             Ed. J. Willis. Leipzig, B. G. Teubner, 1963. W. H. Stahl, *Macro-
             bius:* Commentary on the Dream of Scipio. New York, Columbia

University Press, 1952. Records of Civilization: Sources and Studies, 48.

Saturn.   *Ambrosii Theodosii Macrobii Saturnalia.* Ed. J. Willis. Leipzig, B. G. Teubner, 1963. P. V. Davies, *Macrobius: The Saturnalia.* New York, Columbia University Press, 1969. Records of Civilization: Sources and Studies, 79.

Marcus Aurelius

Marcus Aurelius. With an English trans. by C. R. Haines. LCL.

Martial

Martial. With an English trans. by W. C. A. Ker. 2 vols. LCL.

Martianus Capella

De nupt.   *Martiani Minnei Felicis Capellae De nuptiis Philologiae et Mercurii libri ix.* Ed. A. Dick. Leipzig, B. G. Teubner, 1925. W. H. Stahl and R. Johnson, *Martianus Capella and the Seven Liberal Arts.* Vol. ii: The Marriage of Philology and Mercury. New York, Columbia University Press, 1977. Records of Civilization: Sources and Studies, 84.

Martin of Braga (Bracara *or* Dumiensis)

Martini episcopi Bracarensis opera omnia. Ed. Claude W. Barlow. New Haven, Yale University Press, 1950. Papers and Monographs of the American Academy in Rome, 12.

Matthew of Vendôme

Ars versificatoria. In Faral (1924, as under Geoffrey of Vinsauf). Pp. 109–193. *The Art of Versification.* Trans. with intro. A. E. Galyon. Ames, Iowa State University Press, 1980.

Mirabilia urbis Romae. In R. Valentini and G. Zuchetti, *Codice topografico della città di Roma* (Fonti per la Storia d'Italia, 1940–1953). Vol. iii. *The Marvels of Rome.* Ed. and trans. F. M. Nichols. London, Ellis & Elvey, 1889. Ibid. 2d ed. Ed. by E. Gardner. New York, Italica Press, 1986.

Monumentum Ancyranum. See Res gestae divi Augusti.

Nicholas of Lynn

The Kalendarium of Nicholas of Lynn. Ed. S. Eisner. Athens, University of Georgia Press, 1980.

Nicole Oresme

De commens.   *Tractatus de commensurabilitate vel incommensurabilitate motuum celi: Nicole Oresme and the Kinematics of Circular Motion.* Ed. and trans. E. Grant. Madison, University of Wisconsin Press, 1971. (1971a)

De config.   *De configurationibus: Nicole Oresme and the Medieval Geometry of Qualities and Motions.* Ed. and trans. M. Clagett. Madison,

University of Wisconsin Press, 1968.

De proportionibus proportionum *and* Ad pauca recipientes. Ed. and trans. E. Grant. Madison, University of Wisconsin Press, 1966.

Le Livre du ciel *Le Livre du ciel et du monde*. Ed. and trans. A. D. Menut and A. J. Denomy. Madison, University of Wisconsin Press, 1968.

Odo of Cluny

Coll. *Collationum libri iii. PL* 133 (cf. Manitius, ii [1923], pp. 21–26).

Orosius

Historiarum adversus paganos libri vii. PL 31, cc. 633–1174. *CSEL* 5. Paulus Orosius, *The Seven Books of History against the Pagans*. Trans. R. J. Deferrari. Washington, D.C., Catholic University of America Press, 1964. Fathers of the Church, 50.

Ovid

Am. *Amores*. LCL, Ovid. Vol. i. With an English trans. by G. Showerman.

Ars amat. *Ars amatoria*. LCL, Ovid. Vol. ii. With an English trans. by J. H. Mozley.

Cons. ad Liv. *Consolatio ad Liviam*. Ibid.

Ex pont. *Epistulae ex ponto*. LCL, Ovid. Vol. vi. As *Tristia*, below.

Fasti LCL, Ovid. Vol. v. With an English trans. by J. G. Frazer.

Heroides LCL, Ovid. Vol. i. As *Am*., above.

Metam. *Metamorphoses*. LCL, Ovid. Vols. iii, iv. With an English trans. by F. J. Miller.

Rem. am. *Remedia amoris*. LCL, Ovid. Vol. ii. As *Ars amat*., above.

Tristia LCL, Ovid. Vol. vi. With an English trans. by A. L. Wheeler.

Palladius

Hist. Laus. *Historia Lausiaca, PL* 73. Also ed. Dom Cuthbert Butler. 2 vols. Cambridge, Cambridge University Press, 1898, 1904.

Paul the Deacon

Hist. Lang. *Historia Langobardorum*. In *Scriptores rerum Langobardicarum et Italicarum Saec. vi–ix*. Ed. G. Waitz. Hannover, Hahn, 1878. *Monumenta Germaniae historica* i, 3. Paul the Deacon, *History of the Lombards*. Trans. W. D. Foulke. Ed. E. Peters. Philadelphia, University of Pennsylvania Press, 1974.

Paulus Orosius. *See* Orosius.

Paulus Presbyter

Vita Ambrosii. PL 14, cc. 27–46.

Persius. *See* Juvenal.

Peter Damian
> *Vita S. Romualdi. PL* 144, c. 973.

Peter Lombard
> *Sententiae.* In *Opera S. Bonaventurae* i–iv. Quaracchi, 1892–1896. *See also PL* 192, c. 522.

Petrus Cantor
> *Verbum abbreviatum. PL* 205, cc. 144–147.

The Phoenix. Ed. N. F. Blake. Manchester, Manchester University Press, 1964.

Physiologus latinus versio Y. Ed. F. J. Carmody. *University of California Publications in Classical Philology* 12 (1941), pp. 95–134.

Pierre Bersuire
> *Reductorium morale.* For the Latin text, *see* F. Stegmueller, *Repertorium biblicum medii aevi* (5 vols., Madrid, 1940–1955), nos. 6425–6429, where the Prologue is quoted. The work includes the *Ovide moralisé*, published in a French translation (Bruges, Colaert Mansion, 1484) and for a long time attributed to Thomas Waleys. "L'Ovidius moralizatus." Ed. F. Ghisalberti. *Studi Romanzi* 23 (1933), pp. 5–136.

Piers the Plowman. A Critical Edition of the A-Version. T. A. Knott and D. C. Fowler. Baltimore, Johns Hopkins Press, 1952. *The Vision of William Concerning Piers the Plowman; by William Langland.* Ed. W. W. Skeat. B-Text. Oxford, Clarendon Press, 1869.

Pindar
> *Pindar.* With an English trans. by J. E. Sandys. LCL.

Plato
> LCL, Plato. With English trans. by W. R. M. Lamb, H. N. Fowler, and R. G. Bury. 12 vols.
> [Hamilton (1961).] *The Collected Dialogues of Plato.* Ed. E. Hamilton and H. Cairns. Princeton, Princeton University Press, 1961. Bollingen Series, 71.

Plato latinus   Ed. R. Klibansky. Vol. i: *Meno interprete Henrico Aristippo*, ed. V. Kordeuter and C. Labowsky; vol. ii: *Phaedo interprete Henrico Aristippo*, ed. L. Minio-Paluello and H. J. Drossaart Lulofs; vol. iii: *Parmenides . . . interprete Guillelmo de Moerbeka*, ed. R. Klibansky and C. Labowsky. London, Warburg Institute, 1940, 1950, 1953. For vol. iv, *see* Chalcidius.

Plautus
> LCL, Plautus. With an English trans. by P. Nixon. 5 vols.

Pliny the Elder

Nat. hist.   *Naturalis historia. Natural History.* With English trans. by H. Rackham, W. H. S. Jones, and D. E. Eichholz. 10 vols. LCL.

Pliny the Younger

Ep.   *Letters.* Trans. Melmoth. Rev'd. W. M. L. Hutchinson. 2 vols. LCL.

Pseudo-Pliny (Also attributed to Aurelius Victor.)

De vir. ill.   *Incerti auctoris Liber de Viris illustribus urbis Romae.* In Pichlmayr (1911), Aurelius Victor, above. *Deeds of Famous Men.* Critical text and trans. W. K. Sherwin, Jr. Norman, University of Oklahoma Press, 1973.

Plotinus

LCL, Plotinus. With an English trans. by A. H. Armstrong. 5 vols. to date. LCL. *The Six Enneads.* Trans. S. McKenna and B. S. Page. Chicago, Encyclopaedia Britannica, 1952. Great Books of the Western World, 17.

Plutarch

Moralia   With English trans. by F. C. Babbitt, W. C. Helmbold, P. H. De Lacy, B. Einarson, E. L. Minar, Jr., F. H. Sandbach, H. N. Fowler, L. Pearson, and H. Cherniss. 15 vols. LCL.
The Parallel Lives. With an English trans. by B. Perrin. 11 vols. LCL.

Porphyry

Isagoge. In Aristotele, *Opera* (1590). Vol. i, pp. 1–8. *Porphyrii Isagoge et Liber sex principiarum.* Ed. L. Minio-Paluello. Paris, Desclée, de Brouwer, 1966. *Aristoteles latinus.* Vol. i, 6–7. Porphyry the Phoenician, *Isagoge.* Trans., intro., and notes E. W. Warren. Toronto, Pontifical Institute of Mediaeval Studies, 1975. *Life of Plotinus. See* Plotinus, above.

Possidius

Vita Aug.   *Vita S. Aurelii Augustini. PL* 32, cc. 33–66. *S. Augustini vita scripta a Possidio episcopo.* Ed. with rev. text and trans. H. T. Weiskotten. Princeton, Princeton University Press, 1919.

The Pricke of Conscience. Ed. R. Morris. Berlin, Philological Society, 1863.

Priscian of Caesarea

Inst. gramm.   *Institutionum grammaticarum libri xviii.* Ed. M. Hertz in H. Keil, *Grammatici Latini.* Vols. ii–iii. Leipzig, B. G. Teubner, 1855–1859.

Propertius

With an English trans. by H. E. Butler. LCL.

La Prosa del Duecento. Ed. C. Segre and M. Marti. Milan, Ricciardi, 1959.

Prudentius
>With an English trans. by H. J. Thomas. 2 vols. LCL.

Publilius Syrus
(Sententiae)   LCL, Minor Latin Poets. As *Dicta Catonis*, above.

Quintilian
Inst. orat.   *Institutio oratoriae.* With an English trans. by H. E. Butler. 4 vols. LCL.

Ramon Llull. *See* Bonner (1985), below, III.

Raynardo e Lesengrino. Ed. E. Teza. Pisa, Nistri, 1869.

Res gestae divi Augusti. LCL, Velleius Paterculus. Pp. 331–405.

Richard de Bury
Philobiblon   *The Philobiblon of Richard de Bury, Bishop of Durham, Treasurer and Chancellor of Edward III.* Ed. and trans. E. C. Thomas. London, Kegan Paul, Trench, 1888. New ed. Ed. M. Maclagan. Oxford, Blackwell, 1960.

Robert de Boron
>"The Romance of the Story of the Grail." In Goodrich (1964), chap. 9, as below, III.

Robert Grosseteste
>*Questio de fluxu.* Ed. R. C. Dales. In Grant (1974), as below, III. Pp. 640–644.

Robert Kilwardby
De ortu sci.
>*De ortu scientiarum.* Ed. A. G. Judy. London, British Academy, 1976. Auctores Britannici medii aevi, 4.

Roman de la Rose   Guillaume de Lorris and Jean de Meun, *Le Roman de la Rose.* Ed. E. Langlois. 5 vols. Paris, Didot (vols. 1–2), Champion (vols. iii–v), 1914–1924. Société des ançiens textes français.
Guillaume de Lorris and Jean de Meun, *The Romance of the Rose.* Trans. C. Dahlberg. Princeton, Princeton University Press, 1971.

Le Roman de Renart. Ed. E. Martin. 3 vols. Strasbourg, Truebner, 1882–1887.

Rufinus
Hist. eccl.   *Historia ecclesiastica.* PL 21, cc. 467–540 (cf. Cayre, i [1936], pp. 565–566).

Salimbene. *See* Coulter (1972), below, III.

Sallust
Cat.   *Bellum Catilinae.* LCL, Sallust. With an English trans. by J. C. Rolfe, pp. 2–129.

Jug.　　　　　*Bellum Jugurthinum.* Ibid. Pp. 132–379.

Salutati, Coluccio. *See* below, III.

Scotus Erigena, Johannes

De div. nat.　　*De divisione naturae. PL* 122, cc. 441–1022.

De praedest.　　*De praedestinatione. PL* 122, c. 362.

Super hier.　　*Expositiones super Ierarchiam caelestem S. Dionysii. PL* 122, cc.
　coel.　　　125–266. The missing part of the work, published by H. F.
　　　　　　Dondaine. *Archives d'histoire doctrinale et litteraire du Moyen Âge,*
　　　　　　25–26 (1950–1951). Pp. 245–302.

Seneca (the Philosopher)

Ad Marc.　　*De consolatione ad Marciam. Dial.* vi. In Seneca, *Moral Essays.*
　　　　　　With an English trans. by J. W. Basore. Vol. ii. LCL.

Agamemnon　In Seneca. *Tragedies.* With an English trans. by F. J. Miller. Vol. ii.
　　　　　　LCL.

De benef.　　*De beneficiis.* LCL, Seneca. As *Ad. Marc.,* above. Vol. iii.

De clem.　　*De clementia.* Ibid. Vol. i.

De ira　　　*Dial.* iii–v. Ibid. Vol. i.

De matrim.　*De matrimonio. Fragmenta xiii.* In *L. Annaei Senecae Opera quae*
　　　　　　supersunt. Ed. F. Haase. Vol. iii. Leipzig, Teubner, 1886.

De rem. fort.　*De remediis fortuitorum liber. Ad Gallionem.* Ibid. R. G. Palmer,
　　　　　　Seneca's De remediis fortuitorum *and the Elizabethans.* The 1547
　　　　　　edition of the Latin text and English trans. Chicago, Institute of
　　　　　　Elizabethan Studies, 1953.

De tranqu.　*De tranquillitate animi. Dial.* ix. LCL, Seneca. As *Ad Marc.,* above.
　　　　　　Vol. ii.

De vita　　　*De vita beata. Ad Gallionem. Dial.* vii. Ibid.
　beata

Dial.　　　*L. Annaei Senecae Dialogorum libri xii.* In Seneca, *Moral Essays.*
　　　　　　As above, vols. i, ii.

Ep.　　　　*Ad Lucilium. Epistulae morales.* With an English trans. by R. M.
　　　　　　Gummere. 3 vols. LCL.

Hippolytus　In Seneca. *Tragedies.* As *Agamemnon,* above. Vol. ii.
　　　　　　Ludus de morte Claudii. In *Opera.* As *De matrim.,* above. Vol. i.

Medea　　In Seneca. *Tragedies.* As *Agamemnon,* above. Vol. ii.

Nat. quaest.　*Naturales quaestiones.* With an English trans. by T. H. Corcoran. 2
　　　　　　vols. LCL.

Thyestes　　In Seneca. *Tragedies.* As *Agamemnon,* above. Vol. ii.

Seneca Rhetor

Controv.　　*Controversiae.* LCL, The Elder Seneca. With an English trans. by
　　　　　　M. Winterbottom. Vol. i.

Suas.　　　*Suasoriae.* Ibid. Vol. ii.

Servius Grammaticus

Ad Aen.   *In Vergilii Carmina commentarii*. Ed. G. Thilo and H. Hagen. 3
                 vols. Hildesheim, G. Olms, 1961.

Solinus

Coll.   *C. Iulii Solini Collectanea rerum memorabilium*. Ed. T. Mommsen.
                 Berlin, Weidmann, 1895.

Speculum virginum. See Bernards, below, III.

Statius

Achill.   *Achilleid*. LCL, Statius. With an English trans. by J. H. Mosley.
                 Vol. ii.
Silvae   Ibid. Vol. i.
Theb.   *Thebaid*. Ibid. Vols. i, ii.

Stimulus conscientiae. See The Pricke of Conscience.

Suetonius Tranquillus, Gaius

De gramm.   *De grammaticis*. LCL, Suetonius. With an English trans. by J. C.
                 Rolfe. Vol. ii.
De caes.   *De vita caesarum*. Ibid.
Horace   *Vita Horati*. Ibid. Vol. ii.
Lucan   *Vita Lucani*. Ibid. Vol. ii.
Persius   *Vita Auli Persi Flacci*. Ibid. Vol. ii.
Vergil   *Vita Vergili*. Ibid. Vol. ii.

Suger   *Abbot Suger*: On the Abbey Church of St. Denis and Its Treasures.
                 Ed. and trans. E. Panofsky. Princeton, Princeton University Press,
                 1946.

Sulpicius Severus

Dial.   *Dialogi tres*. In *Sulpitii Severi Opera omnia*. Leiden, Elsevir, 1635.
                 The Works of Sulpitius Severus, trans. A. Roberts. Nicene and post-
                 Nicene Fathers of the Christian Church, Ser. 2, xi, New York,
                 1894.
Sacra hist.   *Sacra historia*. As above. Note also *PL* 19, 20; and B. M. Peebles in
                 Fathers of the Church, 7.

Summa virtutum de remediis anime. Ed. and transl. S. Wenzel. Athens, Ga., Univer-
                 sity of Georgia Press, 1984.

Syrus, Publilius. *See* Publilius Syrus.

Tacitus

Ann.   In Tacitus, *Histories and Annals*. With an English trans. by C. H.
                 Moore and J. Jackson. 4 vols. LCL.
Hist.   *Histories*. Ibid.

Terence

Adelphoë	*The Brothers.* LCL, Terence. With an English trans. by J. Sergeaunt. Vol. ii.
Andria	*The Lady of Andros.* Ibid. Vol. i.
Eun.	*The Eunuch.* Ibid. Vol. i.
Heaut. tim.	*Heauton timorumenos. The Self-Tormentor.* Ibid. Vol. i.
Phormio	Ibid. Vol. ii.

Tertullian

De cultu fem.	*De cultu feminarum. PL* 1, cc. 1304, 1334, *CSEL* 70. Trans. in R. Arbesmann et al., *Disciplinary, Moral, and Ascetical Works.* New York, Fathers of the Church, 1959. Fathers of the Church, 40.
De exh. cast.	*De exhortatione castitatis. PL* 2, cc. 913–930. *CSEL* 70. Trans. in *Treatises on Marriage and Remarriage: To His Wife, An Exhortation to Chastity, Monogamy.* Ed. W. P. LeSaint. Westminster, Md., Newman, 1951. Ancient Christian Writers, 28.

Thomas Aquinas

In Metaph.	*In xii libros Metaphysicorum* . . . Ed. R. Spiazzi. Turin, Marietti, 1950. *Commentary on the Metaphysics of Aristotle.* Trans. J. P. Rowan. 2 vols. Chicago, Regnery, 1961.
In Phys.	*In octo libros De physico auditu sive physicorum Aristotelis commentaria.* Ed. A.-M. Pirotta. Turin, Marietti, 1953. *Commentary on Aristotle's Physics.* Trans. R. J. Blackwell, R. J. Spath, and W. E. Thirlkel. New Haven, Yale University Press, 1963.
In Sent. P. Lomb.	*Scriptum super Sententiis Magistri Petri Lombardi.* Ed. M. F. Moos. 4 vols. Paris, Lethielleux, 1947. Cf. Thomas Aquinas, *Selected Political Writings.* Ed. A. P. D'Entrèves. Trans. J. G. Dawson. Oxford, Blackwell, 1948.
Summa theol.	*Summa theologica* (theologiae). 4 vols. Turin, Marietti, 1948. Trans. Fathers of the Dominican Province. 20 vols. New York, Benzinger, 1911–1923. Sufficient for the general reader is *Basic Writings of Saint Thomas Aquinas.* Ed. A. C. Pegis. 2 vols. New York, Random House, 1945.

Thomas a Celano

  Legenda prima beati Francisci. Ed. E. Alençon. Rome, Desclée, 1906.

Thomas à Kempis. *See De imitatione Christi.*

Ulrich Boner

  Der Edelstein. Ed. F. Pfeiffer. Leipzig, Fues, 1844.

Valerius. *See* Julius Valerius.

Valerius Maximus

Facta et	*Factorum et dictorum memorabilium libri ix.* Ed. C. Kempf. Leip-

dicta   zig, B. G. Teubner, 1888.
mem.

Varro
De ling. Lat.   *De lingua Latina.* With an English trans. by R. G. Kent. 2 vols.
                   LCL.
De re rust.   *De re rustica.* As Cato, *De re rustica,* above.

Vegetius
De re mil.   *De re militari.* Ed. C. Lang. Leipzig, B. G. Teubner, 1885.

Velleius Paterculus
                   Historiae Romanae libri ii. With an English trans. by F. W. Ship-
                   ley. LCL. Includes the *Res gestae divi Augusti.*

Vincent of Beauvais
                   De eruditione filiorum nobilium. Ed. A. Steiner. Cambridge, Mass.,
                   Mediaeval Academy of America, 1938. Publication no. 32.
Spec. hist.   *Speculum historiale.* Venice, Herm. Liechtenstein, 1494. (Cop-
                   inger iii, 6241[4]).
Spec. nat.   *Speculum naturale.* 2 vols. Strassburg, Printer of *Legenda aurea,*
                   1483. (Copinger iii, 6257.)

Virgil
                   Pub. Virgilii Maronis Opera omnia. Ed. C. Schrevelius. Leiden,
                   Franciscus Hackius, 1661.
                   Aeneid. LCL, Virgil. With an English trans. by H. R. Fairclough. 2
                   vols. *The Aeneid*: Virgil. Trans. R. Fitzgerald. New York, Random
                   House, 1983.
Ecl.   *Eclogues.* LCL, Virgil. Vol. i.
Georg.   *Georgics.* Ibid. Vol. i.

Vita di Cola di Rienzo (ca. 1358)
                   The Life of Cola di Rienzo. Trans. with intro. J. Wright. Toronto,
                   Pontifical Institute of Mediaeval Studies, 1975.

Vitruvius Pollio
                   De architectura. With an English trans. by F. Granger. LCL.

Walter Map
De nugis cur.   *De nugis curialium—Courtier's Trifles.* Ed. and trans. M. R. James
                   et al. Oxford, Clarendon Press, 1983.

Walther von der Vogelweide
                   Gedichte. Ed. K. Lachmann. Berlin, G. Reimer, 1875.

III. OTHER PUBLICATIONS

Abert, Hermann. *Die Musikanschauung des Mittelalters und ihre Grundlagen*. Halle, Niemeyer, 1905.

Adler, Guido, ed. *Handbuch der Musikgeschichte*. Frankfurt, Frankfurter Verlags-Anstalt, 1924.

Aerts, W. J., ed. *Alexander the Great in the Middle Ages*. Nijmegen, J. M. Meulenhoff, 1978.

Aiken, Pauline. "The Animal History of Albertus Magnus and Thomas of Catimpré." *Speculum* 20 (1947), pp. 205–225.

Allen, Don Cameron. *Mysteriously Meant*: The Rediscovery of Pagan Symbolism and Allegorical Interpretation in the Renaissance. Baltimore, Johns Hopkins University Press, 1970.

Allen, Judson Boyce. *The Friar as Critic*: Literary Attitudes in the Later Middle Ages. Nashville, Vanderbilt University Press, 1971.

Allers, Rudolf. *Anselm von Canterbury*: Leben, Lehre, Werke. Vienna, Jakob Hegner, 1936.

––––––– . "Microcosmus." *Traditio* 2 (1944), pp. 375–376.

Alsop, Joseph. *The Rare Art Tradition*. New York, Harper & Row, 1982. Bollingen Series, 35, 27.

Anthony, Edgar Waterman. *Romanesque Frescoes*. Princeton, Princeton University Press, 1951.

Apel, Willi. *Gregorian Chant*. Bloomington, Indiana University Press, 1958.

Armstrong, A. H., ed. *The Cambridge History of Later Greek and Early Medieval Philosophy*. Cambridge, The University Press, 1967.

Artelt, W. *Die Quellen der mittelalterlichen Dialogdarstellung*. Berlin, Kunstgeschichtliche Studien, 3 (1934).

Auden, W. H. *A Certain World: A Commonplace Book*. New York, Viking Press, 1970.

Auden, W. H., and N. H. Pearson, eds. *Poets of the English Language*. 5 vols. New York, Viking Press, 1950.

Auer, Albert. *Leidenstheologie des Mittelalters*. Salzburg, Igonta, 1947.

Auerbach, Erich. "Figura"; and "St. Francis of Assissi in Dante's 'Commedia.' " In idem, *Scenes from the Drama of European Literature*. New York, Meridian Books, 1959.

_____ . *Literary Language and Its Public in Late Latin Antiquity and in the Middle Ages*. New York, Pantheon, 1965. Bollingen Series, 74.

Badius Ascensius, Jodocus. (Commentary on Juvenal.) *See* Juvenal (1498), above, II.

Balthasar, Hans Urs von. *A Theological Anthropology*. (American ed. of *Das Ganze im Fragment*, Einsiedeln, Benziger, 1963.) New York, Sheed & Ward, 1968.

_____ . *The von Balthasar Reader*. Ed. M. Kehl & W. Löser. New York, Crossroad, 1982.

Baltrusaitis, Jurgis. *Réveils et prodiges*: La Gothique fantastique. Paris, Armand Colin, 1960.

Baltus, Jean François. *Défense des SS. Pères accusez de Platonisme*. Paris, LeConte & Montalant, 1711.

Baluzius, Stephanus. (*Notae* on *De mort. pers.*) *See* Lactantius, above, II.

Barber, Malcolm. *The Trial of the Templars*. Cambridge, The University Press, 1978.

Barbeu du Rocher, A. "Ambassade de Pétrarque auprès du roi Jean le Bon." Académie des Inscriptions et Belles-Lettres de l'Institut Impérial de France, *Mémoires présentées par divers savants*. Sér. 2, vol. iii (1854), pp. 172–228.

Barlow (1950). *See* Martin of Braga, above, II.

Baron, Hans. *The Crisis of the Early Italian Renaissance*. 2 vols. Princeton, Princeton University Press, 1955. Rev. ed. 1 vol., Princeton, Princeton University Press, 1966.

_____ . *From Petrarch to Leonardo Bruni*: Studies in Humanistic and Political Literature. Chicago, University of Chicago Press, 1968. (1968a)

_____ . *Humanistic and Political Literature in Florence and Venice at the Beginning of the Quattrocento* (1955). Reissued. New York, Russell & Russell, 1968. (1968b)

_____ . *Petrarch's* Secretum: Its Making and Its Meaning. Cambridge, Mass., Medieval Academy of America, 1985.

_____ . *In Search of Florentine Civic Humanism*: Essays on the Transition from Medieval to Modern Thought. 2 vols. Princeton, Princeton University Press, 1988.

Battenhouse, Roy W. *A Companion to the Study of St. Augustine*. New York, Oxford University Press, 1955.

Bauer, Clemens, Laetitia Boehm, and Max Mueller, eds. *Speculum historiale*: Geschichte im Spiegel von Geschichtsschreibung und Geschichtsdeutung. Freiburg, Karl Alber, 1965.

Baxandall, Michael. *Giotto and the Orators*: Humanist Observers of Painting in Italy and the Discovery of Pictorial Composition, 1350–1450. Oxford, Clarendon Press, 1971. Oxford-Warburg Studies.

_____ . *Painting and Experience in Fifteenth Century Italy*. Oxford, Clarendon Press, 1972.

Bedini, Silvio A., and Francis R. Maddison. *Mechanical Universe*: The Astrarium of Giovanni de' Dondi. Transactions of the American Philosophical Society, N.S. 56, 5 (1966).

Beloch, Karl J. *Bevoelkerungsgeschichte Italiens*. Ed. G. DeSanctis. 2 vols. Berlin, 1937–1939.

Benedek, Thomas G., and Gerald P. Rodnan. "Petrarch on Medicine and the Gout." *Bulletin of the History of Medicine* 37 (1963): 397–416.

Berenson, Bernard. *Italian Painters of the Renaissance*. New York, Phaidon; Garden City Books, 1953.

Bergin, Thomas G. *Petrarch*. New York, Twayne, 1970.

———. *Boccaccio*. New York, Viking Press, 1981.

Berman, Harold J. *Law and Revolution*: The Formation of the Western Legal Tradition. Cambridge, Mass., Harvard University Press, 1983.

Bernal, J. D. *Science in History*. 4 vols. Cambridge, Mass., MIT Press, 1971.

Bernardi Perini, Giorgio. "La *Philologia* del Petrarca. Seneca e Marziano Capella." *Atti e mem. dell'Accad. patavina di scienze, lettere ed arti* 83 (1970–1971), pp. 147–169.

Bernardo, Aldo S. *Petrarch, Scipio and the "Africa."* Baltimore, Johns Hopkins University Press, 1962.

———. *Concordance to the* Epistolae familiares *by Francesco Petrarca*. New York, New York State University Press, 1976. Microfiche.

———. *Francesco Petrarca*: Citizen of the World. Padua, Antenore, and Albany, New York State University Press, 1980.

Bernardo (1975), Bernardo (1982), Bernardo (1985). *See* Petrarch, *Fam.*, above, I, iii.

Bernards, Matthaeus. *Speculum virginum*. Koeln, Boehlau, 1955.

Bernath, M. *Die Malerei des Mittelalters*. Leipzig, A. Kroener, 1916.

Bernt & Burdach. *See* Johannes von Tepl, above, II.

Berschin, Walter. *Griechisch-lateinisches Mittelalter*: Von Hieronymus zu Nikolaus von Kues. Bern, Francke, 1980.

Besseler, Heinrich. *Musik des Mittelalters und der Renaissance*. Potsdam, Athenaion, 1931. Bueckens Handbuch der Musikwissenschaft.

Besserman, Lawrence L. *The Legend of Job in the Middle Ages*. Cambridge, Mass., Harvard University Press, 1979.

Biers, William R. *The Archaeology of Greece*. Ithaca, N.Y., Cornell University Press, 1980.

Bigi, Quirino. "Di Azzo da Correggio e dei Correggi." R. R. Deputazioni di storia patria per le provincie modenesi e parmensi. *Atti e memorie* 3 (1866), pp. 211–258.

Billanovich, Giuseppe. "Petrarca e Cicerone." *Miscellanea Giov. Mercati*. Vol. iv. Città del Vaticano, 1946, pp. 88–106.

———. *Petrarca letterato*. i. Lo scrittoio del Petrarca. Rome, Edizioni di Storia e Letteratura, 1947.

———. *Un nuovo esempio delle scoperte e delle letture del Petrarca: L'Eusebio-Girolamo-Pseudo Prospero*. Krefeld, Scherpe, 1954.

———. "Nella biblioteca del Petrarca. i. Il Petrarca, il Boccaccio e le *Ennarrationes in Psalmos* di S. Agostino. ii. Un altro Svetonio del Petrarca (Oxford, Exeter College, 186)." *IMU* 3 (1960), 1–58.

––––––. "Il Petrarca e il Ventoso." *IMU* 9 (1966), pp. 369–401.

––––––. "La Bibliothèque de Pétrarque et les bibliothèques médiévales de France et de Flandre." *L'Humanisme médiéval dans les littératures romanes du XII*[e] *au XIV*[e] *siècles.* Paris, Centre de Philologie et de littératures romanes, 1966, pp. 205–216.

––––––. *La Tradizione del Testo di Livio e le Origini dell' Umanesimo.* 2 vols. Padua, Antenore, 1981, 1985. Studi sul Petrarca, 9.

Binni, Walter, ed. *I classici italiani nella storia della critica.* 2 vols. Florence, La Nuova Italia, 1962.

Biraben, J.-N. *Les hommes et la peste.* 2 vols. The Hague, Mouton, 1975.

Bishop, Morris. *Petrarch and His World.* Bloomington, Indiana University Press, 1963.

––––––. *The Horizon Book of the Middle Ages.* Ed. M. Bishop and N. Kotker. New York, American Heritage; Boston, Houghton Mifflin, 1968.

Bishop (1966). *See* Petrarch, *Fam.*; and *Sen.*, above, I, iii.

(Bishop). *See also* Petrarch, below.

Blake (1964). *See The Phoenix,* above, II.

Bloch, Marc. *Feudal Society.* Chicago, University of Chicago Press, 1961.

––––––. *Slavery and Serfdom in the Middle Ages.* Berkeley, University of California Press, 1975.

Bloomfield, Morton W. *The Seven Deadly Sins.* N.p., Michigan State College Press, 1952.

––––––. *Incipits of Latin Works on the Virtues and Vices, 1108–1500* A.D. Cambridge, Mass., Medieval Academy of America, 1979.

Boardman, John, Jasper Griffin, and Oswyn Murray. *The Oxford History of the Classical World.* Oxford, Oxford University Press, 1986.

Bocheński, I. M. *A History of Formal Logic.* Notre Dame, Ind., University of Notre Dame Press, 1961.

Boitani, Piero, ed. *Chaucer and the Italian Trecento.* Cambridge, The University Press, 1983.

Bolgar, R. R., ed. *Classical Influences on European Culture,* A.D. *500–1500.* Cambridge, The University Press, 1971.

Bonner, Anthony, ed. and trans. *Selected Works of Ramon Llull (1232–1316).* 2 vols. Princeton, Princeton University Press, 1985.

Bosco, Umberto. "Particolari danteschi." *Annali della R. Scuola Normale Superiore di Pisa, Lettere, storia, e filosofia,* ser. 2, xi (1942), pp. 131–147.

Bowder, Diana. *Who Was Who in the Roman World.* Phaidon, Ithaca, N.Y., Cornell University Press, 1980.

Boyde, Patrick. *Dante Philomythes and Philosopher.* Cambridge, The University Press, 1981.

Bradley, Ritamary. "Backgrounds of the Title *Speculum* in Medieval Literature." *Speculum* 29 (1954), pp. 100–115.

Braudel, Fernand. *Civilization and Capitalism, 15th–18th Century*. New York, Harper & Row. Vol. i: The Structures of Everyday Life (1981); vol. ii: The Wheels of Commerce (1982); vol. iii: The Perspective of the World (1984).

Braudy, Leo. *The Frenzy of Renown*: Fame and Its History. New York, Oxford University Press, 1986. —This important book came to my attention too late to be considered here.

Breviarium Romanum . . . 4 vols. Rome, Desclée, 1908.

Brewer, Derek. *Chaucer and His World*. New York, Dodd, Mead & Co., 1978.

Brewer's Dictionary of Phrase and Fable. Ed. I. H. Evans. New York, Harper & Row, 1970.

Brieger, Peter, M. Meiss, and C. S. Singleton. *Illuminated Manuscripts of the Divine Comedy*. 2 vols. Princeton, Princeton University Press, 1969.

Brower, Reuben A., ed. *On Translation*. Cambridge, Mass., Harvard University Press, 1959. Harvard Studies in Comparative Literature, 23.

Bryan and Dempster. *Sources and Analogues of Chaucer's Canterbury Tales*. Ed. W. F. Bryan and G. Dempster. New York, Humanities Press, 1958.

Buchheim, Karl. *Wahrheit und Geschichte*. Leipzig, Jakob Hegner, 1935.

Buck, Carl D. *A Dictionary of Selected Synonyms in the Principal Indo-European Languages*. Chicago, University of Chicago Press, 1949.

Bugenhagen, Johann. *In librum psalmorum interpretatio*. Nuremberg, J. Petreius, 1524.

Burckhardt, Jacob. *The Age of Constantine the Great* (1852). Trans. M. Hadas. New York, Pantheon, 1949.

––––––– . *The Civilization of the Renaissance* (1878). London, Phaidon, 1944.

––––––– . *Der Cicerone* (1907). Leipzig, A. Kroener, 1935.

Burdach, Konrad, ed. *Aus Petrarcas aeltestem deutschen Schuelerkreise*. Berlin, Weidmann, 1929. Vom Mittelalter zur Reformation, 4.

––––––– . *Der Dichter des Ackermann aus Boehmen und seine Zeit*. Berlin, Weidmann, 1926, 1932. Vom Mittelalter zur Reformation, 3, 2.

Burdach, Konrad, and Paul Piur. *Briefwechsel des Cola di Rienzo*. 5 vols. Berlin, Weidmann, 1912–1929. Vom Mittelalter zur Reformation, 2, 1–5.

Burley (1953). *See* Augustine, above, II.

Burrow, J. A. *The Ages of Man*: A Study of Medieval Writing and *Thought*. Oxford, Clarendon Press, 1986.

Burton, Robert. *The Anatomy of Melancholy* (1621). Ed. F. Dell and P. Jordan-Smith. New York, Tudor Publishing, 1948.

Bury, J. B. *A History of Greece to the Death of Alexander the Great* (1913). New York, Random House, n.d. Modern Library.

Butler, Christopher. *Number Symbolism*. London, Routledge & Kegan Paul, 1970.

Caggese, Romolo. *Roberto d'Angiò e i suoi tempi*. 2 vols. Florence, R. Bemporad, 1922–1930.

Calin, William. *A Poet at the Fountain*: Essays on the Narrative Verse of Guillaume de Machaut. Lexington, University Press of Kentucky, 1974.

Campbell, Joseph. *The Mythic Image.* Princeton, Princeton University Press, 1974. Bollingen Series, 100.

Cantor, Norman F. *Medieval History.* New York, Macmillan, 1963.

Carrara, Enrico. *Studi petrarcheschi ed altri scritti.* Turin, Bottega d'Erasmo, 1959.

Cary, G. *The Medieval Alexander.* Cambridge, The University Press, 1956.

Cassell (1975). *See* Boccaccio, *Il Corbaccio,* above, II.

Cassirer, Ernst. *Individuum und Kosmos in der Philosophie der Renaissance* (1927). Darmstadt, Wissenschaftliche Buchgesellschaft, 1963.

Cayré, F. *Manual of Patrology and History of Theology.* 2 vols. Paris, Desclée, 1935, 1940.

Cecchi, Emilio, and Natalino Sapegno. *Storia della Letteratura Italiana.* Vol. i: Le origini e il Duecento; vol. ii: Il Trecento. Milan, Garzanti, 1965.

Ceglar, S. *William of Saint Thierry: The Chronology of His Life.* Washington, D.C., Ph.D. diss., Catholic University of America, 1971.

La Celestina (1499). *Celestina: Tragicomedia de Calisto y Melibea.* By Fernando de Rojas. Ed. Miguel Marciales. 2 vols. Urbana, University of Illinois Press, 1985. Illinois Medieval Monographs, 1.

————. *The Celestina.* Trans. L. B. Simpson. Berkeley, University of California Press, 1955.

Cervone, Antonio. *Constitutionum Regni Siciliarum libri iii, cum commentariis Veterum Jurisconsultorum.* Naples, 1773.

Chandler, S. Bernard, and Julius A. Molinaro. *The Culture of Italy, Mediaeval to Modern.* Toronto, Griffin House, 1979.

Chapman, John Jay. *Lucian, Plato and Greek Morals.* Boston, Houghton Mifflin, 1931.

Chenu, M.-D. *Toward Understanding Saint Thomas* (1950). Chicago, Henry Regnery, 1964.

————. *Nature, Man and Society in the Twelfth Century* (1957). Ed. J. Taylor and L. K. Little. Chicago, University of Chicago Press, 1968.

Chevalier, Ulysse. *Répertoire des sources historiques du Moyen-Âge*: Bio-bibliographie. 2 vols. (1905–1907). New York, Kraus Reprint Corp., 1960.

Chiovenda, L. "Die Zeichnungen Petrarcas." *Archivum Romanicum* 16 (1933), pp. 1–61.

Ciapponi, Lucia A. "Il '*De architectura*' di Vitruvio nel primo Umanesimo." *IMU* 3 (1960), pp. 59–99.

Clark, John W. *The Care of Books.* Cambridge, The University Press, 1902.

Clagett (1968). *See* Nicole Oresme, above, II.

Classical Studies in Honor of B. L. Ullman. 2 vols. Rome, Ediz. di Storia e Letteratura, 1964.

Cochin, Henry. *Un ami de Pétrarque*: Lettres de Francesco Nelli à Pétrarque. Paris, H. Champion, 1892.

————. *Un amico di Francesco Petrarca*: Le lettere del Nelli al Petrarca. Florence, Le Monnier, 1901.

_____ . *Le frère de Pétrarque et le livre Du repos des religieux*. Paris, Bouillon, 1903.

Coffman, G. R. "Old Age from Horace to Chaucer: Some Literary Affinities and Adventures of an Idea." *Speculum* 9 (1934), pp. 249–258.

Cohen, Gustave. *La "Comédie" latine en France au XIIᵉ siècle*. 2 vols. Paris, Société d'Édition "Les Belles-Lettres," 1931. Collection Latine du Moyen Âge.

Cohen, Morris R., and I. E. Drabkin. *A Source Book in Greek Science*. Cambridge, Mass., Harvard University Press, 1948.

Colie, Rosalie L. *Paradoxia Epidemica*: The Renaissance Tradition of Paradox. Princeton, Princeton University Press, 1966.

Colish, Marcia L. *The Mirror of Language*: A Study in the Medieval Theory of Knowledge. New Haven, Yale University Press, 1968.

_____ . "St. Augustine's Rhetoric of Silence Revisited." *Augustinian Studies* 9 (1978), pp. 15–24.

_____ . *The Stoic Tradition from Antiquity to the Early Middle Ages*. 2 vols. Leiden, E. J. Brill, 1985. Studies in the History of Christian Thought, 34–35. —This notable work arrived too late to be included as basic reference in many of my notes.

Coluccio Salutati. *See* Salutati, Coluccio.

Concordantiarum SS. Scripturae Manuale. Paris, V. Lecoffre, 1950.

Contamine, Philippe. *War in the Middle Ages*. Oxford, Blackwell, 1984.

Coogan, Robert. "Petrarch's Latin Prose and the English Renaissance." *Studies in Philology* 68 (1971), esp. pp. 274–275.

_____ . *Babylon on the Rhone*: A Translation of Letters by Dante, Petrarch, and Catherine of Siena on the Avignon Papacy. Madrid, J. Porrúa Turanzas, 1983.

Cooke, Thomas D. *The Present State of Scholarship in Fourteenth-Century Literature*. Columbia, University of Missouri Press, 1982.

Cornelius, Roberta D. *The Figurative Castle*: A Study in the Medieval Allegory of the Edifice with Especial Reference to Religious Writings. Bryn Mawr, Pa., 1930.

Corrigan, B. "Petrarch in English." *Italica* 50 (1973), pp. 400–407.

Cosenza (1910). *See* Petrarch, *Fam.*, above, I, iii.

Cosenza (1913). *Petrarch*: The Revolution of Cola di Rienzo. Chicago, University of Chicago Press, 1913. Repr. New York, Italica Press, 1986.

Cosman, Madeleine P. *Fabulous Feasts*. New York, G. Braziller, 1976.

Cottrell, Leonard. *Wonders of Antiquity*. London, Longmans, Green, 1959.

Coulter, G. G. *Medieval Panorama*. Cambridge, The University Press, 1934.

_____ . *From St. Francis to Dante*: Translations from the Chronicle of the Franciscan Salimbene (1221–1288). Philadelphia, University of Pennsylvania Press, 1972.

Courcelle, Pierre. "Tradition platonicienne et traditions chrétiennes du corps-prison (Phaedon 62b; Cratyle 400c)." *Revue des études latines* 43 (1965), pp. 406–443.

————. *La Consolation de Philosophie dans la Tradition Littéraire*: Antécédents et posterité de Boèce. Paris, Études Augustiniennes, 1967.

Coussemaker, E. de. *Histoire de l'harmonie au Moyen Âge*. Paris, V. Didron, 1852.

Cowell, F. R. *Cicero and the Roman Republic*. New York, Chantecleer, 1948.

Crombie, A. C. *Medieval and Early Modern Science*. 2 vols. New York, Doubleday-Anchor, 1959.

Cunliffe, John W. *See* Gascoigne.

Curtius, Ernst Robert. *European Literature and the Latin Middle Ages*. New York, Pantheon, 1953. Bollingen Series, 36.

————. *Kritische Essays zur europaeischen Literatur*. Bern, Francke, 1950.

Curtius, Ludwig. *Rome*. New York, Pantheon, 1950.

Dahlberg (1971). *See Roman de la Rose*, above, II.

Daumas, Maurice, ed. *Histoire de la science*. Paris, Gallimard, 1957. Encyclopédie de la Pléiade, 5.

Davenport, Millia. *The Book of Costume*. 2 vols. New York, Crown, 1948.

Davies (1968). *See* Macrobius, *Saturn.*, above, II.

Deane (1966). *See* Anselm of Canterbury, above, II.

De Bruyne, Edgar. *Études d'esthétique médiévale*. 3 vols. Brugge, De Tempel, 1946.

Delachenal, Roland. *Histoire de Charles V*. 2 vols. Paris, A. Picard, 1909.

Del Monte, Alberto. "Sul testo del 'De remediis' petrarchescho." *Filologia Romanza* 3 (1956), 84–86.

De Lubac, Henri. *Exégèse médiévale*: Les quatre sense de l'Écriture. Paris, Aubier. Vol. i, 1 and 2, 1959; vol. ii, 1, 1961; vol. ii, 2, 1964.

Demaray, John G. *The Invention of Dante's Commedia*. New Haven, Yale University Press, 1974.

Deyermond, A. D. *The Petrarchan Sources of* La Celestina. Oxford, Oxford University Press, 1961.

Di Benedetto, L. *Da Giacomo da Lentino a Francesco Petrarca*. Naples, Astrea, 1949, pp. 61–62, on *Fam.* vii, 8.

Dick (1925). *See* Martianus Capella, above, II.

Diekstra, F. N. M. *A Dialogue between Reason and Adversity*: A Late Middle English Version of Petrarch's *De remediis*. Assen, Van Gorcum-Prakke, 1968.

Donaldson, E. T. *Speaking of Chaucer*. London, Athlone, 1970.

Doren, A. "Fortuna in Mittelalter und in der Renaissance." *Vortraege der Bibliothek Warburg* 2 (1922–1923), pp. 71–144.

Dornseiff, F. "Literarische Verwendungen des Beispiels." *Vortraege der Bibliothek Warburg* 3 (1924–1925).

Dreves, Guido M., and Clemens Blume. *Ein Jahrtausend lateinischer Hymnendichtung*. 2 vols. Leipzig, O. R. Reisland, 1909.

Dronke, Peter. *Medieval Latin and the Rise of European Love-Lyric*. 2 vols. Oxford, Clarendon Press, 1965, 1966.

————. *The Medieval Lyric*. Cambridge, Cambridge University Press, 1977.

Duby, Georges. *The Chivalrous Society*. Berkeley, University of California Press, 1980. (1980a)

_____ . *The Three Orders*: Feudal Society Imagined. Chicago, University of Chicago Press, 1980. (1980b)

_____ . *The Age of the Cathedrals*. Chicago, University of Chicago Press, 1981.

Duhem Pierre. *Le système du monde*. 10 vols. Paris, Hermann, 1913–1959.

Dumur, Guy. *Histoire des Spectacles*. Paris, Gallimard, 1965. Encyclopédie de la Pléiade, 19.

Durham, Frank, and Robert D. Purrington. *Frame of the Universe*: A History of Physical Cosmology. New York, Columbia University Press, 1983.

Dziedzic, Margarita, et al. "The Binghamton Manuscript of Petrarch." *Manuscripta* 25 (1981), pp. 35–42.

Eco, Umberto. *Postscript* to The Name of the Rose. San Diego, Harcourt, Brace, Jovanovich, 1983.

Elbow, Peter. *Oppositions in Chaucer*. Middletown, Conn., Wesleyan University Press, 1975.

Eliade, Mircea. *The Myth of the Eternal Return*; or, Cosmos and History. Princeton, Princeton University Press, 1954. Bollingen Series, 46.

Elliott, T. J. *A Medieval Bestiary*. British Museum, Arundel 292; Boston, Godine, 1971.

Essling, Victor Masséna, prince d', and Eugène Muentz. *Pétrarque, ses études d'art*. Paris, Gazette des Beaux-Arts, 1902.

Evans, G. R. *Alan of Lille*. Cambridge, The University Press, 1983.

Evans, Joan. *Art in Medieval France, 987–1498*. London, Oxford University Press, 1948.

_____ . *Life in Medieval France*. London, Phaidon, 1969.

Fabricius, Joh. Albert. *Bibliographia antiquaria*. Hamburg, C. Liebezeit, 1716.

_____ . *Bibliotheca latina mediae et infimae aetatis*. 6 vols. Hamburg, Vid. Felgineria, Bohn, 1734–1746.

_____ . *Bibliotheca latina nunc melius delecta* . . . Io. Aug. Ernesti. 3 vols. Leipzig, Weidmann, 1773–1774.

Fallani, Giovanni. " 'D'entro Siratti': Il paragone della lebbra di Costantino." *Lettere italiane* 10 (1958), pp. 55–60.

Fedele, P. "Stefano Colonna." *Nuova antologia*, CD vii (1940), pp. 234–243.

Ferante, Giuseppina. "Lombardo della Setta Umanista Padovano (?–1390)." R. Istituto Veneto di Scienze, Lettere de Arti, *Atti* 93 (1933–1934): 445–487.

Ferguson, George. *Signs and Symbols in Christian Art*. New York, Oxford University Press, 1954.

Ferguson, Wallace K. *The Renaissance in Historical Thought*. Boston, Houghton Mifflin, 1948.

Finke, H. G. *Furcht und Hoffnung als antithetische Denkform in der roemischen Literatur von Plautus bis Tacitus*. Tuebingen, Ph.D. diss., 1951.

Fisher, John H. *John Gower*. New York, New York University Press, 1964.

Fiske, Daniel Willard. "Francis Petrarch's Treatise *De Remediis utriusque Fortunae*." *Bibliographical Notices* 3, Florence, Le Monnier, 1888.

Fleming, John V. *The Roman de la Rose*: A Study in Allegory and Iconography. Princeton, Princeton University Press, 1969.

Fletcher, Angus. *Allegory*. Ithaca, Cornell University Press, 1964.

Flinn, John. *Le Roman de Renart dans la littérature française et dans les littératures etrangères au Moyen Âge*. Paris, Ph.D. diss., 1963.

Focillon, Henri. *The Year 1000*. New York, Ungar, 1969.

Folklore, Myths and Legends of Britain. London, Reader's Digest Assoc. Ltd, 1977.

Fontaine, Jacques. *Isidore de Seville et la culture classique dans L'espagne Wisigothique*. 2 vols. Paris, Études Augustiniennes, 1959.

Foresti, Arnaldo. *Aneddoti della vita di Francesco Petrarca* (1928). Ed. A. T. Benvenuti. Padua, Antenore, 1977.

Fort, George F. *Medical Economy during the Middle Ages* (1883). New York, A. M. Kelley, 1970.

Foster, Kenelm. *Petrarch*: Poet and Humanist. Edinburgh, Edinburgh University Press, 1984. Writers of Italy Series, 9.

Fowler (1952). *See Piers the Plowman*, above, II.

Fowler, Alastair, ed. *Silent Poetry*: Essays in Numerological Analysis. London, Routledge & Kegan Paul, 1970. (1970a)

———. *Triumphal Forms*: Structural Patterns in Elizabethan Poetry. Cambridge, The University Press, 1970. (1970b)

Fowler, Mary. *Cornell University Library Catalogue of the Petrarch Collection Bequeathed by Willard Fiske*. London, Oxford University Press, 1916. *See also* Fucilla.

Fox, Robin Lane. *The Search for Alexander*. Boston, Little, Brown, 1980.

Francon, Marcel. "Petrarch, Disciple of Heraclitus." *Speculum* 11 (1938), pp. 256–271.

Frankl, Paul. *The Gothic*: Literary Sources and Interpretations through Eight Centuries. Princeton, Princeton University Press, 1960.

Frappier, Jean. *Amour courtois et Table Ronde*. Geneva, Droz, 1973.

Fraser, J. T. *The Voices of Time*. New York, Braziller, 1966.

Frey, Dagobert. *Gotik und Renaissance als Grundlagen der modernen Weltanschauung*. Augsburg, B. Filser, 1929.

Friedmann, John Block. *Orpheus in the Middle Ages*. Cambridge, Mass., Harvard University Press, 1970.

———. *The Monstrous Races in Medieval Art and Thought*. Cambridge, Mass., Harvard University Press, 1981.

Fucilla, Joseph G. *Oltre un cinquantennio di scritti sul Petrarca* (1916–1973). Padua, Antenore, 1982.

Gaffurius, Franchinus. *Practica musicae* (1496). Ed. C. A. Miller. Rome, American Institute of Musicology, 1968.

Gardner, E. G. *The Arthurian Legend in Italian Literature*. London, J. M. Dent, 1930.

Gardner, John. *The Life and Times of Chaucer*. New York, A. A. Knopf, 1977.

Garraty, John A., and Peter Gay. *The Columbia History of the World*. New York, Harper & Row, 1972.

Gascoigne, George. *The Complete Works*. Ed. John W. Cunliffe. 2 vols. Cambridge, The University Press, 1907, 1910.

Gasparotto, Giovanni. "Il Petrarca conosceva direttamente Lucrezio. Le fonti dell' egloga ix, 'Querulus' del *Bucolicum carmen*." *Atti e mem. dell' Acad. di scienze, lettere ed arti in Padova* 80 (1967–68), pp. 309–355.

Gautier, Léon. *La chevalerie*. Paris, Ch. Delagrave, 1883.

Gennrich, Friedrich. *Grundriss einer Formenlehre des mittelalterlichen Liedes*. Halle, Niemeyer, 1932.

Gentile, Giovanni. *Studi sul rinascimento*. 2d ed. Florence, Sansoni, 1936.

Gérold, Théodore. *Histoire de la musique des origines à la fin du XIVe siècle*. Paris, Renouard, 1936.

Gerosa, Pietro Paolo. *Umanesimo Cristiano del Petrarca*. Turin, Bottega d'Erasmo, 1966.

Ghellinck, J. de. "Nani et gigantes." *Bulletin du Cange* 18 (1945), pp. 25–29.

———. "Iuventus, gravitas, senectus." In *Studia Medievalia R. J. Martin*. Brugge, De Tempel, 1948.

Gibbon, Edward. *The Decline and Fall of the Roman Empire* (1787–1789). Ed. J. B. Bury. 7 vols. London, Methuen, 1909–1914. New York, Random House, n.d. Modern Library. 2 vols.

Gide, André, ed. *Anthologie de la Poésie Française*. Paris, Gallimard, 1949.

Gilman, Stephen. *The Art of* La Celestina. Madison, University of Wisconsin Press, 1956.

Gilson, Etienne. *Les Idées et les lettres*. Paris, J. Vrin, 1932.

———. *The Spirit of Medieval Philosophy*. New York, Scribner's, 1940.

———. *History of Christian Philosophy in the Middle Ages*. New York, Random House, 1955.

———. *The Christian Philosophy of St. Thomas Aquinas*. New York, Random House, 1956.

———. *Painting and Reality*. New York, Pantheon, 1957. Bollingen Series, 35, 4.

———. *The Christian Philosophy of Saint Augustine*. New York, Random House, 1960.

Gingerich, Owen, ed. *The Nature of Scientific Discovery*. Washington, D.C., Smithsonian Institution Press, 1975.

Glare, P. G. W., ed. *Oxford Latin Dictionary*. Oxford, Clarendon Press, 1982.

Gmelin, Hermann. "Das Prinzip der Imitatio in den romanischen Literaturen der Renaissance." *Romanische Forschungen* 46 (1932).

Godi, C. "L'Orazione del Petrarca per Giovanni il Buono." *IMU* 8 (1965), 45–83. "La 'Collatio laureationis' del Petrarca." *IMU* 13 (1970), 1–27.

Godolphin (1942). *See* Herodotus, above, II.

Goetz, Walter, et al. *Das Mittelalter bis zum Ausgang der Staufer, 400–1250*. Berlin, Propyläen Verlag, 1932. Propyläen Weltgeschichte, 3.

———— . *Das Zeitalter der Gotik und Renaissance, 1250–1500*. Berlin, Propylaeen Verlag, 1932. Propylaeen Weltgeschichte, 4.

Goldstaub, Max, and Richard Wendriner. *Ein Tosco-Venezianischer Bestiarius*. Halle, Niemeyer, 1892.

Goldstein, Bernard R. *The Astronomy of Levi ben Gerson (1288–1344)*. New York, Springer Verlag, 1985. Studies in the History of Mathematics and Physical Sciences, 11.

Gombrich, E. H. *Norm and Form*. London, Phaidon, 1966.

———— . *Symbolic Images*. London, Phaidon, 1972.

Goodrich, Norma L. *The Ways of Love*: Eleven Romances of Medieval France. N.p., Beacon Press, 1964.

Gottfried, Robert S. *The Black Death*: Natural and Human Disaster in Medieval Europe. New York, Free Press, 1983.

Gower, John. *See* above, II.

Grabes, Herbert. *The Mutable Glass*. Cambridge, The University Press, 1982.

Grabmann, Martin. *Mittelalterliches Geistesleben*. 3 vols. Munich, Max Huber, 1926–1956.

Grant, Edward. *Physical Science in the Middle Ages*. Cambridge, The University Press, 1977. (1971b)

———— . *A Source Book in Medieval Science*. Cambridge, Mass., Harvard University Press, 1974.

Grant (1966), Grant (1971a). *See* Nicole Oresme, above, II.

Grant, Michael. *Cities of Vesuvius*: Pompeii and Herculaneum. Harmondsworth, Penguin Books, 1976.

Grant, W. Leonard. *Neo-Latin Literature and the Pastoral*. Chapel Hill, University of North Carolina Press, 1965.

Graves, Robert. *The Greek Myths*. 2 vols. Baltimore, Penguin Books, 1955.

Green, Dennis H. *Irony in the Medieval Romance*. Cambridge, The University Press, 1979.

Green, Louis. *Chronicles into History*: An Essay on the Interpretation of History in Florentine Fourteenth Century Chronicles. Cambridge, The University Press, 1972.

Green, William M. "*Initium omnis peccati superbia*: Augustine on Pride as the First Sin." *University of California Publications in Classical Philology* 13 (1949), pp. 407–432.

Greene, Thomas M. *The Light in Troy*: Imitation and Discovery in Renaissance Poetry. New Haven, Yale University Press, 1982.

Gregorovius, Ferdinand. *Geschichte der Stadt Rom im Mittelalter* (1872). Ed. F. Schillmann. 2 vols. Dresden, W. Jess, 1926.

Group μ. *A General Rhetoric*. Baltimore, Johns Hopkins University Press, 1981.

Gruber, Joachim. "Die Erscheinung der Philosophie in der *Consolatio Philosophiae* des Boethius." *Rheinisches Museum fuer Philologie* 112 (1969), pp. 166–186.

———— . *Kommentar zu Boethius*: De consolatione philosophiae. Berlin, Walter De Gruyter, 1978.

Grupp, Georg. *Kulturgeschichte des Mittelalters.* 6 vols. Paderborn, F. Schoeningh, 1923–1932.

Haase, Friedrich. *Animadversiones ad Senecae libros De rem. fort. et De nat. quaest.* Breslau, Typ. acad., 1859.

Haase (1881); Haase (1886). *See* Seneca, above, II.

Hadas, Moses. *A History of Latin Literature.* New York, Columbia University Press, 1952.

———. *Ancilla to Classical Reading.* New York, Columbia University Press, 1954.

———. *A History of Rome.* Garden City, N.Y., Doubleday-Anchor, 1956.

Hale, William Harlan. *The Horizon Cookbook and Illustrated History of Eating and Drinking through the Ages.* New York, American Heritage, 1968.

Halm (1863). *See* above, II.

Hammerstein, Reinhold. *Die Musik der Engel.* Bern, Francke, 1962.

———. *Diabolus in Musica.* Bern, Francke, 1974.

———. *Tanz und Musik des Todes*: Die mittelalterlichen Totentaenze und ihr Nachleben. Bern, Francke, 1980.

Handschin, Werner. *Francesco Petrarca als Gestalt der Historiographie.* Basel, Helbing & Lichtenhahn, 1964.

Harvey, Paul. *The Oxford Companion to Classical Literature.* Oxford, Clarendon Press, 1974.

Haskins, Charles Homer. *Studies in the History of Mediaeval Science.* Cambridge, Mass., Harvard University Press, 1927.

———. *The Renaissance of the Twelfth Century.* Cambridge, Mass., Harvard University Press, 1933.

Hauréau, B. "Mémoire sur quelques Traductions de *L'Economiques* d'Aristote." Académie des Inscriptions et Belles Lettres, *Mémoires* 30 (1881), part 1, pp. 463–482.

Heitmann, Klaus. "La genesi del *De remediis utriusque fortune* del Petrarca." *Convivium,* N.S. (1957), pp. 9–30.

———. *Fortuna und Virtus*: Eine Studie zu Petrarcas Lebensweisheit. Koeln, Boehlau, 1958.

———. "Augustins Lehre in Petrarcas *Secretum.*" *Bibliothèque Humanisme et Renaissance* 22 (1960), pp. 34–53.

Henschel, A. W. "Petrarcas Urtheil ueber die Medizin und die Aerzte seiner Zeit." *Janus* (Breslau) 1 (1846), pp. 183–223.

Hervieux, Léopold. *Les fabulistes latins.* 5 vols. Paris, Firmin-Didot, 1893–1899.

Hesbert, Dom René-Jean. *Antiphonale Missarum sextuplex.* Brussels, Vromant, 1935.

Hicks, Eric C., and Ezio Ornato. "Jean de Montreuil et le Débat sur le Roman de la Rose." *Romania* 98 (1977), pp. 34–64, 186–219.

Highet, Gilbert. *The Classical Tradition.* New York, Oxford University Press, 1949.

———. *The Anatomy of Satire.* Princeton, Princeton University Press, 1962.

Hillgarth, J. N. *Ramon Llull and Llullism in Fourteenth-Century France.* Oxford, Clarendon Press, 1971.

Hirsch, E. D., Jr. *Validity in Interpretation*. New Haven, Yale University Press, 1967.

Hodgkin, Thomas. *Italy and Her Invaders*. 8 vols. Oxford, Oxford University Press, 1880–1899.

Hohl, E. "Petrarca und der Palatinus 869 der *Historia Augusta*." *Hermes* 11 (1916), pp. 154–159.

Hollander, John. *The Untuning of the Sky*. Princeton, Princeton University Press, 1961.

Hollander, Robert. *Boccaccio's Two Venuses*. New York, Columbia University Press, 1977.

Hollway-Calthrop, H. C. *Petrarch*: His Life and Times. (1907). New York, Cooper Square Pub., 1972.

Holmes, Urban T. *A History of Old French Literature from the Origins to 1300*. New York, F. S. Crofts, 1948.

Holt, Elizabeth Gilmore. *Literary Sources of Art History*. Princeton, Princeton University Press, 1947.

Hortis, Attilio. *Scritti inediti di Francesco Petrarca*. *See* Petrarch, Orations, above, I, ii.

––––––. "Le Additiones al *De remediis fortuitorum* di Seneca . . . " *Archeografo triestino* 6 (1879), fasc. iii. Triest, L. Hermanstorfer, 1879.

Howard, Donald R. *The Three Temptations*. Princeton, Princeton University Press, 1966.

Hubaux, Jean, and Maxime Leroy. *Le mythe du Phénix dan les littératures grecque et latins*. Liège, Bibliothèque du philosophie et lettres de l'Université de Liège, 82, 1939.

Huizinga, J. *Herbst des Mittelalters*. 3d ed. Leipzig, A. Kroener, 1930.

––––––. *Homo ludens*: Versuch einer Bestimmung des Spielelementes der Kultur. Basel, Pantheon, 1938.

Huppé, Bernard F. *Doctrine and Poetry*. Augustine's Influence on Old-English Poetry. Albany, State University of New York, 1959.

Huppé, Bernard F., and D. W. Robertson. *Fruyt and Chaf*: Studies in Chaucer's Allegories. Princeton, Princeton University Press, 1963.

Immerwahr, Henry R. *Form and Thought in Herodotus*. Cleveland, Press of Western Reserve University, 1966. American Philological Society, Monograph 23.

Isaeus, Jos. *Notae in Div. inst. See* Lactantius, above, II.

Jackson, W. T. H. "The Progress of Parzival and the Trees of Virtue and Vice." *Germanic Review* 33 (1958), pp. 118–124. Repr. in idem, *The Challenge of the Medieval Text*, New York, Columbia University Press, 1985, chap. 14.

––––––. "Allegory and Allegorization." *Research Studies* 32 (1964), pp. 161–175. Repr. in idem, *The Challenge of the Medieval Text*, chap. 10.

Jacobs, Jay, ed. *The Horizon Book of Great Cathedrals*. New York, American Heritage, 1968.

Jacobus, Melancthon W., et al. *Funk and Wagnalls New Standard Bible Dictionary*. Garden City, N.Y., Garden City Books, 1936.

Jacquin, A. M. *Histoire de l'Église*. 3 vols. Paris, Desclée, de Brouwer, 1928–1948.

James (1983). *See* Walter Map, above, II.

Jammers, Ewald. *Das koenigliche Liederbuch des deutschen Minnesangs*. Heidelberg, L. Schneider, 1965.

Janson, H. W. *Apes and Ape Lore in the Middle Ages and the Renaissance*. London, Warburg Institute, 1952.

―――― . *History of Art*. Englewood Cliffs, N.J., Prentice Hall, 1962.

Jasenas, Michael. *Petrarch in America*: A Survey of Petrarchan Manuscripts. New York, Pierpoint Morgan Library, 1974.

Javelet, Robert. *Image et ressemblance au douzième siècle*: De Saint Anselme à Alain de Lille. 2 vols. Paris, Letouzey & Ané, 1967.

Jeauneau, E. "*Nani gigantum humeris insidentes*: Essai d'interpretation de Bernard de Chartres." *Vivarium* 5 (1967), pp. 79–99.

Jungmann, Josef Andreas. *Missarum sollemnia*: Eine genetische Erklaerung der roemischen Messe. 2 vols. Vienna, Herder, 1949.

Kahn, Arthur D. *The Education of Julius Caesar*. New York, Schocken Books, 1986.

Kamerbeek, J. "La dignité humaine: Esquisse d'une terminographie." *Neophilologus* 41 (1957), pp. 242–251.

Kantorowicz, Ernst H. *The King's Two Bodies*: A Study in Medieval Political Theology. Princeton, Princeton University Press, 1957. (1957a)

―――― . *Frederick the Second (1194–1250)*. New York, F. Ungar, 1957. (1957b)

Karlinger, Hans. *Die Kunst der Gotik*. Berlin, Propylaeenverlag, 1926. Propylaeen Kunstgeschichte, 7.

Katzenellenbogen, Adolf. *Die Psychomachie in der Kunst des Mittelalters, von den Anfaengen bis zum 13, Jahrhundert*. Hamburg, Ph.D. diss., 1933.

―――― . *Allegories of the Virtues and Vices in Medieval Art, from Early Christian Times to the Thirteenth Century*. London, Warburg Institute, 1939.

Kelly, Louis G. *The True Interpreter*. A History of Translation Theory and Practice in the West. New York, St. Martin's Press, 1979.

Kittredge, G. L. "The Canon's Yeoman's Prologue and Tale." *Transactions of the Royal Society of Literature*, 2d ser., 30 (1910), 87–95.

Klingender, Francis. *Animals in Art and Thought to the End of the Middle Ages*. Cambridge, Mass., MIT Press, 1971.

Koch, Hannesjoachim W. *Medieval Warfare*. London, Bison Books, 1978.

Koerting, Gustav. *Petrarca's Leben und Werke*. Leipzig, Fues, 1878. Geschichte der Litteratur Italiens im Zeitalter der Renaissance, 1.

Konner, Melvin. *The Tangled Wing*. Biological Constraints on the Human Spirit. New York, Holt, Rinehart & Winston, 1982.

Koonce, B. G. "Satan the Fowler." *Mediaeval Studies* (Toronto) 31 (1959), pp. 176–184.

Kornhardt, H. *Exemplum*: Eine bedeutungsgeschichtliche Studie. Goettingen, Ph.D. diss., 1936.

Kraus, Henry. *The Living Theatre of Medieval Art*. Bloomington, Indiana University Press, 1967.

Krautheimer, Richard. *Rome*: Profile of a City, 312–1308. Princeton, Princeton University Press, 1980.

Krautheimer, Richard, and Trude Krautheimer-Hess. *Lorenzo Ghiberti*. 3d ed. Princeton, Princeton University Press, 1982.

Kretzmann, Norman, et al. *The Cambridge History of Later Medieval Philosophy*: From the Rediscovery of Aristotle to the Disintegration of Scholasticism, 1100–1600. Cambridge, The University Press, 1982.

Kristeller, Paul Oskar. *Studies in Renaissance Thought and Letters*. Rome, Ediz. di Storia e Letteratura, 1956.

———— . *Eight Philosophers of the Italian Renaissance*. Stanford, Stanford University Press, 1964.

———— . *Renaissance Philosophy and the Mediaeval Tradition*. Latrobe, Pa., Archabbey Press, 1966. Wimmer Lecture, 15.

———— . *Renaissance Thought and Its Sources*. New York, Columbia University Press, 1979.

———— . *Renaissance Thought and the Arts*. (1965) Princeton, Princeton University Press, 1980.

———— . "Petrarcas Stellung in der Geschichte der Gelehrsamkeit." In Klaus W. Hempfer and Enrico Straub, eds., *Italien und die Romania in Humanismus und Renaissance*. Wiesbaden, F. Steiner, 1983.

Krutch, Joseph Wood. *Herbal*. New York, G. P. Putnam's Sons, 1965.

Kuhn, Reinhard. *The Demon of Noontide*: Ennui in Western Literature. Princeton, Princeton University Press, 1976.

Ladner, Gerhart B. *The Idea of Reform*: Its Impact on Christian Thought and Action in the Age of the Fathers. Cambridge, Mass., Harvard University Press, 1959.

———— . *Ad imaginem Dei*: The Image of Man in Medieval Art. Latrobe, Pa., Archabbey Press, 1965. Wimmer Lecture, 16.

———— . "*Homo viator*: Mediaeval Ideas on Alienation and Order." *Speculum* 42 (1967), pp. 233–259.

———— . "Medieval and Modern Understanding of Symbolism: A Comparison." *Speculum* 54 (1979), pp. 223–256.

Lamer, Hans, et al. *Woerterbuch der Antike*. Leipzig, A. Kroener, 1933.

Langer, William L. *An Encyclopedia of World History*. Boston, Houghton Mifflin, 1940.

Langosch, Karl. *Lyrische Anthologie des lateinischen Mittelalters*. Darmstadt, Wissenschaftliche Buchgesellschaft, 1968.

Landes, David. *Revolution in Time*: Clocks and the Making of the Modern World. Cambridge, Mass., Harvard University Press, 1983.

Latham, R. E. *Revised Medieval Latin Word-List from British and Irish Sources*. London, Oxford University Press, 1965.

Lausberg, Heinrich. *Handbuch der literarischen Rhethorik*. 2 vols. Munich, Max Huber, 1960.

Lechner, Joan Marie. *Renaissance Concepts of the Commonplaces*. New York, Pageant Press, 1962.

Lehmann, Paul. *Erforschung des Mittelalters*. 5 vols. Stuttgart, Hiersemann, 1959–1962.

——— . *Die Parodie im Mittelalter*. Stuttgart, Hiersemann, 1963.

Leibbrand, Werner. *Heilkunde*: Eine Problemgeschichte der Medizin. Freiburg, K. Alber, 1953.

Lerer, Seth. *Boethius and Dialogue*: Literary Method in *The Consolation of Philosophy*. Princeton, Princeton University Press, 1985.

Levi, G. A. "Pensiero classico e pensiero cristiano nel Petrarca." *Atene e Roma* 39 (1937), pp. 77–101.

Levinson, Ronald B. *In Defense of Plato*. Cambridge, Mass., Harvard University Press, 1953.

Lewis, C. S. *The Allegory of Love*. London, Oxford University Press, 1938.

——— . *The Discarded Image*: An Introduction to Medieval and Renaissance Literature. Cambridge, The University Press, 1964.

Lewis (1978). *See* Innocent III, above, II.

Leyser, Polycarp. *Historia poetarum et poematum medii aevi*. Halle, Nov. Bibliop., 1721.

Liber usualis . . . Tournai, Desclée, 1950.

Liebeschuetz, Hans. *Fulgentius metaforalis*: Ein Beitrag zur Geschichte der antiken Mythologie in Mittelalter. Leipzig-Berlin, 1926. Studien der Bibliothek Warburg, 4.

Lietzmann, Hans. *From Constantine to Julian*. New York, Charles Scribner's Sons, 1952. A History of the Early Church, 3.

Lindsay (1911). *See* Isidore of Seville, above, II.

Lippmann, E. O., von. "Petrarca ueber die Alchemie." *Archiv fuer Geschichte der Naturwissenschaften* 6 (1913), pp. 236–240.

The Liturgy of the Hours: According to the Roman Rite. 4 vols. New York, Catholic Book Publishing, 1975.

Lloyd, G. E. R. *Aristotle*: The Growth and Structure of His Thought. Cambridge, The University Press, 1968.

Lonergan, Bernard J. F. *Insight*: A Study of Human Understanding. New York, Longmans, Green, 1957.

Lottin, Odon. *Psychologie et morale aux XIIe et XIIIe siècles*. 6 vols. Gembloux, Louvain, J. Ducolot, 1942–1960.

Luce, Siméon. *Histoire de la jacquerie*. Paris, H. Champion, 1894.

Luebke, Wilhelm. *Die Kunst des Mittelalters*. Stuttgart, Paul Neff, 1923. Luebke-Semrau, Grundriss der Kunstgeschichte, 2.

Lydgate, John. *The Fall of Princes*. Ed. H. Bergen. EETS, E.S., 121–124. Oxford, 1924–1927.

Machabey, Armand. *Guillaume de Machault, 130?–1377*: La vie et l'œuvre musical. 2 vols. Paris, Richard Masse, 1955.

Majno, Guido. *The Healing Hand*: Man and Wound in the Ancient World. Cambridge, Mass., Harvard University Press, 1975.

Mâle, Emile. *Religious Art in France*: The Twelfth Century. Princeton, Princeton University Press, 1978. Bollingen Series, 90, 1.

————. *Religious Art in France*: The Thirteenth Century. Princeton, Princeton University Press, 1984. Bollingen Series, 90, 2.

————. *Religious Art in France*: The Late Middle Ages. Princeton, Princeton University Press, 1986. Bollingen Series, 90, 3.

Mallett, Michael E. *Mercenaries and Their Masters*: Warfare in Renaissance Italy. London, Longwood, 1974.

Malory, Sir Thomas. *The Works of Sir Thomas Malory*. Ed. E. Vinaver. 3 vols. Oxford, Clarendon Press, 1947.

————. *Caxton's Malory*: A New Edition of Sir Thomas Malory's *Le Morte Darthur* [1485]. Ed. J. W. Spisak and W. Matthews. 2 vols. Berkeley, University of California Press, 1983.

————. *Tales of King Arthur*. Ed. Michael Senior. New York, Schocken, 1981.

Malraux, André. *The Psychology of Art*. Trans. S. Gilbert. Vol. i: Museum without Walls; vol. ii: The Creative Act; vol. iii: The Twilight of the Absolute. New York, Pantheon, 1949–1950. Bollingen Series, 24.

————. *The Metamorphosis of the Gods*. Garden City, N.Y., Doubleday, 1960.

Manitius, Max. *Geschichte der lateinischen Literatur des Mittelalters*. 3 vols. Munich, Beck, 1911, 1923, 1931.

Mann, Nicholas. "La Fortune de Pétrarque en France: Recherches sur le 'De remediis.' " *Studi francesi* 37 (1969), pp. 9–13.

————. "The Manuscripts of Petrarch's 'De remediis': A Checklist." *IMU* 14 (1971), pp. 57–90.

————. *Petrarch Manuscripts in the British Isles*. Padua, Antenore, 1975. Censimento dei Codici Petrarcheschi, 6.

————. *Petrarch*. Oxford, Oxford University Press, 1984.

————. *A Concordance to Petrarch's* Bucolicum Carmen. Quaderni petrarcheschi ii. Pisa, Nistri-Lischi, 1984.

Manuel, Frank E., and Fritzie P. Manuel. *Utopian Thought in the Western World*. Cambridge, Mass., Harvard University Press, 1979.

Manzalaoui, M. A. " 'Ars longa, vita brevis.' " *Essays in Criticism* 12 (1962), pp. 221–224.

Marciales (1985). *See La Celestina* (1499).

Marković, M. "Odakle Seneki: *Ducunt volentem fata, nolentem trahunt?*" *Ziva Antika* (Skoplje), 1951, pp. 245–248.

Marrou, Henri-Irenée. *Saint Augustin et la fin de la culture antique*. Paris, E. de Boccard, 1938–1949.

————. *A History of Education in Antiquity*. New York, Sheed & Ward, 1956.

Marsh, David. *The Quattrocento Dialogue*: Classical Tradition and Humanist Innovation. Cambridge, Mass., Harvard University Press, 1980.

Martellotti, Guido. Francesco Petrarca, *Laura occidens. Bucolicum carmen X*: Testo, traduzione e commento. Rome, Ediz. di Storia e Letteratura, 1968.

──────. *Scritti petrarcheschi*. Ed. M. Feo and S. Rizzo. Padua, Antenore, 1983.

Martinelli, Bartolo. *Il "Secretum" conteso*. Naples, Federico Ardia, 1982.

Masi (1983). *See* Boethius, *De inst. arith.*, above, II.

Masnovo, O. "Francesco Petrarca e Azzo da Correggio." *Parma e Francesco Petrarca*. Parma, M. Fresching, 1934, pp. 181–224.

Maurer, Armand A. *Medieval Philosophy*. New York, Random House, 1962.

Maurer, Friedrich. *Leid*. Bern, Francke, 1951.

Mayer, Cornelius. *Augustinus-Lexikon*. Vol. i. Basel, Schwabe & Co., 1986.

Mazzaro, Jerome. *The Figure of Dante*: An Essay on the *Vita Nuova*. Princeton, Princeton University Press, 1981.

Mazzeo, Joseph Anthony. *Renaissance and Revolution*. New York, Pantheon, 1965.

Mazzolani, Lidia Storoni. *Empire without End*: Three Historians of Rome. New York, Harcourt, Brace, Jovanovich, 1976.

Mazzoni, F. "Per il 'topos' della gazza e del pappagallo." *IMU* 2 (1959).

Mazzotta, Giuseppe. *Dante, Poet of the Desert*. Princeton, Princeton University Press, 1979.

McCall, Andrew. *The Medieval Underworld*. London, Hamish Hamilton, 1979.

McClure, George W. "A Little Known Renaissance Manual of Consolation: Nicolaus Modrussiense's *De consolatione* 1465–1466." *Supplementum Festivum* Studies in Honor of Paul Oskar Kristeller. Ed. James Hankins et al. Binghamton, N.Y., Medieval and Renaissance Texts and Studies, 1987, pp. 247–277.

McDermott, William C. *The Ape in Antiquity*. Baltimore, Johns Hopkins University, 1938. Johns Hopkins Studies in Archaeology, 27.

McGinn, Bernard. *Visions of the End*: Apocalyptic Traditions in the Middle Ages. New York, Columbia University Press, 1979. Records of Civilization: Sources and Studies, 96.

McKinney, Loren. *Medical Illustrations in Medieval Manuscripts*. Berkeley, University of California Press, 1965.

McNeill, William H. *Venice, the Hinge of Europe, 1081–1797*. Chicago, University of Chicago Press, 1974.

──────. *Plagues and Peoples*. New York, Doubleday, 1976.

──────. *The Human Condition*. Princeton, Princeton University Press, 1980.

──────. *The Pursuit of Power*. Chicago, University of Chicago Press, 1982.

Meinel, P. *Seneca ueber seine Verbannung*. Ph.D. diss., Erlangen. Bonn, 1972.

Meiss, Millard. *Painting in Florence and Siena after the Black Death*. Princeton, Princeton University Press, 1951.

──────. *The Painter's Choice*: Problems in the Interpretation of Renaissance Art. New York, Harper & Row, 1976.

──────. *Francesco Traini*. Ed. H. B. J. Maginnis. Washington, D.C., Decatur House Press, 1983.

Menut (1968). *See* Nicole Oresme, above, II.

Merrins, E. M. "The Deaths of Antiochus IV, Herod the Great, and Herod Agrippa I." *Bibliotheca Sacra* 61 (1904), pp. 561–562.

Merton, Robert K. *On the Shoulders of Giants*: A Shandean Postscript. New York, Free Press, 1965.

Meyer-Baer, Kathi. *Music of the Spheres and the Dance of Death*: Studies in Musical Iconology. Princeton, Princeton University Press, 1970.

MGG. Die Musik in Geschichte und Gegenwart. Ed. F. Blume. 14 vols. Kassel, Baerenreiter, 1949–1968.

Milne, Lorus and Margery. *The Audubon Society Field Guide to North American Insects and Spiders*. New York, A. A. Knopf, 1980.

Minio-Paluello, L. "Il Fedone latino con note autografe del Petrarca." *Rendiconti*. Acc. Lincei, Cl. Sc. mor. viii, 4, 1949, pp. 107–113.

Minnis, A. J. *Medieval Theory of Authorship*. 2d ed. Philadelphia, University of Pennsylvania Press, 1988.

A Mirour for Magistrates: Being a true chronicle historie of the untimely fall of such unfortunate Princes and men of note . . . London, Felix Kyngston, 1610.

Misch, Georg. *Geschichte der Autobiographie*. 4 vols. in 8. Frankfurt, Schulte-Bulmke, 1949–1979.

Missale Romanum . . . Regensburg, F. Pustet, 1913.

Moé, Émile van. *Un ms. à peintures de Boèce*. Paris, Editions du Cerf, 1937.

Momigliano, Arnaldo. "Notes on Petrarch, John of Salisbury and the Institutio Traiani." [1949.] *Contributo alla storia degli studi classici*. Rome, Ediz. di Storia e Letteratura, 1955, pp. 377–379.

Mommsen, Theodor E. "Petrarch and the Decoration of the *Sala virorum illustrium* in Padua." *Art Bulletin* 34 (1952), pp. 95–116.

Mommsen (1957). *See* Petrarch, Testament, above, I, ii.

Morey, Charles Rufus. *Medieval Art*. New York, Norton, 1942.

Morhof, Daniel Georg. *Polyhistor, literarius, philosophicus et practicus*. Editio iv. Ed. Joh. Albert Fabricius. 2 vols. Luebeck, P. Boeckmann, 1747.

Mueller, C., ed. *Reliqua Arriani, et Scriptorum de rebus Alexandri Magni fragmenta*; Pseudo-Callisthenis Historiam fabulosam Itinerarium Alexandri. Paris, Firmin Didot, 1846.

Murdoch, John E., and Edith D. Sylla. *The Cultural Context of Medieval Learning*. Dordrecht, D. Reidel, 1975.

Murphy, James J. *Rhetoric in the Middle Ages*. Berkeley, University of California Press, 1974.

———. *Medieval Eloquence*. Studies in the Theory and Practice of Medieval Rhetoric. Berkeley, University of California Press, 1978.

Nelson, Benjamin. *The Idea of Usury*. Chicago, University of Chicago Press, 1969.

Nestle, Wilhelm. "Die Fabel des Menenius Agrippa." *Klio* 21 (1926–1927), pp. 350–360.

Neugebauer, Otto. *A History of Ancient Mathematical Astronomy*. 3 vols. New York and Heidelberg, Springer Verlag, 1975. Studies in the History of Mathematics and Physical Sciences, 1.

Nichols (1889). *See Mirabilia Urbis Romae*, above, II.

Niermeyer, J. F. *Mediae latinitatis lexicon minus*. 2 vols. Leiden, E. J. Brill, 1976.

Nida, Eugene A. *Toward a Science of Translating*. Leiden, E. J. Brill, 1964.

Nisbet, Robert. *History of the Idea of Progress*. New York, Basic Books, 1980.

Nolhac, Pierre de. *Pétrarque et l'humanisme* (1907). 2 vols. Paris, H. Champion, 1965.

Norton-Smith, J. *Geoffrey Chaucer*. London, Routledge, Keagan Paul, 1974.

Norwich, John J. *A History of Venice*. New York, A. A. Knopf, 1982.

Oates (1938). *See Greek Drama*, above, II.

Oates (1940). *See Epicurus*, above, II.

Oates (1948). *See Augustine*, above, II.

Oesterley (1872). *See Gesta Romanorum*, above, II.

Olschki, Leonardo. *The Genius of Italy*. New York, Oxford University Press, 1949.

Olson, Glending. *Literature as Recreation in the Later Middle Ages*. Ithaca, N.Y., Cornell University Press, 1982.

Omont, H. "Les sept merveilles du monde au moyen âge." *Bibliothèque de l'école des Chartes* (1882), pp. 40–59.

Ong, Walter J. *Ramus*: Method, and the Decay of Dialogue. Cambridge, Mass., Harvard University Press, 1958.

———. *The Presence of the Word*. New Haven, Yale University Press, 1967.

Owen, D. D. R. *Noble Lovers*. New York, New York University Press, 1975.

Owen, G. E. L. *Aristotle on Dialectic*. Oxford, Clarendon Press, 1968.

Padoan, Giorgio. " 'Colui che fece per viltà il gran rifiuto.' " *Studi danteschi* 38 (1961), pp. 75–128.

Panofsky, Erwin. *Early Netherlandish Painting*. 2 vols. Cambridge, Mass., Harvard University Press, 1953.

———. *Meaning in the Visual Arts*. Garden City, Doubleday-Anchor, 1955.

———. *Renaissance and Renascences in Western Art*. Stockholm, Almqvist & Wiksell, 1960.

———. *Studies in Iconology*. (1939) New York, Harper & Row, 1962.

Panofsky (1946). *See Suger*, above, II.

Paré, G., A. Brunet, and P. Tremblay. *La Renaissance du XIIe siècle*: Les écoles et l'enseignement. Ottawa, Institut d'Études Médiévales, 1933.

Pareyson, L. "Studi sul l'estetica del Settecento I: La dottrina vichiana del ingegno." *Atti del l'Acc. delle Scienze di Torino, Classe di Scienze Morali* . . . 81–83 (1947–1949), pp. 82–115.

Pascal, Blaise. *Pensées*. Trans. W. F. Trotter. New York, Random House, 1941. Modern Library.

Pasquazi, Silvio. "San Francesco in Dante." *Studi in onore di Alberto Chiari*. Vol. ii. Brescia, Paidea, 1973, pp. 939–970.

Passmore, John. *The Perfectibility of Man*. New York, Charles Scribner's Sons, 1970.

Patch, Howard R. *The Goddess Fortuna in Medieval Literature*. Cambridge, Mass., Harvard University Press, 1927.

_____ . *The Tradition of Boethius*. New York, Oxford University Press, 1935.

_____ . *On Rereading Chaucer*. Cambridge, Mass., Harvard University Press, 1939.

_____ . *The Other World According to Descriptions in Medieval Literature*. Cambridge, Mass., Harvard University Press, 1950.

Pelikan, Jaroslav. *The Christian Tradition*: A History of the Development of Doctrine. 4 vols. to date. Chicago, University of Chicago Press, 1971–.

Percy, Thomas. *Reliques of Ancient English Poetry* (1794). Ed. H. B. Wheatley. 3 vols. London, Allen & Unwin, 1927.

Perelman, Ch., and L. Olbrechts-Tyteca. *The New Rhetoric*: A Treatise on Argument. Notre Dame, Ind., University of Notre Dame Press, 1969.

Pertusi, Agostino. "La scoperta di Euripide nel primo Umanesimo." *IMU* 3 (1960).

Petrarch: Catalogue of the Petrarch Collection in Cornell University Library. Introduction by Morris Bishop. Millwood, N.Y., Kraus-Thomson, 1974. *See also* Fowler, Mary.

Petrucci, Armando. *La scrittura di Francesco Petrarca*. Città del Vaticano, Biblioteca apostolica vaticana, 1967. Studi e testi, 248.

Petrus Bonus Lombardus. *Pretiosa margarita novella*. Ed. Janus Lacinius. Venice, Aldine, 1546. Ed. Michael Toxites. Montbéliard, Jacques Foillet, 1602. English paraphrase by Arthur E. Waite. London, B. Quaritch, 1894. (Cf. Sarton [1975], iii, pp. 750–752; and Thorndike, iii [1934], chap. 9.)

Pickering, F. P. *Literature and Art in the Middle Ages*. Coral Gables, Fla., University of Miami Press, 1970.

Pitkin, Hanna F. *Fortune Is a Woman*. Berkeley, University of California Press, 1984.

Piur, Paul. *Petrarcas Briefwechsel mit deutschen Zeitgenossen*. Berlin, Weidmann, 1933. Vom Mittelalter zur Reformation, 7.

Piur (1925). *See* Petrarch, SN, above, I, ii.

Plater, W. E., and H. J. White. *A Grammar of the Vulgate*. Oxford, Clarendon Press, 1926.

Platner, S. B., and T. Ashby. *A Topographical Dictionary of Ancient Rome*. Oxford, Oxford University Press, 1929.

Pohlenz, Max. *Die Stoa*. 2 vols. Goettingen, Vandenhoeck & Ruprecht. Vol. i, 1959; vol. ii, 1955.

Polydore Vergil. *De rerum inventoribus libri viii*. Basel, Isengrim, 1546.

Popper, Karl R. *The Open Society and Its Enemies*. Princeton, Princeton University Press, 1950.

Popper, Karl R., and John C. Eccles. *The Self and Its Brain*. New York and Heidelberg, Springer Verlag, 1977.

Post, Gaines. "Petrarch and Heraclitus Once More." *Speculum* 12 (1938), pp. 343–350.

_____ . *Studies in Medieval Legal Thought*. Princeton, Princeton University Press, 1964.

Powell (1971). *See* Frederick II, above, II.

Powicke, F. M., and A. B. Emden, eds. *The Universities of Europe in the Middle Ages.* By the late Hastings Rashdall. 3 vols. Oxford, Oxford University Press, 1936.

Praetorius, Michael. *Syntagma musicum.* 3 vols. Vol. i: Wittenberg, 1614–1615; vols. ii, iii: Wolfenbuettel, 1619. Facsimile. Ed. W. Gurlitt. Basel, Baerenreiter Verlag, 1958–1959.

Prete, Sesto. "Il frammento della 'Philologia' di F. Petrarca." *Studi petrarcheschi* 1 (1948), pp. 141–144.

Previté-Orton, C. W. *The Shorter Cambridge Medieval History.* 2 vols. Cambridge, The University Press, 1952.

Printz, Wolfgang Caspar. *Historische Beschreibung der edelen Sing und Klingkunst.* Dresden, Joh. Christ. Mieth, 1690.

La prosa del Duecento. See above, II.

Putnam, George H. *Books and Their Makers during the Middle Ages.* 2 vols. (1896–1897). New York, Hillary House, 1962.

Quaglio, Antonio Enzo. *Francesco Petrarca.* Milan, Garzanti, 1967.

Quinones, Ricardo J. *The Renaissance Discovery of Time.* Cambridge, Mass., Harvard University Press, 1972.

Rabbow, P. *Antike Schriften ueber Seelenheilung und Seelenleitung.* Leipzig, Teubner, 1914.

———. *Seelenfuehrung.* Methodik der Exerzitien in der Antike. Munich, Koesel Verlag, 1954.

Raby, F. J. E. *A History of Secular Latin Poetry in the Middle Ages.* 2 vols. Oxford, Clarendon Press, 1934.

———. *A History of Christian-Latin Poetry:* From the Beginnings to the Close of the Middle Ages. 2d ed. Oxford, Clarendon Press, 1953.

Rand, Edward K. *Founders of the Middle Ages.* Cambridge, Mass., Harvard University Press, 1941.

Randall, John H. *Aristotle.* New York, Columbia University Press, 1960.

Rashdall, Hastings. *See* Powicke, F. M., above.

Rawski, Conrad H. "Notes on Aribo Scholasticus." In *Natalicia Musicologica Knud Jeppesen.* Ed. B. Hjelmborg and S. Sørensen. Copenhagen, Hansen, 1962, pp. 19–29.

———. *Petrarch: Four Dialogues for Scholars.* Cleveland, Press of Western Reserve University, 1967.

———. "Petrarch's Dialogue on Music." *Speculum* 46 (1971), pp. 302–317.

———. "Notes on the Rhetoric in Petrarch's *Invective contra medicum.*" In Scaglione (1975), pp. 249–277.

———. *Petrarch's Latin Prose Works and the Modern Translator.* Cleveland, School of Library Science, Case Western Reserve University, 1977.

Razzolini (1874, 1879). *See* Petrarch, *De vir. ill.,* above, I, ii.

Reedy (1978). *See* Boccaccio, above, II.

Reese, Gustave. *Music in the Middle Ages.* New York, Norton, 1940.

Ricci, Pier Giorgio. "*Cretico* non *critico.*" *Rinascimento* 3 (1952), pp. 371–372.

————. "Sulla tradizione manoscritta del *De Remediis*." *Rinascimento* 6 (1955), pp. 163–166.

Rico, Francisco. "Petrarca y el *De vera religione*." *IMU* 17 (1974), pp. 313–364.

————. *Vida u obra de Petrarca*. Vol. i: *Lectura del* Secretum. Chapel Hill, University of North Carolina, 1974. North Carolina Studies in the Romance Languages and Literatures, Essays, 33. Also published, Padua, Antenore, 1974. Studi sul Petrarca, 4.

————. "Precisazioni di cronologia petrarchesca: Le Familiares viii, 2–5, i rifacimenti del 'Secretum.'" *Giornale Storico della Letteratura Italiana* 155 (1978).

————. "Sobre la cronologia del *Secretum*: Las viejas leyendas y el fantasma nuevo de un lapsus biblico." *Studi petrarcheschi*, N.S., 1 (1984), pp. 51–102.

Rickert, Edith. *Chaucer's World*. New York, Columbia University Press, 1948.

Rilke, Rainer Maria. *Die Weise von Liebe und Tod des Cornets Christoph Rilke*. Leipzig, Insel-Verlag, n.d. Insel Buecherei, 1 (1926).

Rimanelli, G., and K. J. Atchity. *Italian Literature: Roots and Branches*. New Haven, Yale University Press, 1976.

Robertson, D. W., Jr. *A Preface to Chaucer*. Princeton, Princeton University Press, 1963.

————. *Abelard and Heloise*. New York, Dial Press, 1972.

Robertson (1958). *See* Augustine, *De doct.*, above, II.

Robertson, D. W., Jr., and B. F. Huppé. *Piers Plowman and Scriptural Tradition*. Princeton, Princeton University Press, 1951.

Robinson, D. M. "The Wheel of Fortune." *Classical Philology* 41 (1946), pp. 207–216.

Robinson, James H., and Henry W. Rolfe. *Petrarch: The First Modern Scholar and Man of Letters*. New York, G. P. Putnam's Sons, 1914.

Rohde, Erwin. *Psyche*: Seelenkult und Unsterblichkeitsglaube der Griechen (1897). Leipzig, A. Kroener, n.d.

Rojas, Fernando de. *See La Celestina* (1499).

Roppen, Georg, and Richard Sommer. *Strangers and Pilgrims*: An Essay on the Metaphor of Journey. Oslo, Norwegian Universities Press, 1964. Norwegian Studies in English, 11.

Rose, H. J. *A Handbook of Latin Literature*: From the Earliest Times to the Death of St. Augustine. London, Methuen, 1949.

Ross, D. J. A. *Alexander historiatus*. London, Warburg Institute, 1963.

Rossi, Vittorio. *Scritti di critica litteraria*. 3 vols. Florence, Sansoni, 1930.

Rotondi, G. "Note alle Familiari del Petrarca." *Rendiconti*. Istit. Lombard., 86 (1942–1943).

Rowland, Beryl. *Blind Beasts*: Chaucer's Animal World. Kent, O., Kent State University Press, 1971.

————. *Animals with Human Faces*. Knoxville, University of Tennessee Press, 1973.

Russell, Josiah C. *Late Ancient and Medieval Population.* Philadelphia, Transactions of the American Philosophical Society. N.S., 48 (1958), pt. 3.

Sabbadini, R. *Le scoperte dei codici latini e greci ne'secoli xiv e xv.* Florence, Sansoni, 1905. (Vol. i.)

———. *Le scoperte dei codici latini e greci ne'secoli xiv e xv.* Florence, Sansoni, 1914. (Vol. ii.)

Sachs, Curt. *World History of the Dance.* New York, Norton, 1937.

Salutati, Coluccio. *De laboribus Herculis.* Ed. B. L. Ullman. 2 vols. Zurich, Thesaurus mundi, 1947.

———. *Epistolario.* Ed. F. Novati. 4 vols. in 5. Rome, Istituto storico italiano, 1891–1911.

Sambin, P. "Libri del Petrarca presso suoi discendenti." *IMU* 1 (1958), 359–369.

Sandys, John. *A Companion to Latin Studies.* Cambridge, The University Press, 1929.

Sarton, George. *Introduction to the History of Science* (1927–1948). 3 vols. in 5. Huntington, N.Y., Krieger Publ. Co., 1975.

———. "Second Preface to Volume Forty: In Defense of Petrarca's Book on the Remedies for Good and Evil Fortune." *Isis* 40 (1949), pp. 95–98.

———. *A Guide to the History of Science.* Waltham, Mass., Chronica Botanica, 1952. (1952a)

———. *A History of Science*: Ancient Science through the Golden Age of Greece. Cambridge, Mass., Harvard University Press, 1952. (1952b)

———. *A History of Science*: Hellenistic Science and Culture in the Last Three Centuries B.C. Cambridge, Mass., Harvard University Press, 1959.

———. *Six Wings*: Men of Science in the Renaissance. Bloomington, Indiana University Press, 1957.

Saville, Jonathan. *The Medieval Erotic Alba*: Structure as Meaning. New York, Columbia University Press, 1972.

Saxl, F. *Lectures.* 2 vols. London, Warburg Institute, 1957.

Scaglione, Aldo. *The Classical Theory of Composition from Its Origins to the Present.* Chapel Hill, University of North Carolina Press, 1972.

———. *Francis Petrarch, Six Centuries Later.* Chapel Hill, University of North Carolina, 1975. North Carolina Studies in the Romance Languages and Literatures, Symposia, 3.

Schapiro, Meyer. *Romanesque Art.* New York, Braziller, 1977.

———. *Late Antique, Early Christian and Mediaeval Art.* New York, Braziller, 1979.

———. *The Sculpture of Moissac* (1929). New York, Braziller, 1985.

Scheidig, Walther. *Die Holzschnitte des Petrarca-Meisters zu Petrarcas Werk*: Von der Artzney bayder Glueck des guten und widerwaertigen—*Augsburg 1532.* Berlin, Henschelverlag, 1955.

Schevill, Ferdinand. *History of Florence*: From the Founding of the City through the Renaissance. New York, Ungar, 1961.

Schlosser, Julius. *La letteratura artistica*: Manuale delle fonti della storia dell' arte moderna. Florence, La Nuova Italia, 1964.

Schmeller (1847). *See Carmina Burana*, above, II.

Schoenbaum, S. *Shakespeare's Lives*. Oxford, Clarendon Press, 1970.

———. *William Shakespeare*: A Documentary Life. New York, Oxford University Press, 1975.

Schottlaender, Rudolf, ed. and trans. *Francesco Petrarcha*: De remediis utriusque Fortunae. Munich, W. Fink, 1975. (Text selections in Latin and German trans. Contains *DR* i, Pref., and dialogues 21, 43, 44, 101, 102, 105, 106; *DR* ii, Pref., and dialogues 85, 88, 93, 106, 118.)

Schuetz, L. *Thomas Lexikon*. Paderborn, F. Schoeningh, 1895.

Schwab, Gustav. *Gods and Heroes*: Myths and Epics of Ancient Greece. New York, Pantheon, 1946.

Seigel, Jerrold E. *Rhetoric and Philosophy in Renaissance Humanism*. Princeton, Princeton University Press, 1968.

Seung, T. K. *Cultural Thematics*: The Formulation of the Faustian Ethos. New Haven, Yale University Press, 1976.

Seward, Desmond. *The Hundred Years' War*: The English in France, 1337–1453. New York, Atheneum, 1978.

Seyffert, Oskar. *Dictionary of Classical Antiquities*. Ed. H. Nettleship and J. E. Sandys. Cleveland, World, 1956.

Seznec, Jean. *The Survival of the Pagan Gods*. New York, Pantheon, 1953. Bollingen Series, 38.

Shakespeare, William. *Comedies, Histories, & Tragedies*. Facsimile of the First Folio (1623). Ed. H. Koekeritz. New Haven, Yale University Press, 1954.

Sheridan (1973). *See* Alain de Lille, *Anticlaud.*, above, II.

Siciliano, Italo. *François Villon et les thèmes poétiques du Moyen Âge*. Paris, Nizet, 1934.

Simson, Otto von. *The Gothic Cathedral*. New York, Pantheon, 1956. Bollingen Series, 48.

Singer, Charles, et al. *A History of Technology*. 5 vols. Oxford, Clarendon Press, 1954–1958.

Singleton (1955), Singleton (1974), Singleton (1982). *See* Boccaccio, *Decameron*, above, II.

Singleton (1970–1975), and *Commentary*. *See* Dante Alighieri, *Div. Comm.*, above, II.

Skeat, Walter W. *Early English Proverbs*. Oxford, Oxford University Press, 1910.

Smalley, Beryl. *The Study of the Bible in the Middle Ages*. Oxford, Blackwell, 1952.

———. *English Friars and Antiquity in the Early Fourteenth Century*. Oxford, Blackwell, 1960.

Smith, F. Joseph. "A Medieval Philosophy of Number: Jacques de Liège and the *Speculum musicae*." *Arts liberaux et philosophie au Moyen Âge*. Actes de Quatrième Congrès international de philosophie médiévale. Montréal, Institut d'Études Médiévales, 1969, pp. 1023–1039.

Smith, Macklin. *Prudentius'* Psychomachia: *A Reexamination*. Princeton, Princeton University Press, 1976.

Smits van Waesberghe, Jos. *School en Muziek in de Middeleeuwen*. Amsterdam, Uitgeversmaatschappij Holland, 1949.

Snyder, George Sergeant. *Maps of the Heavens*. New York, Abbeville Press, 1984.

Snyder, S. "The Left Hand of God: Despair in Medieval and Renaissance Tradition." *Studies in the Renaissance* 12 (1965), pp. 18–59.

Sohm, Rudolph, and Ludwig Mitteis. *Institutionen*: Geschichte und System des roemischen Privatrechts. Ed. L. Wenger. Munich, Duncker & Humblot, 1931.

Souter, Alexander. *A Glossary of Later Latin to 600 A.D.* Oxford, Clarendon Press, 1949.

Spearing, A. C. *Criticism and Medieval Poetry*. New York, Barnes & Noble, 1972.

Spence, Jonathan D. *The Memory Palace of Matteo Ricci*. New York, Viking Press, 1984.

Spenser, Edmund. *The Faerie Queene*. 2 vols. London, J. M. Dent, 1910. Everyman's Library, 443, 444.

Spitzer, Leo. *Romanische Literaturstudien, 1936–1956*. Tuebingen, N. Niemeyer, 1959.

——— . *Classical and Christian Ideas of World Harmony*. Ed. A. G. Hatcher. Baltimore, Johns Hopkins University Press, 1963.

Stahl (1952). *See* Macrobius, *Comm.*, above, II.

Stahl (1977). *See* Martianus Capella, *De nupt.*, above, II.

Stammler, Wolfgang, ed. *Deutsche Philologie im Aufriss*. 3 vols. Berlin, Erich Schmidt, 1957–1962.

Stegner, Hugo. *David Rex Propheta*. Nuremberg, Hans Carl, 1961.

Steinbuechel, Theodor. *Christliches Mittelalter*. Leipzig, Jakob Hegner, 1935.

Steiner, George. *After Babel*: Aspects of Language and Translation. New York, Oxford University Press, 1975.

——— . *Antigones*: How the Antique Legend Has Endured in Western Literature, Art, and Thought. New York, Oxford University Press, 1984.

Stock, Brian. *Medieval Latin Lyrics*. Boston, D. Godine, 1971.

——— . *Myth and Science in the Twelfth Century*. Princeton, Princeton University Press, 1972.

——— . "*Antiqui* and *Moderni* as 'Giants' and 'Dwarfs': A Reflection of Popular Culture?" *Journal of Modern Philology* 76 (1979), pp. 370–374.

——— . *The Implications of Literacy*: Written Language and Models of Interpretation in the Eleventh and Twelfth Centuries. Princeton, Princeton University Press, 1983.

Stolfi, Casimiro. *Fioretti de rimedi contro fortuna di messer Fr. Petrarca, volgarizzati per D. Gio Dassaminiato* . . . Bologna, G. Romagnoli, 1867.

——— . *De' rimedii dell' una e dell' altra fortuna di messer Francesco Petrarca volgarizzati nel buon secolo della lingua per D. Giovanni Dassaminiato monaco degli Angeli*. 2 vols. Bologna, G. Romagnoli, 1867–1868.

Strunk, Oliver. *Source Readings in Music History.* New York, Norton, 1950.

Suchomski, Joachim. Delectatio *und* Utilitas: Ein Beitrag zum Verstaendnis mittel-alterlicher komischer Literatur. Bern, Francke, 1975.

Sudre, Léopold. *Les sources du Roman de Renart.* Paris, Bouillon, 1893.

Susemihl, F. *See* Aristotle, *Oeconomica*, above, II.

Szöverffy, Josef. *Die Annalen der lateinischen Hymnendichtung.* 2 vols. Berlin, Erich Schmidt, 1964–1965.

Tateo, Francesco. *Dialogo interiore e polemica ideologica nel "Secretum" del Petrarca.* Florence, Le Monnier, 1965.

Tatham, E. H. R. *Francesco Petrarca, the First Modern Man of Letters*: His Life and Correspondence. 2 vols. London, The Sheldon Press, 1925–1926.

Taton, René, ed. *History of Science.* 4 vols. New York, Basic Books, 1963–1966.

Taylor, Henry Osborne. *The Medieval Mind.* 2 vols. London, Macmillan (1925), 1938.

Taylor (1961). *See* Hugh of St. Victor, *Didasc.*, above, II.

Temkin, Owsei. *Galenism.* Ithaca, N.Y., Cornell University Press, 1973.

Ten Brink, Bernhard. *Geschichte der Englischen Litteratur.* 2 vols. Strasbourg, K. J. Truebner, 1893, 1899.

Tentler, Thomas N. *Sin and Confession on the Eve of the Reformation.* Princeton, Princeton University Press, 1977.

Tester, S. J. *A History of Western Astrology.* Woodbridge, Suffolk, Boydell Press, 1987.

Thompson, David, ed. *Petrarch*: A Humanist among Princes: An Anthology of Petrarch's Letters and of Selections from His Other Works. New York, Harper & Row, 1971.

———. *The Idea of Rome*: From Antiquity to the Renaissance. Albuquerque, University of New Mexico Press, 1972.

Thompson, James Westfall. *An Economic and Social History of the Middle Ages (300–1300).* New York, Century, 1928.

———. *A History of Historical Writing.* 2 vols. New York, Macmillan, 1942.

Thorndike, Lynn. *A History of Magic and Experimental Science.* 8 vols. New York, Columbia University Press, 1923–1958.

———. "Invention of the Mechanical Clock about 1271 A.D." *Speculum* 16 (1941), pp. 242–245.

Toffanin, Giuseppe. *Storia dell' Umanesimo.* 4 vols. Bologna, Zanichelli, 1964.

Toynbee, Paget, and Charles S. Singleton. *A Dictionary of Proper Names and Notable Matters in the Works of Dante.* Oxford, Clarendon Press, 1968.

Trimpi, Wesley. *Muses of One Mind*: The Literary Analysis of Experience and Its Continuity. Princeton, Princeton University Press, 1983.

Trinkaus, Charles E. *Adversity's Noblemen.* New York, Columbia University Press, 1940.

———. *In Our Image and Likeness.* 2 vols. Chicago, University of Chicago Press, 1970.

———. "Renaissance Idea of the Dignity of Man." In Wiener (1973). Vol. iv, pp. 136–147.

———. *The Poet as Philosopher*: Petrarch and the Formation of Renaissance Consciousness. New Haven, Yale University Press, 1979. ("Petrarch and Classical Philosophy" also in Bernardo [1980], pp. 249–274.)

———. *The Scope of Renaissance Humanism*. Ann Arbor, University of Michigan Press, 1983.

Tripet, Arnaut. *Pétrarque ou la connaissance de soi*. Geneva, Droz, 1967.

Trompf, G. W. *The Idea of Historical Recurrence in Western Thought*: From Antiquity to the Reformation. Berkeley, University of California Press, 1979.

Trotter (1941). *See* Pascal.

Tschan, Francis J. *Saint Bernward of Hildesheim*. 3 vols. Notre Dame, Ind., University of Notre Dame, 1942–1952. Publications in Medieval Studies, 6, 12, 13.

Tubach, Frederic C. *Index exemplorum*. Helsinki, Suomaleinen Tiedeakatemia, 1969. FF Communications, 204.

Tuchman, Barbara W. *A Distant Mirror*. New York, A. A. Knopf, 1978.

Tuve, Rosemond. *Allegorical Imagery*. Princeton, Princeton University Press, 1966.

Ullman, B. L. *Studies in the Italian Renaissance*. Rome, Ediz. di Storia e Letteratura, 1955.

———. *The Humanism of Coluccio Salutati*. Padua, Antenore, 1963.

Ullman (1947). *See* Salutati.

Ullmann, Walter. "The Influence of John of Salisbury on Medieval Italian Jurists." *English Historical Review* 59 (1944), pp. 384–393.

———. *Medieval Foundations of Renaissance Humanism*. Ithaca, N.Y., Cornell University Press, 1977.

———. "John of Salisbury's *Policraticus* in the Later Middle Ages." In *Geschichtsschreibung und geistiges Leben im Mittelalter*. Ed. K. Hauck and H. Mordek. Cologne, 1978, pp. 519–545.

Underwood, P. A. "The Fountain of Life in Manuscripts of the Gospels." *Dumbarton Oaks Papers* 5 (1950), pp. 41–138.

Upjohn, Everard M., et al. *History of World Art*. New York, Oxford University Press, 1949.

Ussani, Vincenzo. "Il Petrarca e Flavio Giuseppe." *Rendiconti della Pontificia accad. romana di archeologia* 20 (1943–1944), pp. 447–465.

Vacant, A., E. Mangenot, and E. Amann. *Dictionnaire de théologie catholique*. 15 vols. Paris, Letouzey, 1909–1950.

Voigt, Georg. *Die Wiederbelebung des classischen Alterthums*. 2 vols. Berlin, Reimer, 1880–1881.

Von den Steinen, Wolfram. *Notker der Dichter und seine geistige Welt*. 2 vols. Bern, Francke, 1948.

———. *Der Kosmos des Mittelalters*. Bern, Francke, 1959.

———. *Homo caelestis*: Das Wort der Kunst im Mittelalter. 2 vols. Bern, Francke, 1965.

———. *Menschen im Mittelalter*. Ed. Peter von Moos. Bern, Francke, 1967.

Von Moos, P. *"Consolatio*: Studien zur mittellateinischen Trostliteratur ueber den Tod und zum Problem der christlichen Trauer." *Muenstersche Mittelalter-Schriften* 3 (1971–1972), parts 1–4.

Voretzsch, Karl. *Einfuehrung in das Studium der altfranzoesischen Literatur.* Halle, Niemeyer, 1925.

Waegner, Wilhelm. *Rom.* Ed. O. E. Schmidt. Berlin, Neufeld & Henius, 1923.

Wagner, Peter. *Einfuehrung in die gregorianischen Melodien.* 3 vols. Leipzig, Breitkopf & Haertel, 1911–1921.

Wallach, Luitpold, ed. *The Classical Tradition*: Literary and Historical Studies in Honor of Harry Kaplan. Ithaca, N.Y., Cornell University Press, 1966.

Wallace, William A. *Causality and Scientific Explanation.* 2 vols. Ann Arbor, University of Michigan Press, 1972, 1974.

Walshe, Maurice O'C. *Mediaeval German Literature.* Cambridge, Mass., Harvard University Press, 1962.

Walshe (1951). *See* Johannes von Tepl, *Ackerm.*, above, II.

Walther, Hans. *Proverbia sententiaeque latinitatis medii aevi.* Goettingen, Vandenhoeck & Rupprecht, 1963–1969.

Wantzloeben, Sigfrid. *Das Monochord als Instrument und als System.* Halle, Niemeyer, 1911.

Wattenbach, W. *Das Schriftwesen im Mittelalter.* Leipzig, S. Hirzel, 1896.

Webb (1909). *See* John of Salisbury, *Policrat.*, above, II.

Weiss, Roberto. *Il primo secolo dell' umanesimo.* Rome, Ediz. di Storia e Letteratura, 1949.

———. *Humanism in England during the Fifteenth Century.* Oxford, Blackwell, 1957. Medium Aevum Monographs, 4.

———. *Medieval and Humanist Greek.* Padua, Antenore, 1977. Medioevo e Umanesimo, 8.

Wellendorffer, Virgilius. *Heptalogium.* Leipzig, M. Lotter, 1502.

Welter, Jean Th. *L'exemplum dans la littérature religieuse et didactique du Moyen Âge.* Paris, Occitania, 1927.

Wenzel, Siegfried. "Petrarch's Accidia." *Studies in the Renaissance* 8 (1960), pp. 36–48.

———. *The Sin of Sloth*, Acedia, in Medieval Thought and Literature. Chapel Hill, University of North Carolina Press, 1967.

Wenzel (1984). *See Summa virtutum* . . . , above, II.

West, Delmo C., and Sandra Zimdars-Swartz. *Joachim of Fiore*: A Study in Spiritual Perception and History. Bloomington, Indiana University Press, 1983.

Wetherbee, Winthrop. *Platonism and Poetry in the Twelfth Century*: The Literary Influence of the School of Chartres. Princeton, Princeton University Press, 1972.

Whicher, George F. *The Goliard Poets.* Cambridge, Mass., n.p., 1949.

White, Lynn, Jr. "Cultural Climates and Technological Advance in the Middle Ages." *Viator* 2 (1971), pp. 171–201.

White, T. H. *The Book of Beasts* (Cambridge, ii, 4, 26). New York, G. P. Putnam's Sons, 1954.

Whiting, Bartlett Jere. *Proverbs, Sentences, and Proverbial Phrases*: From English Writings Mainly before 1500. Cambridge, Mass., Harvard University Press, 1968.

Wiener, Philip P., ed. *Dictionary of the History of Ideas*. 5 vols. New York, Charles Scribner's Sons, 1973–1974.

Wiesen, David S. *St. Jerome as a Satirist*. Ithaca, N.Y., Cornell University Press, 1964.

Wilkins, Eliza Gregory. Know Thyself *in Greek and Latin Literature*. Ph.D. diss., University of Chicago, 1917.

Wilkins, Ernest Hatch. *The Making of the Canzoniere and Other Petrarchan Studies*. Rome, Ediz. di Storia e Letteratura, 1951.

––––––. *A History of Italian Literature*. Cambridge, Mass., Harvard University Press, 1954. Rev. T. G. Bergin. Ibid., 1974.

––––––. *Studies in the Life and Works of Petrarch*. Cambridge, Mass., Medieval Academy of America, 1955.

––––––. *Petrarch's Eight Years in Milan*. Cambridge, Mass., Medieval Academy of America, 1958. (1958a)

––––––. *Petrarch at Vaucluse*. Chicago, University of Chicago Press, 1958. (1958b)

––––––. *Petrarch's Later Years*. Cambridge, Mass., Medieval Academy of America, 1959.

––––––. *Petrarch's Correspondence*. Padua, Antenore, 1960. Medioevo e umanesimo, 3.

––––––. *Life of Petrarch*. Chicago, University of Chicago Press, 1961.

––––––. *Studies on Petrarch and Boccaccio*. Ed. A. S. Bernardo. Padua, Antenore, 1978.

Wilkins (1962). *See* Petrarch, *Triumphs*, above, I, iii.

Wilks, Michael, ed. *The World of John of Salisbury*. Oxford, Blackwell, 1984. Studies in Church History. Subsidia, 3.

Willard, Charity Cannon. *Christine de Pizan*: Her Life and Works. New York, Persea Press, 1984.

Willcock, Malcolm M. *A Companion to the Iliad*. Chicago, University of Chicago Press, 1976.

Wille, Guenther. *Musica Romana*: Die Bedeutung der Musik im Leben der Roemer. Amsterdam, P. Schippers, 1967.

Williman, Daniel, ed. *The Black Death*: The Impact of the Fourteenth-Century Plague. Binghamton, Center for Medieval and Early Renaissance Studies, 1982. Medieval and Renaissance Texts and Studies, 13.

Wilson, Edward O. *The Insect Societies*. Cambridge, Mass., Harvard University Press, 1971.

Wolohojian, Albert M. *The Romance of Alexander the Great by Pseudo-Callisthenes*. New York, Columbia University Press, 1969. Records of Civilization, Sources and Studies, 82.

Wright, Thomas. *The Anglo-Latin Satirical Poets and Epigrammatists of the Twelfth Century*. 2 vols. London, Longman and Co., 1872.

Wright (1975). See *Vita di Cola di Rienzo*, above, II.

Yates, Frances A. "Charles Quint et l'idée d'empire." *Les Fêtes de la Renaissance*. Ed. J. Jacquot. Vol. ii. Paris, Éditions du Centre National de la Recherche Scientifique, 1960.

——— . *Giordano Bruno and the Hermetic Tradition*. London, Routledge & Kegan Paul, 1964.

——— . *The Art of Memory*. Chicago, University of Chicago Press, 1966.

Young, Karl. *The Drama of the Medieval Church*. 2 vols. Oxford, Clarendon Press, 1933.

Young, Robert, and Donald Guthrie. *Young's Analytical Concordance to the Bible*. Nashville, Tenn., Thomas Nelson, 1982.

Zacour (1973). See Petrarch, SN, above, I, iii.

Zeydel, Edwin H. *Vagabond Verse*: Secular Latin Poems of the Middle Ages. Detroit, Wayne State University Press, 1966.

Ziegler, J. G. *Die Ehelehre der Poenitentialsummen von 1200–1350*. Regensburg, F. Pustet, 1956.

Ziegler, Leopold. *Ueberlieferung*. Leipzig, Jakob Hegner, 1936.

Ziegler, Philip. *The Black Death*. London, Pelican Books, 1970.

Zumthor, Paul. *Histoire littéraire de la France médiévale*. Paris, Presses Universitaires de France, 1954.

Indexes

LATIN TITLES

*Indicates 1581 title variants.

ENGLISH TITLES

INCIPITS

		DR
Avaricie stimulis urgeor	ii,	105
Aves varias in aviario conclusi	i,	64
Bello quatimur civili	ii,	74
Bello victoriam spero	i,	102
Bello vinci metuo	ii,	70
Beneficia multos contulisse gaudeo	i,	93
Cantu delector ac fidibus	i,	23
Carcere claudor indigno	ii,	64
Casta mihi est filia	i,	74
Celebrior sum: quam vellem: notiorque	ii,	88
Choreis gaudeo	i,	24
Classem habeo instructam	i,	98
Conviviis glorior	i,	19
Cum res fortunasque hominum cogito: incertosque & subitos rerum motus	i,	Pref.
De amicis queror	ii,	27
De inimici morte laetus sum	i,	104
Delector histrionum iocis	i,	28
Delector variis spectaculis	i,	30
Delicata nimis est filia	ii,	23
Dentium vexor aegritudine	ii,	94
Discesserunt servi	ii,	30
Discipulum habeo indocilem	ii,	41
Dominum bonum habeo	i,	85
Dormire non possum	ii,	86
Dote auctus sum opima	i,	68
Durum iter pedibus meis ago	ii,	57
Durum patior parentem	ii,	43
Ecce autem iure Rex sum	i,	96
Egisse mecum nimis illiberaliter naturam queror:	ii,	1
Eloquium deest	ii,	102
Equo agili delector	i,	31
Est mihi filius vir fortis	i,	73
Est mihi magister militiae inconsultus	ii,	72
Est mihi praeceptor indoctus	ii,	40
Estu quatior libidinae	ii,	110
Etas florida est	i,	1
Et (quod morte gravius). Qui meus credebatur alienus est filius	ii,	50
Ex aedificiis gloriam spero	i,	118

		DR
Quid quod linguam et loquelam perdidi	ii,	103
Quid quod valitudo prospera est	i,	3
Quisquis ego sum:	i,	11
Rebus rite compositis tranquillus ago	i,	90
Regno excidi	ii,	79
Regnum est mihi non filius	ii,	78
Relligione glorior perfecta	i,	13
Repulsam passus indignor	ii,	38
Sapientiam consecutus sum	i,	12
Scabie premor importuna	ii,	85
Secundas nuptias celebrabo	i,	76
Sed abundo opibus	i,	53
Sed amisi filium	ii,	48
Sed contemnor	ii,	36
Sed ignominiosa mors est	ii,	122
Sed inveni magnam gloriam	i,	92
Sed irascor	ii,	107
Sed memoria inopi & infirma sum	ii,	101
Sed pernicitas multa est	i,	6
Sed violenta morte pereo	ii,	121
Senui	ii,	83
Serenus est aer: ac iocundus	i,	86
Sero promissa complentur	ii,	37
Servus in hanc vitam intravi	ii,	7
Signis gemma expressis mulceor	i,	39
Simia delectabilis est mihi	i,	61
Sine filiis morior	ii,	131
Somniis inquietor	ii,	87
Spero aeternam vitam	i,	122
Spero alchimiae prosperos exitus	i,	111
Spero filii reditum	i,	114
Spero gloriam ex convictu	i,	119
Spero pacem	i,	105
Spero tempora meliora	i,	115
Sponsam mihi sententia iudicialis erripuit	ii,	17
Sterilis uxor est mihi	ii,	22
Sterilitate premor annua	ii,	58
Stultum habeo: ac temerarium collegam	ii,	71
Suavibus delector odoribus	i,	22
Sum foelix	i,	108
Sunt mihi elephantes	i,	60

RES ET VERBA: SUBJECTS, TOPICS AND MAXIMS

SUBJECTS

(As a rule, only the first mention of a given subject in a dialogue is recorded. All noun entries apply to singular as well as plural.)

	Book	Dial.	Line
abduction	2	20	
abundance	1	43	19
	1	43	130
accident	1	2	6
acclaim	2	26	28
aconite	1	9	92
acting, theatrical	1	28	17
action, human	1	58	66
	2	Pref.	300
	2	4	12
actors	1	30	29
adamas	1	37	63
adiaphora. *See* indifferents			
adjudication	1	47	33
administrator, royal	1	47	6
adolescents. *See* youth			
adoption	1	79	
	2	131	11
adulation, Achaean	1	19	116
adultery	1	24	51
	1	65	46
	2	6	69
	2	21	34
	2	66	

	Book	Dial.	Line
aspiration	1	80	31
association. *See* company			
astrologers	1	112	26
astrology	1	6	21
	1	112	
	2	114	210
attainments	1	90	17
	1	120	49
auguries from birds	1	112	97
augurs	1	112	78
aureus	1	37	16
austerity	1	18	20
	1	22	28
	1	106	
	2	8	5
	2	10	53
authors. *See* writers			
autumn	2	Pref.	8
avarice. *See* greed			
aviaries	1	64	
ballistae	1	99	20
ballplaying	1	25	
banquets. *See* feasts			
barrenness	1	57	63
	2	22	
	2	58	
basilisk	2	Pref.	62
bastard	2	50	
bears	1	32	47
	2	90	8
	2	97	28
beasts. *See* animals			
beauty	1	Pref.	246
	1	2	
	1	3	2
	1	20	33
	1	37	56
	1	66	5
	1	68	3
	1	72	2
	1	84	60
	2	1	9

	Book	Dial.	Line
blaspheming	1	27	62
	1	87	25
blindness	1	96	264
	2	79	48
	2	83	178
	2	96	
	2	97	4
	2	120	85
blood relationship	2	50	26
boar	2	121	41
boasting	1	91	37
body	1	3	17
	1	4	
	1	6	18
	1	29	4
	1	48	21
	1	120	13
	2	1	
	2	2	
	2	99	
body and mind	1	3	
	1	5	
	1	24	8
	1	24	63
	1	25	5
	2	Pref.	382
	2	1	
	2	2	
	2	3	
body as lodging of the soul	1	5	53
	1	24	8
	2	2	34
beauty of	1	2	69
deformed	2	1	
goods of	2	6	48
health of	1	3	
	1	4	
	1	5	2
master of man	1	29	4
body odor	1	18	100
body, shape of	1	2	
	1	5	2
	1	65	11

	Book	Dial.	Line
strength of	1	5	
weakness of	2	2	
books	1	Pref.	62
	1	43	
	1	44	82
bookseller	1	43	149
booty	1	37	106
born poor	2	11	
born rich	1	17	
botheration	2	Pref.	209
	2	90	
	1	24	25
	1	5	
	1	29	63
	2	2	11
bread and water	2	10	10
brevity	1	Pref.	73
	2	Pref.	403
brevity, memory's best friend	1	Pref.	73
bride, loss of a	2	17	
bridle curbing insolence	2	4	52
brotherhood of man	2	50	20
brothers	1	52	17
	1	84	
	2	Pref.	114
	2	45	
	2	51	
brothers, love between	1	84	39
	2	45	3
	2	45	22
brothers. *See also* siblings			
building materials	1	118	2
	2	Pref.	334
building projects	1	118	
buildings, ancient Roman	1	118	
bull	2	Pref.	87
burial. *See* funeral			
bushwhackers	1	21	77
	2	90	122
business matters	1	57	45
	1	89	24
	2	13	187
	2	15	31

	Book	Dial.	Line
children	1	18	10
	1	66	35
	1	67	1
	1	70–	
	1	74	
	1	77	18
	1	79	
	1	81	36
	1	82–	
	1	83	
	1	84	6
	1	85	17
	1	105	32
	1	120	34
	2	Pref.	116
	2	Pref.	360
	2	12	
	2	17	36
	2	18	50
	2	22	14
	2	24	45
	2	50	12
	2	53	23
	2	127	
	2	131	
children, death of	2	48–	
	2	49	
loyalty of	1	81	36
many	2	12	
punishment of	2	43	2
treasures	2	12	7
child's love	1	82	36
	1	83	3
chimera, three-shaped	1	81	27
	2	114	50
choral dance	1	24	15
circus	1	30	6
citizens	1	15	15
	1	97	10
	2	38	30
cities	1	14	2
	1	15	
	2	4	12

	Book	Dial.	Line
crossbow	1	48	50
crowd, vulgar, *esp.*	1	11	6
	1	11	63
	1	11	84
	1	12	47
	1	19	38
	1	30	110
	1	40	47
	1	41	23
	1	42	34
	1	44	106
	1	46	86
	1	49	17
	1	94	
	1	109	48
	2	Pref.	219
	2	8	19
	2	13	64
	2	13	161
	2	25	
	2	34	
	2	35	14
	2	36	
	2	90	150
	2	119	128
crows	2	Pref.	40
cruelty	1	30	7
	1	101	111
	1	103	2
	2	39	20
	2	43	2
	2	65	
	2	114	316
	2	122	16
cuckoo	2	Pref.	43
cups, precious	1	18	12
	1	37	109
	1	38	
	1	42	49
	1	43	3
	2	116	28
cure by contraries	1	69	229

	Book	Dial.	Line
	1	120	17
	2	11	10
	2	33	26
	2	46–	
	2	49	
	2	51–	
	2	53	
	2	86	2
	2	117–	
	2	132	
death, as creditor	1	4	23
certainty of	2	48	3
fear of	2	Pref.	369
	2	117	
meditation on	1	90	50
of infants	1	78	20
	2	49	
power of	2	48	67
	2	51	16
privilege of	2	51	28
shameful	1	18	108
	2	122	
sudden	1	78	19
	2	49	17
	2	120	
without burial	1	112	106
	2	132	
deathbed	1	90	74
	2	131	55
debt	1	4	23
	1	56	30
debtor	1	4	23
	1	56	29
decay	1	16	57
decay, moral	1	22	28
	1	105	49
	1	116	18
	2	10	54
	2	21	103
	2	44	40
deceit	1	23	12
	1	45	18
	1	46	38

	Book	Dial.	Line
	2	9	116
disloyalty	1	84	6
	2	27	7
disrepute	1	51	33
	2	6	
	2	24–	
	2	25	
	2	36	
dissipation	1	115	12
distinction. *See* fame			
distress	2	12	82
divination	1	112	50
divorce	1	65	31
dizziness	2	10	38
doctors of the Church	1	112	57
dog	1	32	11
	1	32	45
	1	48	13
	2	Pref.	23
	2	97	28
doing nothing	2	52	15
dolphin	1	23	
	1	98	21
domain, human	1	96	260
donkey	2	17	40
	2	97	28
dowry	1	68	
	2	12	105
drawing, art of	1	41	12
dreaming	1	90	56
	2	87	
drought	1	114	98
	2	58	
drum	2	50	49
drinking, *esp.*	1	18	11
	2	10	71
drunkenness	1	18	11
	1	19	32
	1	24	73
	1	38	39
	2	115	14
duck	2	Pref.	97
dukes	1	20	60

	Book	Dial.	Line
effeminacy	1	22	94
	1	24	8
	2	53	29
	2	114	36
elders	2	36	10
elements, the four	1	18	100
	1	86	2
	2	Pref.	5
	2	Pref.	279
	2	Pref.	388
	2	121	76
elephant	1	5	10
	1	30	40
	1	60	23
	2	Pref.	63
	2	2	45
	2	41	44
eloquence	1	9	
	1	43	122
	1	46	81
	1	62	19
	1	64	64
	2	7	36
	2	25	72
	2	102	
eloquence, Cicero's definition of	1	9	33
emblems	1	45	18
	1	46	59
Emperor, Holy Roman	1	96	59
emperors	1	97	41
empires	2	4	12
end	1	17	31
	1	18	121
	1	94	4
	1	103	12
	2	11	10
endorsements	2	26	
enemies	1	33	
	1	91	29
	1	97	16
	1	100	25
	1	101	72
	1	103	27

	Book	Dial.	Line
	1	14	16
	1	15	140
	1	16	113
	1	24	66
	1	40	4
	1	63	41
	1	89	13
	1	96	192
	1	101	92
	1	108	77
	1	110	39
	1	119	4
	2	13	65
	2	14	49
	2	21	61
exercise	1	7	26
	1	24	55
	1	25	4
	1	29	6
	1	44	88
	2	101	10
excess	1	5	12
	1	22	21
	1	43	26
executioner	1	97	46
	2	62	46
	2	65	25
	2	114	318
	2	122	
exertion	1	10	44
	1	45	10
exile	1	Pref.	105
	1	8	19
	1	37	31
	1	37	51
	2	67	
expectation	1	110	
	1	113–	
	1	116	
experience	1	Pref.	104
	2	13	65
	2	45	19
	2	58	73

	Book	Dial.	Line
	2	73	32
extramarital arrangement	1	76	9
	2	131	42
extravagance	1	38	90
	1	96	121
	2	8	19
eyes	1	12	61
	1	22	7
	1	30	116
	2	53	16
	2	73	32
	2	79	50
	2	94	29
	2	96	
face, human	1	40	25
	2	96	16
facts	2	38	29
fainting spells	2	113	
fairness	2	32	33
	2	42	5
faith	1	109	70
	1	122	9
faithfulness	1	68	28
	2	12	113
falcon	1	32	
	2	93	168
fall. See autumn			
fame	1	9	80
	1	16	7
	1	44	112
	1	60	39
	1	117–	
	1	120	
	2	4	10
	2	5	7
	2	25	15
	2	35	
	2	88	
	2	130	
fame. See also glory; reputation			
family	1	16	
	1	18	1

	Book	Dial.	Line
	1	65–	
	1	68	
	1	70–	
	1	79	
	1	82–	
	1	84	
	1	114	
	2	5	
	2	6	
	2	53	23
	2	127–	
	2	128	
farmers	1	43	102
	1	57	17
	2	Pref.	204
	2	58	
	2	59	6
fashion	1	20	
	1	66	20
fasting	1	18	12
fate	1	101	103
	2	33	35
father	1	16	18
	1	18	116
	1	70	34
	1	77	47
	1	82	
	1	83	3
	1	84	3
	2	Pref.	123
	2	42	2
	2	43	
	2	44	2
	2	46	
	2	51	72
father, duties of	2	23	30
	2	43	32
	2	44	36
holy	1	19	99
	1	20	14
	1	112	57
father-in-law	1	77	35
fatigue	2	10	38

	Book	Dial.	Line
fife	2	50	49
fire	1	91	11
	2	Pref.	11
	2	18	70
	2	55	
	2	74	11
	2	90	150
	2	121	62
fire, ekpyrosis	2	55	43
firmament. *See* heaven			
first cause eternal	1	23	76
fish	1	20	22
	1	37	177
	1	41	85
	1	63	
fishermen	2	Pref.	34
	2	Pref.	47
	2	41	41
fishponds	1	63	
flattery	1	11	21
	1	19	113
	1	28	52
	1	49	22
	1	85	18
	1	110	65
	2	9	186
fleas	2	Pref.	53
	2	90	45
flies	2	82	67
	2	119	43
flight from people	2	31	20
	2	35	15
	2	88	46
flight from people, *note*	1	16	30
	1	17	13
	1	46	57
	1	92	48
flocks and herds. *See* livestock			
flood and ebb. *See* tides			
floods	2	Pref.	204
flowers	1	40	52
foliage	2	Pref.	198

	Book	Dial.	Line
	1	91	20
	1	96	80
	1	107	48
	2	79	47
fortune-tellers	1	37	216
	1	38	66
	1	105	51
	1	112	
	2	90	284
	2	91	6
	2	96	50
forum, noises of the	2	Pref.	226
fountain of life	1	16	71
	2	12	73
fowl	1	62	23
	2	Pref.	40
	2	Pref.	91
fowler	1	23	17
	1	65	81
	2	Pref.	47
fowling	1	49	16
fox	2	Pref.	34
fratricides	1	52	38
	1	84	10
	2	45	5
fraud. *See* deception			
freedom	1	89	2
	1	91	17
freedom, personal	1	65	35
	1	66	28
	1	68	10
	1	89	
	2	7	
	2	64	
	2	68	60
	2	78	21
freedom, personal. *See also* liberty			
freeman	1	27	56
	2	38	29
frenzy	1	24	46
	1	112	53
	2	115	35
frenzy. *See also* madness			

	Book	Dial.	Line
	2	13	166
frui-uti	1	10	50
	1	21	6
funeral	1	20	45
	1	23	32
	1	90	96
	1	110	60
	1	120	51
	2	11	16
	2	18	2
	2	33	52
	2	92	24
	2	122	5
	2	132	25
	2	132	81
furniture, precious. *See* precious furniture			
fury, public	1	Pref.	159
	1	89	20
	2	34	15
	2	74	
future	1	Pref.	8
	1	90	112
	1	112	27
	1	121	20
future, *note also*	1	109–	
	1	115	
gallows	1	104	11
	2	122	19
gambling	1	26–	
	1	27	
	2	16	
gameboard, precious. *See* precious gameboard			
garments. *See* apparel			
geese	2	Pref.	97
gemstones. *See* precious stones			
generations, growth of	1	78	5
generosity	1	93	
	2	1	17
	2	45	42
gentleness	1	96	218
	1	101	85
geomancers	1	112	78

	Book	Dial.	Line
gold	1	15	11
	1	35	19
	1	37	107
	1	42	59
	1	52	65
	1	54	
	1	111	24
	2	9	10
	2	9	113
	2	11	11
	2	12	2
	2	13	14
	2	81	12
	2	117	74
	2	129	23
gold, thirst for	1	111	
	2	Pref.	55
trial of	1	84	23
Golden House of Nero	1	96	148
good life, the	1	34	13
	1	90	
	1	96	121
good name	2	13	154
	2	25	
goodness. *See* virtue			
goods	1	8	8
	1	109	77
	1	110	73
	2	9	43
	2	13	15
	2	51	22
goods of the mind	2	13	15
goods. *See also* things			
gown, academic	1	46	94
gout	2	10	38
	2	84	
governance	2	7	72
graduation	1	12	86
grandchildren	1	78	
grandparents	2	10	71
	2	78	16
grasshoppers	2	Pref.	165
	2	25	81

	Book	Dial.	Line
gratitude	1	93	
	2	28	
grave	1	23	38
	1	34	30
	1	103	18
	1	120	53
	2	63	35
	2	95	39
	2	132	
greatness	1	7	34
	1	41	32
	1	64	47
	1	92	2
	2	4	12
greed	1	27	21
	1	35	10
	1	36	14
	1	37	40
	1	38	82
	1	41	79
	1	43	6
	1	46	104
	1	54	16
	1	55	6
	1	57	14
	1	59	14
	1	64	92
	1	68	20
	1	83	29
	1	85	22
	1	93	18
	1	111	10
	1	115	12
	1	121	10
	2	8	19
	2	9	10
	2	9	86
	2	10	24
	2	13	166
	2	38	51
	2	81	92
	2	105	

	Book	Dial.	Line
	1	40	52
	1	41	85
	1	42	3
	1	90	64
	2	Pref.	4
	2	67	60
	2	90	289
	2	93	52
	2	96	76
hedgehog	2	Pref.	173
heirs	1	16	26
	1	90	89
	1	110	
hell	1	13	4
	1	27	93
	1	54	41
	2	132	140
hens. *See* fowl			
herbs	1	3	18
	1	9	92
herdsmen	1	43	89
	1	44	58
	1	59	17
	2	4	40
	2	5	23
	2	41	48
high-mindedness	1	73	14
	2	81	101
historians	1	23	7
	1	29	57
	1	32	40
	1	96	174
homeland. *See* native country			
honesty. *See* probity			
honey	1	62	37
honor, limits of	1	8	19
	1	101	7
honors, *esp.*	1	11	
	1	12	86
	1	45	
	1	46	
	1	92	
	1	96	

	Book	Dial.	Line
	1	36	1
	1	114	96
	2	Pref.	328
	2	19	13
	2	63	
human condition	1	13	72
	1	58	
	1	90	12
	1	101	92
	1	104	10
	1	121	31
	2	17	11
	2	31	
	2	49	3
	2	79	82
	2	93	
	2	111	
human condition, *note*	1	Pref.	
	2	Pref.	
humans, *esp.*	1	5	30
	1	89	11
	1	97	27
	2	32	32
	2	33	25
	2	39	20
	2	51	64
humility	1	10	17
	1	12	109
	1	13	22
	1	46	32
	2	5	156
	2	9	183
	2	12	113
	2	42	13
humors	1	18	98
	2	Pref.	384
	2	75	14
hunger	1	18	12
	1	19	34
	1	116	18
	2	10	43
hunting	1	32	55
	1	49	16

	Book	Dial.	Line
incest	1	52	31
	1	52	54
	2	6	68
incontinence	1	18–	
	1	19	
	1	22	5
	2	108	
	2	110	
indecision	2	76	
indifferents	1	69	80
	2	117	163
indigence. *See* poverty			
indigestion	1	18	101
	1	64	22
indolence	2	100	
inequality	2	2	48
infamy	1	16	37
	1	19	119
	1	42	38
	2	6	43
	2	21	127
	2	24	4
	2	25	
	2	26	10
	2	36	
	2	100	16
infancy	1	115	12
infatuation	2	53	33
infection	2	13	11
inferiors	2	36	10
ingratitude	1	81	51
	1	83	23
	1	93	2
	1	93	40
	2	9	2
	2	28	
ingratitude, twofold root of	2	37	6
inheritance	1	28	14
	1	90	90
	1	110	
	2	13	111
	2	62	39
inheritance, *note*	1	16	

	Book	Dial.	Line
	1	43–	
	1	46	
	2	40	12
	2	51	15
	2	96	97
knowledge, *note*	1	7	
	1	8	
	1	80	
	1	81	
	2	41	
	2	100	
	2	101	
labor	1	5	17
	2	9	126
	2	56	
	2	100	27
labor. *See also* toil			
lamprey. *See* eel			
language	1	9	
	1	33	27
	1	101	115
	2	25	67
	2	50	23
	2	102–	
	2	103	
land	1	57	
	1	114	96
	2	58	
	2	59	8
Last Judgment	2	47	7
laughter, idiotic	2	Pref.	219
	2	90	282
	2	97	28
laws	1	25	15
	1	26	4
	1	48	43
	1	84	32
	2	21	26
	2	43	49
lawyers	1	46	91
	1	90	90
	2	Pref.	318

	Book	Dial.	Line
mediocrity (being average)	1	10	44
	2	52	31
melancholy	1	44	95
	2	93	17
	2	115	38
melancholy, *note*	2	Pref.	388
	2	89	
melancholy. *See also* madness			
memory	1	Pref.	4
	1	Pref.	62
	1	8	
	1	18	9
	1	22	8
	1	30	113
	1	43	13
	1	92	8
	1	101	29
	2	11	5
	2	33	29
	2	51	53
	2	52	51
	2	101	
memory, artificial	1	8	2
	1	8	40
men-at-arms	1	16	75
	1	48	22
	1	99	48
	1	105	55
	1	106	19
	2	96	32
men-at-arms. *See also* military, the			
mercenaries	1	21	60
mercenaries, *note*	1	48	
merchandise	1	21	60
	1	46	38
	1	90	17
	1	120	29
	2	Pref.	230
mercury (metallic)	1	111	57
mercy	1	38	54
	1	85	27
	1	96	114
	1	96	222

Book	Dial.	Line
1	Pref.	225
1	Pref.	238
1	2	69
1	3	17
1	4	7
1	5	18
1	6	16
1	7	
1	8	24
1	9	59
1	21	4
1	27	55
1	28	36
1	29	8
1	30	112
1	35	34
1	40	12
1	42	89
1	43	3
1	43	112
1	46	53
1	48	21
1	55	21
1	56	27
1	57	51
1	60	39
1	63	18
1	86	8
1	90	64
1	106	3
1	112	22
1	121	
2	1	45
2	1	73
2	2	12
2	2	28
2	6	2
2	6	48
2	13	15
2	15	52
2	32	8
2	33	29
2	41	12

	Book	Dial.	Line
	2	43	2
	2	51	67
	2	70	24
	2	83	230
	2	86	8
	2	96	48
	2	99	21
	2	114	147
mine and thine	1	45	44
mining	1	54	
	2	2	5
mirror	1	Pref.	203
	1	Pref.	212
	1	2	60
	2	1	12
misery	1	Pref.	9
	1	27	7
	1	27	93
	1	88	14
	1	95	83
	1	106	71
	1	108	3
	1	108	54
	1	109	82
	1	116	8
	2	35	22
	2	39	35
	2	93	
mob. *See* crowd			
moderation	1	Pref.	98
	1	2	75
	1	5	15
	1	9	14
	1	14	48
	1	18	94
	1	22	18
	1	22	31
	1	38	54
	1	41	38
	1	42	59
	1	50	20
	1	55	11
	1	66	14

	Book	Dial.	Line
	2	Pref.	270
moon	1	40	20
	2	93	56
mortals. *See* humans			
mother	1	73	19
	1	83	
	2	12	15
	2	47	
	2	48	22
mother-in-law	1	65	35
moth	2	Pref.	155
mountain, golden	1	37	113
mourning	1	90	8
	2	18	
	2	46–	
	2	49	
	2	51–	
	2	52	
	2	83	252
	2	92	24
mourning. *See also* funeral			
multitude. *See* crowd			
murder, *esp.*	1	23	17
	1	27	60
	1	49	22
	1	52	
	1	56	52
	1	65	74
	1	77	43
	1	84	14
	2	19	17
	2	59	36
	2	83	134
music	1	23	
	1	28	2
	2	Pref.	230
	2	Pref.	277
	2	18	5
	2	50	49
	2	97	
	2	122	27
mutiny	1	97	30
Myrrhine ware	1	38	122

	Book	Dial.	Line
	2	87	
niké	1	103	47
nimbleness	1	6	
	1	120	11
	2	1	57
nimbleness, *note*	2	99	
nobility	1	15–	
	1	16	
	2	4	2
	2	5	
obesity	2	99	
obscurity	1	15	24
	1	16	
	1	92	47
	2	5	
	2	6	17
ocean, a monster	1	87	6
	1	98	22
	2	76	14
	2	90	153
octopus	1	23	18
odor. *See* scent			
Office, divine	2	109	17
old age	1	1	30
	1	2	16
	1	3	4
	1	5	18
	1	6	5
	1	29	50
	1	110	
	1	115	12
	1	120	15
	2	Pref.	369
	2	13	199
	2	15	10
	2	68	60
	2	83	
	2	86	39
	2	101	
	2	119	5
	2	120	41
old age. *See also* senescence			

	Book	Dial.	Line
	2	50	12
parricide	1	52	21
parrot	1	64	56
	1	65	2
passions	1	Pref.	236
	1	26–	
	1	27	
	1	69	
	1	84	51
	2	Pref.	386
	2	15	52
	2	26	31
	2	32	12
	2	38	51
passions, *note*	1	34	
	1	91	
	2	105–	
	2	111	
passwords	1	35	11
past	1	Pref.	7
	1	43	57
	1	112	27
	2	14	22
	2	83	134
	2	114	40
pastimes	1	23–	
	1	28	
	1	32	
	1	115	12
pastimes, *note*	1	61	
	1	64	
	1	84	39
patience	1	Pref.	6
	1	Pref.	149
	2	7	81
	2	12	113
	2	19	23
	2	31	20
	2	42	18
	2	84	48
	2	95	28
patrimony	1	66	23
	1	84	22

	Book	Dial.	Line
physician	1	Pref.	168
	1	23	16
	1	46	91
	1	90	89
	2	Pref.	320
	2	16	4
	2	20	6
	2	65	23
	2	93	188
	2	95	31
physician, the heavenly	1	Pref.	171
	2	3	26
	2	126	68
pictures	1	37	97
	1	39	3
	1	40	
	1	41	5
pigeons	1	62	39
	2	Pref.	40
	2	Pref.	145
pipes, musical	1	23	60
	1	24	2
plague	1	116	18
	2	92	
planets	1	15	3
	2	93	52
	2	114	208
planets, *note*	1	112	145
plasticen. See art, plastic			
playing ball. *See* ballplaying			
pleasure	1	18	53
	1	19	130
	1	22	7
	1	38	70
	1	69	
	1	90	29
	2	10	10
	2	10	59
	2	12	83
	2	28	5
	2	32	8
	2	53	29

	Book	Dial.	Line
	1	107	1
	1	109	89
	2	63	294
port, *note*	2	54	
port. *See also* metaphor, nautical; navigation; shipwreck; voyage			
portraiture	1	40	25
posterity	1	Pref.	127
	1	16	4
	1	32	77
	1	40–	
	1	41	
	1	43	28
	1	44	99
	1	120	57
	2	78	17
	2	88	
	2	97	46
	2	130	20
posterity, *note*	1	117	
	2	12	
	2	130–	
	2	131	
poverty	1	Pref.	105
	1	8	17
	1	18	36
	1	19	36
	1	33	87
	1	37	31
	1	53	9
	1	100	19
	1	111	7
	2	8	
	2	9	58
	2	10	34
	2	11	
	2	12	36
	2	13	142
	2	84	32
power, *esp.*	1	85	
	1	91	
	1	96	
	1	101	7

	Book	Dial.	Line
	2	59	15
	2	64	13
	2	83	181
	2	91	59
	2	114	200
	2	117	127
pride	1	10	1
	1	13	21
	1	17	24
	1	35	10
	1	38	24
	1	59	
	1	65	15
	1	66	11
	1	68	2
	1	68	41
	1	83	29
	1	93	16
	1	103	2
	1	106	69
	2	8	28
	2	10	30
	2	12	18
	2	29	41
	2	59	
	2	65	17
	2	77	23
	2	78	32
	2	79	83
	2	82	6
	2	111	
	2	117	91
	2	118	56
prime of life	1	1–	
	1	9	
	2	48	
	2	120	
prime of life, *note*	1	69	
princes	1	Pref.	156
	1	14	21
	1	16	80
	1	17	42
	1	19	99

	Book	Dial.	Line
	1	69	229
	1	121	25
	2	18	50
	2	83	
	2	99	1
	2	106	29
senescence. *See also* old age			
senses, bodily	1	18	80
	1	22	4
	1	23	71
	2	51	51
	2	96–	
	2	97	
separation of lovers	1	69	95
separation of lovers, *note*	1	86	30
	2	53	67
Septuagint	1	43	36
	1	43	142
serfdom. *See* servitude			
serpent. *See* viper			
servants	1	29–	
	1	30	
	1	33	
	1	34	9
	1	43	112
	1	53	25
	1	101	63
	2	Pref.	112
	2	7	
	2	9	186
	2	24	34
	2	29–	
	2	30	
	2	90	26
servants. *See also* servitude; slaves			
service, divine	1	38	13
	1	42	43
service, military. *See* military, the			
servitude	1	8	18
	1	105	55
	1	116	5
	2	7	
	2	29	53

	Book	Dial.	Line
slaves, into kings	1	14	29
	1	16	78
	2	5	74
	2	7	15
	2	7	113
of Sabinus	1	43	112
slaves. *See also* servants			
sleep	1	21	22
	1	105	9
	1	112	20
	1	115	10
	2	29	58
	2	52	15
	2	82	15
	2	86	
	2	100	6
	2	109	20
	2	115	14
	2	117	44
	2	119	162
sloth	1	21	11
	1	106	9
	2	3	30
	2	15	57
	2	83	245
	2	90	153
	2	98	
	2	109	20
	2	114	199
	2	120	96
smaragd	1	37	71
	1	39	21
smell. *See* scent			
snakes. *See* vipers			
soldiers. *See* military, the			
solitude	1	28	6
	1	32	65
	1	58	15
	2	18	54
	2	31	50
	2	40	22
	2	88	45

	Book	Dial.	Line
son	1	16	18
	1	16	116
	1	17	42
	1	52	17
	1	71	
	1	72	5
	1	73	
	1	77	34
	1	81	1
	1	82–	
	1	83	
	1	114	1
	2	5–	
	2	6	
	2	12	106
	2	43–	
	2	50	
	2	78	
son-in-law	1	75	
	2	23	42
soothsayers	1	112	76
sophist	1	Pref.	104
	1	7	14
	1	26	36
	1	43	20
sorrow, *esp.*	1	Pref.	9
	1	23	2
	1	71	2
	1	90	8
	1	103	16
	1	109	32
	1	111	16
	1	113	16
	2	42	2
	2	93	
	2	96	
soul, *esp.*	1	5	48
	1	18	29
	1	18	77
	1	107	5
	2	49	6
	2	119	100
soul. *See also* mind			

	Book	Dial.	Line
spectacles (shows)	1	30	
spices	1	22	13
spider	1	7	15
	1	22	13
	1	23	16
	2	Pref.	153
	2	82	67
	2	119	43
sport, *note*	1	6	
	1	25	
	1	29	
	1	31–	
	1	32	
spurs	1	48	50
stability-instability	1	Pref.	156
	1	1	88
	1	14	31
	1	16	58
	1	17	13
	1	86	6
	1	87	9
	1	90	4
	1	90	31
	1	91	20
	2	5	80
	2	79	4
	2	111	
stadium	1	29	55
stars	1	15	3
	1	24	44
	1	39	21
	1	40	52
	1	41	85
	1	42	3
	1	112	142
	2	Pref.	4
	2	93	52
	2	114	210
statues	1	37	109
	1	41	
	1	43	3
	2	117	77
stature	2	1	56

	Book	Dial.	Line
stepchildren	1	79	
stepfather	1	79	28
stepmother	1	65	35
	1	72	22
	1	76	8
	2	42	
stepson	1	79	28
	2	42	
stepson, stepmother. *See also* lust			
sterility	2	22	
	2	58	
	2	78	
stork	2	Pref.	55
strength, physical	1	Pref.	166
	1	5	
	1	7	10
	1	120	23
	2	2	
	2	3	2
	2	83	241
strife, *esp.*	1	2	40
	1	33	12
	1	50	98
	1	65	43
	1	66	
	1	84	8
	1	116	18
	2	Pref.	
	2	13	143
	2	19	
	2	20	11
	2	31	
	2	41–	
	2	45	
	2	50	52
	2	51	5
	2	75–	
	2	76	
	2	80	5
	2	90	306
	2	128	27
string instruments	1	23	9
	1	24	18

	Book	Dial.	Line
	1	72	23
	1	111	42
	2	1	
	2	77	28
	2	83	81
	2	89	
	2	94	36
	2	99	4
	2	110	25
	2	122	
ungodliness	1	27	56
	1	101	104
usury	1	27	25
	1	56	
	2	16	2
values, perversion of	1	21	66
	1	30	128
	1	33	73
	1	39	28
	1	59	9
	1	89	11
	1	90	17
	1	107	73
	1	109	48
	1	112	22
	1	116	37
	1	121	14
	1	122	3
	2	2	51
	2	9	123
	2	10	16
	2	13	65
	2	67	87
	2	79	
	2	83	92
	2	89	
	2	104	31
vengeance	1	96	102
	1	96	216
	1	101	
	1	120	21
	2	32	12

	Book	Dial.	Line
	2	Pref.	63
	2	Pref.	135
	2	90	42
virtue	1	Pref.	19
	1	Pref.	126
	1	Pref.	208
	1	1	51
	1	5–	
	1	7	
	1	9–	
	1	12	
	1	14–	
	1	15	
	1	19	130
	1	21	81
	1	24	98
	1	27	75
	1	29	65
	1	35	51
	1	37	31
	1	37	167
	1	43	122
	1	46	6
	1	46	101
	1	49–	
	1	50	
	1	52–	
	1	53	
	1	55	9
	1	57	19
	1	64	6
	1	69	92
	1	81	24
	1	91–	
	1	92	
	1	97	6
	1	100–	
	1	101	
	1	104	30
	1	108	54
	1	112	23
	1	115	8
	1	119	12

	Book	Dial.	Line
	1	122	6
	2	Pref.	275
	2	1	39
	2	3–	
	2	10	
	2	12–	
	2	13	
	2	15	71
	2	21	5
	2	21	127
	2	24–	
	2	28	
	2	32	3
	2	41	9
	2	44–	
	2	45	
	2	48	50
	2	51–	
	2	53	
	2	67	
	2	102	43
	2	104	

virtue. *See also* courage

voyage	Book	Dial.	Line
	1	1	58
	1	31	76
	1	54	
	1	87	
	1	88	5
	1	90	2
	1	91	28
	1	98	2
	2	Pref.	347
	2	2	5
	2	48	7
	2	76	14
	2	79	60
	2	83	294
	2	90	256
	2	97	22
	2	121	67

voyage. *See also* metaphor, nautical; navigation;
   port; shipwreck

	Book	Dial.	Line
wakefulness	1	21	41
	1	31	2
	1	32	27
	1	35	10
	1	48	25
	1	65	57
	2	18	67
	2	86	
	2	90	53
	2	100	8
walls	1	35	5
	1	99	14
	2	5	23
	2	11	16
	2	68	60
	2	82	19
warfare	1	Pref.	18
	1	31	71
	1	33	4
	1	35	19
	1	48	
	1	49	17
	1	95–	
	1	106	
	1	116	18
	2	Pref.	301
	2	32	26
	2	68–	
	2	74	
	2	77	37
	2	125	20
wasps	2	Pref.	50
weakness	1	5	16
	1	7	11
	1	106	70
	2	2	
	2	81	113
wealth, *esp.*	1	Pref.	180
	1	17	
	1	18	36
	1	19	36
	1	21	79
	1	28	44

	Book	Dial.	Line
	1	77	15
	1	114	102
	2	Pref.	225
	2	17	22
	2	18–	
	2	22	
	2	24	
	2	42	
	2	50	
	2	81	69
	2	128	
will, *esp.*	2	81	12
	2	104	119
wine	1	18	52
	1	24	85
	1	38	54
	2	84	44
	2	90	154
	2	90	283
wisdom	1	Pref.	36
	1	7	13
	1	9	13
	1	12	
	1	13	29
	1	14	47
	1	21	79
	1	43	19
	1	46	13
	1	49	27
	1	64	13
	2	7	17
	2	13	34
	2	36	2
	2	86	18
	2	102	20
	2	117	131
witness, false	1	47	34
wolf	1	95	47
	2	Pref.	39
	2	Pref.	81
	2	49	33
	2	97	28
wolffish	1	63	68

	Book	Dial.	Line
youth	1	1	23
	1	2	35
	1	29	50
	1	32	2
	1	69	
	1	71	
	1	80–	
	1	81	
	1	92	66
	1	115	12
	1	119	7
	2	Pref.	361
	2	12	
	2	40–	
	2	50	
	2	83	
	2	120	114
	2	131	12

TOPICS AND MAXIMS

English	Book	Dial.	Line
Adversity the best teacher	2	73	36
Apocalyptic return	1	114	88
	2	6	77
Appearance and reality. *See* Examine the things . . .			
As one nail drives out another	1	69	221
	2	84	40
As if Epicurus were watching you. *See* tanquam spectet Epicurus			
Attending to the business of others	1	47	passim
	2	13	187
	2	15	31
Beauty and chastity seldom dwell together	1	65	11
	1	66	14
	1	72	5
	2	1	22
	2	21	17
	2	128	33
Being as one professes to be	1	46	115

	Book	Dial.	Line
Enjoy what is difficult	2	99	23
Envy denigrates glory	2	130	29
Even the smallest thing requires effort	2	88	31
	2	104	37
Every age complains about its ways	1	115	33
Everything exists by strife	2	Pref.	passim
Everything is getting worse	1	115	21
	2	28	59
	2	96	22
	2	130	21
Examine the things, not their shadows. *See also* larva *and* opinionum perversitas	1	46	109
	1	108	73
	1	121	31
	2	122	32
Examples console, reassure, challenge. *See also* imitatio	1	Pref.	158
	1	16	104
	1	20	27
	1	29	63
	1	96	192
	2	13	65
	2	21	96
	2	35	6
	2	57	62
	2	67	32
	2	88	64
	2	114	43
Fame is a liar	2	130	48
Forgetful of the human condition	1	Pref.	112
	1	38	70
	1	58	60
	2	49	3
	2	79	82
	2	83	226
	2	111	14
	2	117	189
	2	118	16
Fortune helps the brave	2	28	22
	2	73	23
Forward-backward	1	117	2

	Book	Dial.	Line
at home wherever life is good	2	67	69
	2	125	27
besieged everywhere	2	68	31
deceive themselves	1	11	52
	1	50	17
	1	51	37
	1	101	4
	1	109	48
	1	112	22
	2	51	39
	2	104	24
desiring what is harmful	1	21	66
	1	30	128
	1	33	73
	1	39	28
	1	59	9
	1	89	11
	1	109	48
	1	109	73
	1	112	22
	1	116	37
	1	121	14
	1	122	3
	2	2	51
	2	9	123
	2	10	16
	2	13	65
	2	67	87
	2	73	6
	2	79	91
	2	83	92
	2	83	132
	2	104	31
given to complaints	2	9	190
	2	83	103
	2	92	17
	2	93	16
	2	120	39
imprisoned	2	64	10
making evil what is good	1	21	66
	2	90	54
mortal	1	1	28
	2	69	21

	Book	Dial.	Line
	1	71	2
	1	103	16
	1	113	16
Just a pinprick	1	6	13
	1	92	4
	1	96	253
	2	68	36
Kings: from slaves, slaves from kings	1	14	29
	1	16	78
	2	5	74
	2	7	15
prone to betrayal	2	80	10
public servants	1	96	14
should govern like a parent	1	96	107
	1	99	4
Know thyself. *See* nosce te ipsum			
Ladder. *See* scala			
Learning-experience	2	13	72
	2	45	18
	2	58	74
by juxtaposing contraries	2	6	46
	2	58	2
	2	71	23
from one's errors. *See also* utilia	2	26	37
non discuntur gratis	2	73	17
Leaves, blossoms, and fruit	1	46	2
	1	71	31
Life: an unsavory playlet	2	83	205
a kind of death. *See* vita: mors			
a prison	2	121	6
as exile	2	67	74
	2	125	30
	2	129	2
as torture	2	12	93
	2	65	13
full of dreams and false opinions	1	90	59
full of toil and grief	1	90	13
progress gradual, its end sudden and unex-pected	1	90	108
	2	75	36

	Book	Dial.	Line
just a pinprick. *See* Just a pinprick			
must share human circumstances	2	38	52
	2	50	3
	2	118	18
	2	119	12
	2	125	96
rational, mortal creature	1	18	82
	2	117	25
Many-few. *See* multi-pauci			
Mercy ennobles	1	96	114
	1	101	37
Merry for an hour, sorry forever	1	30	120
Metempsychosis	1	15	74
	2	83	236
Might makes right	2	28	22
Migration of souls. *See* Metempsychosis			
Mind: -body	2	2	26
	2	75	14
easily deceived. *See* Humans: deceive themselves			
must be bridled	1	Pref.	149
	1	6	37
	1	9	60
	1	30	113
	1	35	34
	1	89	31
	2	125	172
nothing more admirable	1	40	12
weakened by riches. *See* Riches weaken the mind			
Mine-thine	2	45	43
Mirror	1	Pref.	203
	1	Pref.	212
Money is round: it rolls	1	27	30
	1	110	73
	2	13	8
	2	127	26
Most evil member of the human body is the tongue	1	9	86
	2	26	14
	2	103	passim
Mother Earth	1	17	8
	1	83	26

	Book	Dial.	Line
Not necessary, but superfluous	1	39	28
	1	50	20
	1	90	60
One art enough for one mind	1	46	75
One learns by making errors. *See also* utilia	2	26	37
non discuntur gratis	2	60	19
	2	73	17
	2	73	33
One of a few	1	1	49
	1	19	130
	2	83	27
	2	102	22
	2	114	49
Opportunity makes thieves	2	60	7
Order of things. *See* ordo naturae			
Pain not an ill	2	114	6
Past, present, and future	1	Pref.	27
	2	87	16
Patience overcomes all violence	2	67	82
Peace fosters moral decay	1	105	49
	1	106	8
	2	32	26
Peasants, the worst kind of people	1	57	14
	2	59	passim
Perverse opinion. *See* opinionum perversitas			
Physician, lord over the human body	2	115	8
Pleasure of revenge is momentary, of mercy perpetual	1	101	32
Point to with the finger	1	29	23
	1	117	26
	2	35	12
Poisons are mixed in precious cups	2	116	27
Power corrupts	2	79	67
Presence diminishes one's appeal	1	51	18
	1	92	56
	2	52	8
	2	53	66
Proving oneself	2	67	117
Proximity and prosperity are the parents of envy	2	106	20

	Book	Dial.	Line
	2	79	4
Stop admiring base things	1	1	82
	1	42	2
	1	54	9
	1	55	21
	1	86	17
	1	117	53
Strive and rise up. *See* assurgere			
Stupidity. *See also* stulti-docti	1	93	20
	1	94	33
	2	12	69
	2	34	15
	2	97	66
	2	100	45
	2	118	52
Stupid laughter	2	Pref.	223
	2	90	282
	2	97	28
Stupid old men (puer-senex *inverted*)	1	26	19
	2	83	152
	2	109	24
Surety, be a, but ruin stands near you	2	14	47
Swan song	1	23	27
	2	119	72
Sword of Damocles	1	95	54
	2	39	28
Teaching those that can be taught	1	81	47
	2	41	9
The three goods. *See also* vera bona	1	109	77
Thinking to be where one is not	1	10	30
Time: cannot be lost unwillingly	2	15	24
cannot be recovered	1	115	7
	2	15	4
	2	83	9
is fleeting	1	1	passim
	1	2	3
	2	14	19
	2	15	25
	2	83	9
Tossing and turning	2	75	45
Traitor injures himself. *See also* Injustice hurts the perpetrator	2	80	30

	Book	Dial.	Line
	2	76	14
	2	77	58
	2	114	103
	2	118	97
is difficult	2	5	7
	2	9	24
	2	10	10
	2	24	42
	2	56	passim
	2	100	27
	2	104	39
	2	104	62
	2	114	29
	2	117	226
may spur body unto death	2	51	18
must be willed	1	119	12
	2	81	14
	2	100	38
	2	104	18
	2	109	5
	2	114	66
no safeguard for the body	1	73	passim
	2	51	16
nothing sweeter than	2	104	40
	2	109	10
	2	118	46
preferable to learning. *See also* Reading for action	1	43	122
	1	44	50
	1	46	31
	2	8	42
	2	41	9
	2	58	73
	2	97	66
	2	100	38
the only good. *See also* vera bona *and* virtus in medio	1	109	76
	2	64	2
	2	82	52
	2	114	6
	2	118	49
the only way to happiness	1	21	33
	1	115	38

	Book	Dial.	Line
Without a teacher	1	45	6
	1	80	12
	2	40	15
Work is hard	2	56	43
World just a pinprick. *See* Just a pinprick			
World upside down	1	12	85
	1	63	59
	1	64	47
Worthless mind, a, loves gold	2	13	167
You have it, it has you	1	85	2
	1	114	104
	2	13	7
	2	18	9
	2	79	67
You waste money, it wastes you	2	13	7

Latin and Greek
ad altum niti. *See* assurgere

	Book	Dial.	Line
ἀδιάφορον	1	69	80
aegritudo animi	2	93	182
aemulatio	1	44	6
aequalitas	2	2	47
	2	75	17
aequanimitas	1	89	31
	2	68	76
	2	75	70
	2	114	298
	2	118	92
	2	120	62
aleatores	1	112	94
alieno gloriari	1	2	80
	1	16	passim
	1	58	21
	1	79	30
	1	80	2
	2	6	17
	2	9	2
	2	13	17
	2	79	94
	2	81	60
	2	127	60
animi morbus	2	114	128

	Book	Dial.	Line
	2	100	8
	2	104	43
auxilium Dei. *See* With God's help			
avarus: avidus auri	1	38	83
	1	64	94
avis. *See* rara avis			
bene vivere. *See* Live well			
bona. *See also* vera bona	1	109	77
	2	9	53
	2	9	62
	2	13	15
bona mea omnia mecum porto	2	9	43
	2	55	10
	2	73	64
brevitas	1	Pref.	71
	1	40	43
	2	Pref.	407
caritas. *See also* Mercy ennobles *and* Pleasure of revenge . . .	1	19	27
caste, sobrie, modeste. *See also* sobrie et modeste	1	2	77
	1	65	53
	2	82	21
cingulum militare	1	48	1
commessatio	1	19	82
commoda. *See* incommoda			
concordia discors/concordia ex contrariis orta	1	11	67
	2	93	40
conditionis oblivio. *See* Forgetful of the human condition			
confirmatio	2	114	258
consuetudo	1	40	47
	1	69	123
	2	10	16
	2	41	41
	2	58	62
contentio	2	114	234
conversatio interna. *See* sermo intimus			
convivium	1	19	74
copia-inopia	1	43	130

	Book	Dial.	Line
	1	23	23
	1	91	20
	1	96	79
	1	107	54
	2	5	83
exercitatio animi	1	29	6
	1	41	87
	1	44	88
	2	2	16
experientia magistra rerum	2	13	75
	2	45	19
	2	58	73
	2	73	32
faeces populi	2	90	290
fenestrae animi, —exteriorum sensuum	1	30	114
	2	96	30
	2	97	2
fiducia	1	9	59
fons aquae vitae	1	16	74
fons curarum	1	70	9
	1	77	18
fortitudo	1	Pref.	209
	1	73	1
	2	28	24
	2	69	29
	2	73	25
	2	90	165
	2	91	67
	2	114	27
fortes Fortuna adiuvat. *See* Fortune helps the brave			
frugalitas. *See also* modestia, sobrietas, *and* temperantia	1	41	38
	1	96	197
	2	84	39
frui-uti	1	10	50
	1	21	6
hic est	1	29	23
hinc-illinc	1	18	20
	1	23	76

	Book	Dial.	Line
	2	5	10
	2	13	65
	2	21	61
	2	24	42
	2	25	46
	2	66	25
	2	77	71
	2	118	152
	2	119	128
imperium	1	96	passim
	1	116	22
in altum niti. *See* assurgere			
incommoda	1	15	117
	2	44	21
	2	94	29
	2	95	25
	2	114	174
inimicus familiaris	1	2	40
	1	33	passim
	1	50	98
	1	84	8
	2	51	5
	2	80	5
in magnis ingeniis magni errores	1	7	35
	1	15	53
insolentia: iuvenilis	2	43	64
	2	44	11
prosperitatis	1	17	35
	2	42	21
	2	58	58
intentio. *See* contentio			
inter os atque offam	1	110	69
intestina discordia	2	Pref.	390
	2	75	passim
	2	109	passim
intus in anima. *See also* sermo intimus; veritas	1	4	7
in silentio; *and* In your own bosom			
	1	11	40
	1	48	20
	2	29	35
	2	40	10
	2	77	74
	2	97	42

	Book	Dial.	Line
	2	49	2
	2	51	39
	2	59	15
	2	64	13
	2	83	181
	2	91	59
	2	113	39
	2	114	200
	2	117	127
	2	117	151
parsimonia	2	81	12
pater patriae	1	96	108
	1	99	6
	2	108	17
patientia	2	7	50
	2	19	24
	2	24	36
	2	28	40
	2	31	20
	2	39	77
	2	42	18
	2	43	83
	2	57	63
	2	58	15
	2	59	12
	2	61	21
	2	64	13
	2	65	52
	2	66	22
	2	67	81
	2	81	150
	2	84	48
	2	85	16
	2	88	68
	2	90	135
	2	95	28
	2	97	6
	2	98	10
	2	114	21
	2	114	128
	2	114	262
	2	117	226
	2	118	passim

	Book	Dial.	Line
sermo intimus. *See also* intus in anima *and* veritas in silentio	2	114	228
	2	114	312
servus servorum	1	107	95
similitudo	1	66	5
	1	94	15
	1	119	8
	2	56	44
	2	93	35
si vis amari, ama	1	50	54
	2	42	31
sobrie et modeste. *See also* caste, sobrie . . .	1	57	3
	1	122	29
	2	82	22
sobrietas. *See also* frugalitas; modestia, *and* temperantia	1	57	3
	1	122	29
somnus mortis consanguineus, —imago. *See* Sleep . . .			
speculum —velut in speculo	1	Pref.	212
stulti-docti. *See also* Stupidity	1	12	47
	1	19	130
	1	38	66
	1	93	20
	2	12	70
	2	36	3
	2	90	54
	2	97	66
	2	114	185
	2	117	56
surdo canere	2	13	211
	2	41	40
	2	73	33
	2	90	192
taedium vitae	2	98	passim
	2	118	45
tanquam spectet Epicurus	2	53	48
temperamentum	2	75	17
temperantia. *See also* frugalitas; modestia; *and* sobrietas	1	Pref.	96
torpor animi	2	109	passim
	2	114	262

EXAMPLES AND STORIES

Examples	Book	Dial.	Line
Armies of the Spaniards			
Armies of the Ligurians			
Armies of the Gauls			
Armies of the Teutones			
Armies of the Cimbri			
Navies of the Carthaginians			
Navies of the Athenians			
Crews on ships before Marseilles			
Salamis			
Marathon			
Jewish wars			
Scyths			
Amazones			
Arabs			
Parthians			
Medes			
Victims of Alexander the Great			
Victims of savage animals (Dicaearchus!)			
Victims of tempests			
Victims of shipwrecks			
Victims of fires			
Victims of civil war			
Castles: and courage	1	35	40
Julius Caesar			
the two *Africani*			
Pompey			
Marius			
Alexander the Great			
Pyrrhus			
Hannibal			
Stefano Colonna			
Castles: none impregnable	1	35	21
Tarpeian citadel			
Tarentinian citadel			
Locri			
Ilion			
Byrsa			
Corinth			
Praeneste			
Castles: suspected by the people	1	35	14
Publicola			

Examples	Book	Dial.	Line
Assyria—Sardanapalus	2	39	51
Persia—Cyrus			
Greece & —Alexander			
Asia—Nabis			
Sicily—Dionysii, Phalaris, Agathocles			
Sparta—Cleomenes, Nabis			
Cities: besieged	2	68	2
Troy			
Tyre			
Carthage			
Jerusalem			
Numantia			
Corinth			
Rome			
Tarentum			
Syracuse			
Athens			
Veii			
Cities: destroyed	2	69	4
Tyre			
Thebes			
Persepolis			
Troy			
Saguntum			
Carthage			
Numantia			
Jerusalem			
Milan			
Troy	2	132	88
Jerusalem			
Carthage			
Corinth			
Numantia			
Saguntum			
twelve cities in Asia			
Cities: destroyed, that rose again	2	69	25
Saguntum			
Milan			
Jerusalem			
Carthage			
[Tortona *or* Cremona?]			
Cities: enslaved	2	14	52
Sparta			

Examples	Book	Dial.	Line
Athens			
Jerusalem			
Rome			
Cities: great, have small (insignificant, mean) inhabitants, small towns have great ones	2	4	6
Romulus			
Catiline			
Bias			
Pythagoras			
Anacharsis			
Democritus			
Aristotle			
Theophrastus			
Cicero			
Philitas			
Hippocrates			
Phidias			
Apelles			
Cities: small, do not prevent greatness of their citizens	2	4	6
Numa Pompilius			
Caligula			
Aeacides			
Alexander the Great			
Cities not always conquered by weaponry	1	99	11
Julius Caesar			
Brutus			
City, safeguarding one's native	2	68	44
Archimedes			
City's (Country's) glory: and one's own	1	15	44
Themistocles and the Seriphian			
Plato			
Epaminondas			
Alcibiades			
Critias			
City's (Country's) glory: increases individual's infamy	1	15	28
Catilina			
Caligula			
Nero			
Civil war: advocates of peace, liberty, and justice	2	74	19
Menenius Agrippa			
Porcius Cato			
Co-commanders, rash	2	71	4
Terentius Varro			

Examples	Book	Dial.	Line
Death: kinds of	2	121	48
Plotinus			
Euripides			
Lucretius			
Herod			
Hadrian			
Death: mitigated when suffered at the hands of distinguished enemies	2	121	31
Pompey at the hands of Julius Caesar			
Ipseus at the hands of Capaneus			
Lausus at the hands of Aeneas			
Ornytus at the hands of Camilla			
Death: "paying one's debt"	2	120	17
Spartan dying under the laws of Lycurgus			
Death: place of, does not matter	2	121	78
(sailor story)			
Death: shameful	2	122	40
Jesus Christ			
Death: sudden, most desirable	2	113	35
	2	123	14
Julius Caesar			
Death: stand up when dying	2	119	75
Vespasian			
Death: suffering valiantly	2	119	131
Cato of Utica (suicide)			
Defeat: followed by victory	2	73	7
Marcellus			
Julius Caesar			
Defeat: gallantry in	2	73	70
Leonidas at Thermopylae			
Deiphobus			
Pompey's legions in Thessaly			
Last battle with Hannibal			
Defrauded, men who were	2	62	37
Canius by Pytius			
Augustus by one Marius			
Dentition, abnormal	2	94	28
King Robert of Sicily			
Daughter of Mithridates, King of Pontus			
Prusias, King of Bithynia			
Zenobia			
Depending on a weakling	1	71	20
Hadrian			

Examples	Book	Dial.	Line
eighty castles			
Effort, zealous	2	100	29
Socrates			
Demosthenes			
Eloquence: danger of	1	9	77
Demosthenes			
Cicero			
Antony			
ii Reg. 1, 1–6	2	103	26
Cicero			
Demosthenes			
Eloquence: without wisdom	1	9	18
Catiline			
Enemy: complaining about the flight of the	2	30	21
Julius Caesar			
Enemy: lamenting the death of an	1	104	32
Metellus lamenting Scipio the Younger			
Julius Caesar lamenting Pompey			
Alexander the Great lamenting Darius			
Exiles: great	2	67	34
Camillus			
Rutilius			
Metellus			
Marcellus the Younger			
Cicero			
Exiles: voluntary			
Scipio Africanus	2	66	68
Cornelians			
Pythagoras	2	67	24
Solon			
Lycurgus			
the three Scipios: Africanus, Nasica, Lentulus			
Fame: cannot be concealed	2	88	50
Dandamus			
Diogenes the Cynic			
Scipio Africanus (at Liternum)			
Titus Livius			
Anchorites			
Solomon			
Fame: harmful	1	117	36
Cicero			
Demosthenes			

Examples	Book	Dial.	Line
Aeneas			
Elijah			
Fire: perishing in a	2	55	2
Alcibiades			
Tullus Hostilius			
Carus			
Fortune-tellers lie	1	112	97
Pompey			
Crassus			
Julius Caesar			
Freed by the eternal master	2	7	27
Malchus			
Friends among one's enemies			
Massinissa	1	51	3
Scipio Africanus			
Augustus	2	52	44
Frugality	1	18	20
Curius			
Fabricius			
Coruncanius			
Serranus			
Cato Censorius			
Paul the Hermit			
Saint Anthony			
Augustus			
Julius Caesar			
Saints (clothing)	1	20	13
Augustus (clothing)			
Aelius Tubero (dishes)	1	42	49
Glory crumbles. *See* Where are they now?			
Going underground	1	54	13
Nero			
Goods that cannot be taken away			
Aristippus	2	9	43
Bias/Stilbo	2	55	10
Gout does not make one unfit for mental work	2	84	54
Septimius Severus			
Grandchildren	1	78	45
Pacuvius			
Commodus			
Romulus and Remus			
Ancus Martius			

Examples	Book	Dial.	Line
Livestock, troubles of keeping	1	59	35
Job			
Lordship: leads to disaster	1	95	8
Alexander Phaereus			
Dionysius of Syracuse			
Phalaris of Agrigentum			
Hanno of Carthage			
Clearchus of Heraclea			
Aristotimus of Epirus			
Nabis of Sparta			
Hipparchus of Athens			
Cassius			
Maelius			
Manlius			
Catiline			
Gracchi			
Apuleius			
Caligula			
Nero			
Domitian			
Commodus			
Bassianus			
Lose the battle, win the war	1	103	9
Rome vs. Carthage, Gauls			
Love	1	69	52
Julius Caesar			
Hannibal			
Jupiter			
Hercules			
Byblis			
Procris			
Pyramus			
Iphis			
Trojan war			
Love of precious cups	1	38	107
Nero			
Pompey			
Love of Corinthian vessels	1	42	21
Augustus			
Love of fish	1	63	31
Sergius Orata			
Licinius Murena			
Philip			

Examples	Book	Dial.	Line
Nero			
Strength, physical			
Milo	1	5	21
	1	29	55
	2	2	20
Hercules	1	5	36
	2	2	20
Strife, advocate of peace in	2	75	32
Menenius Agrippa			
Strongholds. *See* Castles			
Struck down by his tongue	2	103	5
the liar in ii Reg. 1, 1–16			
Successors worse than their predecessors	2	78	17
Hieronymus of Syracuse			
Iugurtha			
Suicide			
Cato of Utica	2	98	15
	2	118	102
Sword of Damocles. *See* Tyrants are wretched			
Talking birds	1	64	13
Laelius Strabo			
Augustus			
Teacher and pupil	1	80	13
Horace and Lucius Orbilius			
Marcus Cicero and Cratippus			
Plato and Socrates			
Plutarch and Trajan	1	81	16
Quintilian and the sons of Domitilla			
Seneca and Nero			
Socrates			
Alexander the Great and Aristotle (?)	2	41	28
Theater builders	1	30	88
Curio			
Scaurus			
Tongue. *See* Struck . . .			
Tyrants are wretched			
Dionysius (Sword of Damocles)	1	95	54
	2	39	28
Ubi sunt? See Where are they now?			
Underground shelter as protection against thunder- storms	2	91	7

Examples	Book	Dial.	Line
Wounds sustained	2	77	37
Horatius Cocles			
Writers, prolific	1	44	72
Cicero			
Varro			
Livy			
Pliny			
Origen			
Youth: not sighing for one's lost	2	83	149
Socrates			
Plato			
Fabius			
Cato			
Youth: sighing for one's lost	2	83	147
Evander			
Youth: trying to pretend	2	83	154
Applicant and Hadrian			

Stories	Book	Dial.	Line
Father and son sentenced to be boiled alive	2	90	165
Florentine patrician and the mechanic	2	72	26
The Fox and the fishermen	2	Pref.	34
Italian patrician and his covetous son	2	13	199
Man who hated birds	2	90	100
Nobleman suspicious of the origin of his son	2	50	32
Old man dreading retirement	2	83	253
Old man prohibited to leave Arezzo	2	68	60
Old Samnite tortured	2	114	313
Sailor whose forebears died at sea	2	121	78
Stefano Colonna and the stranger	1	35	45
and his tower officer	2	118	129
The Talking raven and Augustus	1	64	34
and the cobbler's neighbor	1	64	39
Themistocles and the Seriphian	1	15	44
Tower officer and Stefano Colonna	2	118	129
Woman with eleven illegitimate sons	2	50	67
"You are getting old"	2	83	209

NAMES, AUTHORS, AND WORKS REFERRED TO IN THE TRANSLATION

(As a rule, only the first mention of each entry in a dialogue is recorded. The annotations are mostly based on Boardman [1986], Harvey [1974], and Previté-Orton [1952]. The title abbreviations of individual works are listed in the Bibliography, II.)

	Book	Dial.	Line	
Abdalonymus	2	5	82	Gardner made king of Sidon by Alexander the Great 332 B.C.
	2	9	161	
Abdera	2	4	24	
Abel	2	45	6	
Abigail	2	128	49	Widow of Nabal
Abraham	1	78	6	
Accius, Lucius	2	125	78	170–ca. 85 B.C.; Roman tragic poet
Achaia	1	88	17	Region of ancient Greece in northern part of the Peloponnesus
	1	96	144	
	2	91	33	
Achilles	1	72	61	Chief Greek hero in Trojan war
	1	73	18	
	1	117	49	
	2	4	35	
	2	25	76	
	2	35	28	
	2	36	16	
aconite	1	9	92	

Book	Dial.	Line	
	Book	*Dial.*	*Line*	
	1	69	53	
	2	9	98	
	2	73	74	
	2	125	52	
	2	125	129	
Africans	2	128	14	
Africanus	1	63	35	
Agamemnon	1	52	50	Brother of Menelaus: husband of Clytemnestra; father of Orestes and Electra; leader of Greeks before Troy
	1	65	75	
	2	21	73	
	2	69	7	
	2	80	13	
Agathocles	2	39	54	317–289 B.C.; tyrant of Syracuse
Agis IV	2	81	73	*See* Nabis
Agrippa	1	79	14	Grandson of Emperor Augustus
Agrippa, Marcus	1	75	7	Son-in-law of Emperor Augustus
	1	118	33	
	2	21	80	
Agrippina II	1	52	28	Nero's mother
	1	75	13	
Ajax	2	115	30	Son of Telamon; Argive hero before Troy
Alboin	1	65	76	Died A.D. 572; king of the Lombards
Alcaeus of Lesbos	1	69	130	7th–6th c. B.C.; lyric poet
Alcibiades	1	15	102	Ca. 450–404 B.C.; Athenian statesman and general
	1	23	55	
	1	78	40	
	1	26	25	
	2	35	25	
	2	55	3	
Alcides	2	6	70	*See* Hercules
Alexander	2	9	167	Son of Priam
Alexander of Epirus	2	125	106	Slain 326 B.C.; king of Epirus
Alexander of Pherae	1	95	10	Nephew of Jason; tyrant of Pherae, ca. 369–358 B.C.

	Book	Dial.	Line	
	2	125	15	
Alexander the Great	1	15	86	356–323 B.C.; King of Macedon
	1	18	67	
	1	31	31	
	1	35	41	
	1	37	138	
	1	39	6	
	1	41	16	
	1	49	30	
	1	58	41	
	1	85	49	
	1	104	33	
	1	108	30	
	2	Pref.	27	
	2	1	82	
	2	4	37	
	2	5	81	
	2	6	72	
	2	9	162	
	2	25	75	
	2	39	52	
	2	41	26	
	2	43	56	
	2	58	70	
	2	69	4	
	2	80	13	
	2	81	75	
	2	83	126	
	2	88	51	
	2	90	185	
	2	106	27	
	2	116	38	
	2	125	105	
	2	132	79	
Alexander, teacher of	2	41	28	
Alexandria	1	43	29	
	1	69	54	
	2	125	105	
Alps	1	51	23	
	1	58	24	
	1	88	23	
	2	91	39	

	Book	Dial.	Line	
Antipater	1	52	28	Macedonian ruler, ca. 315 B.C.
	2	96	63	
Antium	2	4	35	
	2	125	78	
Antonia	1	63	64	Wife of Drusus
Antoninus Pius	1	75	8	(Titus Aurelius Fulvius Boionius Arrius Antoninus) Roman emperor, A.D. 138–161.
	1	78	47	
	1	96	98	
	1	131	24	
Antony, Mark	1	9	78	Ca. 82–30 B.C.; Roman politician, military commander; defeated at Actium 31 B.C.
	1	37	41	
	1	42	28	
	1	58	45	
	1	118	20	
	2	36	16	
	2	75	75	
Apelles of Colophon	1	41	15	First half of 4th c. B.C.; greatest painter of Antiquity
	2	4	27	
	2	96	90	
Apennines	1	58	26	
	2	91	50	
Aper	1	75	22	Father-in-law, slayer of Numerian
Apicius, Q. Gavius	2	56	34	Gourmet during reign of Tiberius
Apollo	1	37	155	God of prophecy, music, healing
	2	119	74	
Apollo, Oracle of	1	12	83	
Apollo, Temple of	1	118	23	In Rome
Apollonides	1	39	11	
Apostles	2	57	37	
	2	66	39	
	2	125	42	
Appius Claudius	1	72	32	Decemvir, 449 B.C.; infatuated with Virginia

	Book	Dial.	Line	
Appius Claudius Caecus	2	12	50	Blind Roman censor, 312–308 B.C.
	2	90	298	
	2	96	107	
Apuleius, Lucius	2	Pref.	188	Fl. A.D. 155; author, teacher from Madaura
	1	2	66	*Florida* 10, 5
	2	17	40	*Metam.* 6, 29–30
Apuleius, Saturninus	1	95	14	Slain 100 B.C.; promoter of Gracchan proposals
Apulia	1	69	57	
	2	125	73	
Aquae Sextiae	2	132	65	
Aquinum	2	125	77	
Arabia	1	64	99	
Arabia, Kings of	2	31	41	
Arabs	1	22	31	
	2	132	78	
Arcady	2	125	73	
Archemorus	2	49	13	"Beginner of doom"—name given to infant Opheltes, who was killed by a snake
Archimedes	1	99	34	287–212 B.C.; Greek mathematician, physicist, inventor
	2	68	45	
Archytas of Tarentum	2	59	42	Fl. ca. 400 B.C.; Pythagorean philosopher
	2	107	42	
Arezzo	2	68	60	
Arginusae islands	1	98	31	
Argives	2	39	54	*See* Greeks
Argonauts	1	117	40	
Arimasps	2	Pref.	56	
Arion	1	23	6	Legendary Greek poet, singer
Aristides the Just	1	94	9	D. ca. 468 B.C.; Athenian statesman
	2	66	27	
Aristippus of Cyrene	2	9	42	Pupil of Socrates
Aristophanes	2	39	68	Ca. 448–380 B.C.; Athenian comic poet
Aristotimus of Epirus	1	95	11	

	Book	*Dial.*	*Line*	
	1	23	46	*Conf.* 10, 33
	2	118	159	*De civ. Dei* 1, 23
	2	Pref.	402	*De civ. Dei* 14, 8
	1	62	16	*De civ. Dei* 21, 4
	2	93	84	*De vera rel.* 16, 30
Augustus	1	18	38	(Gaius Julius Caesar Octavianus) Roman emperor, 27 B.C.–A.D. 14
	1	20	15	
	1	21	51	
	1	25	13	
	1	26	3	
	1	30	26	
	1	32	50	
	1	37	189	
	1	39	7	
	1	41	26	
	1	42	22	
	1	64	34	
	1	75	8	
	1	79	13	
	1	85	35	
	1	93	12	
	1	96	73	
	1	96	109	
	1	96	228	
	1	108	37	
	1	110	48	
	1	114	36	
	1	114	75	
	1	117	49	
	1	118	37	
	2	1	82	
	2	4	33	
	2	5	43	
	2	5	105	
	2	19	44	
	2	23	2	
	2	23	43	
	2	24	50	
	2	36	16	
	2	52	44	
	2	62	39	

Book	Dial.	Line	
1	101	48	Eccli. 28, 3–4
1	101	97	Eccli. 28, 6
1	18	112	Eccli. 37, 32–34
2	23	27	Eccli. 42, 11
2	103	73	Ex. 3, 1
2	55	31	Ex. 3, 2
2	102	67	Ex. 4, 10–16
2	103	75	Ex. 14, 15
2	90	41	Gen. 1, 31
2	59	23	Gen. 3, 18
2	81	49	Hab. 1, 9–10
2	59	23	Hebr. 6, 8
2	67	72	Hebr. 13, 14
1	76	19	i Cor. 7, 8–9
1	44	52	i Cor. 8, 1
1	11	20	ii Cor. 1, 12
1	69	95	ii Cor. 4, 18
2	96	40	
2	126	92	Ioan. 11, 39
2	126	10	Is. 38, 17
2	33	39	Jac. 1, 20
2	26	18	Jac. 3, 2
2	26	21	Jac. 3, 8
2	84	78	Job.
1	60	35	Job. 1, 3
1	59	35	Job. 1, 13–15
2	118	37	Job. 5, 7
1	48	16	Job. 7, 1
1	21	28	Job. 7, 14
2	86	20	
2	17	12	Job. 14, 2
2	114	340	Job. 19, 21
2	13	108	Job. 27, 19
1	13	30	Job. 28, 28
1	46	17	
1	86	19	Job. 31, 26–28
1	22	78	Luc. 7, 37–38
2	126	60	Luc. 7, 49
2	36	33	Mal. 2, 10
2	91	69	Mal. 3, 6
2	127	14	Matth. 7, 24–27
2	126	91	Matth. 8, 2–3
2	13	128	Matth. 13, 2–9

Book	Dial.	Line	
2	126	11	Mich. 7, 19
1	78	8	Num. 1, 45–46
1	12	33	Phil. 3, 12
1	12	38	Phil. 3, 13
1	64	104	Prov. 1, 22
1	64	106	Prov. 1, 23
2	103	44	Prov. 4, 23
2	95	9	Prov. 4, 25
2	14	57	Prov. 6, 1–5
1	11	18	Prov. 10, 7
2	13	52	Prov. 11, 4
2	13	126	Prov. 11, 28
1	23	23	Prov. 14, 13
2	95	13	Prov. 15, 21
1	23	24	Prov. 16, 18
1	9	84	Prov. 18, 21
1	11	11	Prov. 22, 1
1	22	88	Prov. 27, 9
2	13	44	Prov. 28, 20
2	126	103	Ps. 10 (H), 15
1	46	22	Ps. 2, 4
2	114	156	Ps. 5, 6
2	90	252	Ps. 10, 7
2	103	65	Ps. 11, 3
1	24	50	Ps. 11, 9
2	127	17	Ps. 26, 10
2	117	167	Ps. 33, 22
2	58	38	Ps. 36, 3–5
2	12	108	Ps. 36, 5
2	103	33	Ps. 38, 2
2	13	112	Ps. 38, 7
2	90	287	Ps. 45, 5
1	56	9	Ps. 48, 19
2	58	45	Ps. 54, 23
2	39	6	Ps. 57, 12
2	13	122	Ps. 61, 11
2	58	36	Ps. 65, 5
1	56	21	Ps. 72, 7
1	53	47	Ps. 75, 6
1	31	84	Ps. 75, 7
2	77	25	Ps. 88, 11
1	1	19	Ps. 89, 10
2	40	12	Ps. 93, 10

	Book	Dial.	Line	
	2	83	115	Ps. 102, 5
	2	126	12	Ps. 102, 12
	1	107	15	Ps. 106, 23–27
	1	13	31	Ps. 110, 10
	2	130	38	Ps. 111, 7
	2	58	35	Ps. 114, 5
	2	117	167	Ps. 115, 15
	2	119	122	Ps. 137, 8
	2	103	68	Ps. 138, 15
	1	12	40	Ps. 138, 16
	2	12	75	Ps. 144, 16
	2	119	123	Ps. 144, 18
	2	66	44	Ps. 145, 7
	2	90	234	i Reg. 2, 10
	2	55	30	iv Reg. 1 and 2
	2	114	119	Rom. 9, 20–21
	1	Pref.	228	Rom. 10, 17
	1	46	25	Rom. 11, 34
	1	19	86	Rom. 13, 13
	2	23	37	Sap. 8, 21
	2	104	56	
	1	Pref.	246	Sap. 11, 21
	2	111	33	Sap. 15, 14
	2	64	12	Sap. 18, 4
	1	42	95	i Thess. 4, 4–5
	2	13	121	i Tim. 6, 10
Bithynia	1	125	150	
Black Sea	2	90	19	
Black Sea region	1	37	48	
Bologna	2	125	57	
Boötes	1	15	3	
Brahmans	2	88	50	
Brindisi	1	96	143	
Britain	1	20	24	
	1	69	52	
	2	78	30	
Britons	1	114	90	
Brundisium	2	125	70	
Brutus, Decimus	1	99	16	(Decimus Junius Brutus) One of Caesar's commanders; conqueror of Marseilles
Brutus, Julius	1	78	41	Nephew of King Tarquinius Superbus

	Book	Dial.	Line	
Brutus, L. Junius	1	102	24	Roman consul 509 B.C.
	2	36	49	
Brutus, Marcus Junius	1	Pref.	89	Ca. 78–42 B.C.; one of Caesar's assassins
	2	117	155	
Brutus	2	118	106	
Bryaxis	2	88	15	4th c. B.C. Greek sculptor
Byblis	1	69	62	Consumed by incestuous love for her brother, Caunus
Byrsa fortress	1	35	25	
	1	118	11	
Byzantium	1	96	143	
Caeculus	2	55	26	Son of Vulcan; founder of Praeneste
Caelius Rufus, M.	2	107	20	Orator of Ciceronian times
Caesius Scaeva	2	77	84	
Caieta	1	58	43	
	2	125	67	
Cain	2	45	6	
Calabria	2	125	73	
Caligula	1	15	29	(Gaius Claudius Nero Caesar Germanicus) Roman emperor, A.D. 37–41
	1	20	29	
	1	23	65	
	1	42	66	
	1	95	18	
	1	96	82	
	1	96	127	
	1	96	140	
	1	110	18	
	2	4	34	
	2	22	23	
	2	24	50	
	2	39	49	
	2	63	25	
	2	81	88	
Calpurnius Flamma	2	72	14	Roman commander in First Punic War 258 B.C.
Calvisius Sabinus	1	43	112	Acquaintance of Seneca the Philosopher
Camilla	2	121	35	In Virgil's Aeneid

	Book	Dial.	Line	
Camillus, Marcus Furius	1	35	23	Early 4th c. B.C. Roman hero
	1	94	7	
	1	105	27	
	2	56	9	
	2	66	27	
	2	66	68	
	2	67	34	
	2	71	5	
Campania	2	12	18	
	2	53	49	
	2	91	33	
	2	125	57	
	2	125	139	
Cannae	1	63	63	Scene of Hannibal's rout of Romans 216 B.C.
	1	69	56	
	2	72	3	
	2	132	62	
Capaneus	2	121	34	In Statius, *Thebaid*
Caphareus mountain	1	98	30	
Capitol	1	60	10	In Rome
	1	114	64	
	1	118	23	
	2	67	35	
Cappadocia	1	52	36	
Capri	1	58	11	
Capua	2	58	71	
	2	68	6	
Caracalla	1	95	18	(Marcus Aurelius Antoninus Bassianus Caracallus) Roman emperor, A.D. 211–217
	1	96	83	
	2	22	23	
	2	24	49	
	2	39	50	
	2	44	18	
	2	84	56	
Caria	2	88	16	
Carneades	2	Pref.	311	213–129 B.C.; Greek philosopher
Carnulus	1	101	122	
Carrhae	2	5	124	Scene of Roman defeat under Crassus 53 B.C.

	Book	Dial.	Line	
	1	24	69	
	1	24	101	
	1	29	69	
	2	38	59	
	2	74	23	
	2	98	16	
	2	118	102	
	2	118	146	
	2	119	133	
	2	125	114	
Cato the Censor	1	7	19	234–149 B.C.; Roman statesman; enemy of Carthage
	1	9	31	
	1	12	75	
	1	15	138	
	1	18	23	
	1	24	101	
	1	56	52	
	1	57	24	
	1	110	53	
	1	112	77	
	2	2	22	
	2	5	64	
	2	7	21	
	2	19	46	
	2	25	79	
	2	27	31	
	2	48	15	
	2	63	21	
	2	81	139	
	2	83	149	
	2	101	25	
Catos	2	56	12	
Catullus, Gaius Valerus	1	59	18	Ca. 84–54 B.C.; Roman poet
	1	69	132	
	2	Pref.	221	
	2	125	78	
Cerberus	1	Pref.	31	Watchdog of Hades
Chalcis	1	96	143	In Euboea, Greece
Chaldaeans	1	112	79	
	1	112	103	
Charmadas	1	101	29	Greek with remarkable memory

	Book	Dial.	Line	
Charybdis	1	93	54	
	2	90	20	
Chimera	1	81	31	Monster with head of a lion, body of a goat, tail of a dragon
	2	114	52	
Christ	1	13	2	
	1	22	77	
	2	9	141	
	2	25	53	
	2	36	18	
	2	57	44	
	2	59	23	
	2	66	38	
	2	79	103	
	2	80	19	
	2	114	383	
	2	117	47	
	2	121	14	
	2	122	43	
	2	126	91	
Christian Fathers	1	18	17	
Chrysippus	2	88	95	Unknown philosopher in Seneca, *Ep.* 56, 3
Chrysippus of Soli	2	101	18	Ca. 280–204 B.C.; Stoic philosopher
	2	132	131	
Chrysostom, John	2	77	10	Ca. A.D. 347–407; Greek Doctor of the Church
Cicero, Marcus	1	80	17	Son of Marcus Tullius Cicero
	2	24	49	
	2	119	133	
Cicero, Marcus Tullius	1	9	78	106–43 B.C.; Roman author, orator, statesman; father of Marcus Cicero
	1	15	139	
	1	16	106	
	1	19	44	
	1	28	20	
	1	29	19	
	1	32	40	
	1	32	79	
	1	43	75	

Book	Dial.	Line	
1	44	73	
1	46	99	
1	58	6	
1	80	16	
1	86	26	
1	112	37	
1	112	103	
1	117	36	
2	4	25	
2	5	56	
2	7	111	
2	15	56	
2	18	1	
2	24	49	
2	25	79	
2	36	17	
2	38	61	
2	40	16	
2	48	15	
2	53	62	
2	66	28	
2	67	49	
2	75	64	
2	90	291	
2	93	153	
2	103	26	
2	107	40	
2	114	194	
2	114	345	
2	117	71	
2	118	190	
2	125	13	
2	125	66	
1	61	5	*Ad Att.* 6, 1, 25
2	53	40	*Ad Quintum* 1, 16, 45–46
2	117	155	Brutus letters 6, 6
1	Pref.	89	Brutus letters 17, 6
2	120	117	*De amic.* 3, 1
2	52	28	*De amic.* 4, 15
2	Pref.	127	*De amic.* 6, 20
2	Pref.	122	*De amic.* 8, 26
2	32	37	*De amic.* 16, 59
1	50	15	*De amic.* 17, 64

Book	Dial.	Line	
2	27	31	*De amic.* 21, 76
1	112	51	*De div.* 1, 1
2	125	12	*De div.* 1, 25, 53
2	126	24	*De div.* 1, 30, 63
2	40	5	*De div.* 1, 38
1	112	126	*De div.* 1, 46, 103
1	112	31	*De div.* 2, 13, 30
1	112	77	*De div.* 2, 24, 51
1	12	80	*De fin.* 2, 3
2	43	76	*De fin.* 2, 19, 60, (1, 7, 23)
2	43	76	*De fin.* 2, 32, 105
2	36	17	*De fin.* 3, 20, 66
1	12	26	*De fin.* 5, 21, 58
1	9	71	*De inv.* 1, 1
2	61	5	*De off.* 1, 13, 41
1	19	45	*De off.* 1, 15
2	13	57	*De off.* 1, 20, 68
2	13	175	
2	105	29	
2	98	15	*De off.* 1, 31, 112
2	118	102	
1	34	2	*De off.* 1, 39, 139
1	114	25	*De off.* 2, 5, 16
2	132	82	
1	95	72	*De off.* 2, 7, 23
2	82	37	
2	82	42	*De off.* 2, 7, 25
2	110	16	*De off.* 2, 10, 37
1	11	76	*De off.* 2, 12, 43
1	19	40	*De off.* 2, 18, 64
1	56	52	*De off.* 2, 25, 89
2	62	36	*De off.* 3, 14, 58–60
2	43	76	*De off.* 3, 31, 112
1	Pref.	153	*De sen.* 1, 2
2	123	7	*De sen.* 7, 24
2	101	16	*De sen.* 8, 26
2	12	52	*De sen.* 11, 37
2	108	22	*De sen.* 14
2	101	16	*De sen.* 14, 50
2	9	42	*De re pub.* 1, 17, 29
2	28	26	*De re pub.* 3, 8–28
2	80	23	*De re pub.* 6, 14
2	118	110	*De re pub.* 6, 15

Book	Dial.	Line	
2	107	10	*Tusc. disp.* 4, 23, 52
1	69	214	*Tusc. disp.* 4, 31, 76
1	69	142	*Tusc. disp.* 4, 33, 72
1	69	148	
1	95	58	*Tusc. disp.* 5, 21, 61–62
2	83	125	*Tusc. disp.* 5, 34, 97
1	18	102	*Tusc. disp.* 5, 34, 100
2	10	61	*Tusc. disp.* 5, 35, 10
1	21	31	*Tusc. disp.* 5, 35, 102
1	19	80	*Tusc. disp.* 5, 38, 111
2	96	63	*Tusc. disp.* 5, 38, 111–112
2	96	103	*Tusc. disp.* 5, 38, 112
2	96	97	*Tusc. disp.* 5, 39, 113
2	96	143	
2	97	43	*Tusc. disp.* 5, 117

	Book	Dial.	Line	
Cicero, Quintus Tullius	2	53	41	Ca. 102–43 B.C.; brother of Marcus Tullius Cicero
Cimbri	2	132	66	
Cimon	1	94	9	Successor of Themistocles
Cincinnatus, Lucius Quinctius	1	18	23	5th C. B.C.; Roman patriot, field commander
Cineas	1	101	29	Envoy of King Pyrrhus to Rome 280 B.C.
Claudia	2	90	298	Sister of Appius Claudius
Claudia, Gens	1	15	138	
Claudian	2	125	79	(Claudius Claudianus) Late 4th c. A.D.; Latin poet
	1	51	19	*De bello Gild.* 385
	1	92	55	
	1	107	56	*In Rufin.* 1, 22–23
Claudius	1	42	66	(Tiberius Claudius Nero Caesar Drusus) Roman emperor, A.D. 41–54
	1	52	51	
	1	72	41	
	1	75	11	
	1	79	37	
	1	96	82	
	1	110	18	
	2	21	85	
	2	116	39	
Claudius Aesopus	1	28	16	1st c. B.C. Roman tragic actor
	2	99	5	

	Book	Dial.	Line	
Cleanthes	2	9	127	Ca. 330–231 B.C.; Greek Stoic philosopher
	2	114	275	
Clearchus of Heraclea	1	95	11	Executed 401 B.C.
Clement of Alexandria	2	57	42	(Titus Flavius Clemens) Ca. A.D. 150–215; teacher of Origen
Cleomenes	2	39	54	Fl. ca. 550 B.C.; king of Sparta
Cleopatra	2	21	73	69–30 B.C.; wife of her brother, Ptolemy XII
Clodius Pulcher, Publius	1	16	107	D. 52 B.C.; adversary of Cicero
	2	66	29	
	2	66	79	
Clytemnestra	1	52	27	Wife of Agamemnon
	2	19	16	
	2	21	73	
Cocles. *See* Horatius Cocles				
Cola di Rienzo	1	89	16	Ca. 1313–1354; self-styled tribune of Sacred Roman Republic
Colchis	1	18	45	Black Sea country; destination of the Argonauts
	1	117	41	
Colonna, Stefano the Elder	1	35	45	Head of Colonna family to ca. 1350
	1	76	15	
	2	118	129	
Colosseum	1	96	165	In Rome
Commodus	1	78	46	(Lucius Aelius Marcus Aurelius Antoninus Commodus) Roman emperor, A.D. 180–192
	1	95	18	
	1	96	83	
	1	110	19	
	2	22	23	
	2	24	48	
	2	39	50	
	2	131	26	
Concordia, Temple of	1	37	191	In Rome

	Book	Dial.	Line	
Dandamus	2	88	50	
Danube river	2	90	19	
Darius III	1	104	33	King of Persia, 336–330 B.C.; defeated by Alexander the Great
	2	80	13	
	2	83	124	
David	1	24	36	Biblical king
	1	56	20	
	2	44	17	
	2	48	20	
	2	51	69	
	2	90	278	
	2	127	17	
	2	128	48	
Decemvirs	1	72	31	
Decii	2	72	14	
	2	125	125	
Decius	1	96	88	(Gaius Messius Quintus Traianus Decius) Roman emperor, A.D. 249–251
	1	96	231	
	2	39	51	
Deiotarus	1	112	114	King of Armenia Minor; friend of Cicero
Deiphobus	1	52	51	Married to Helen of Troy
	1	65	75	
	2	19	17	
	2	73	72	
Delphic oracle	1	12	83	Oracle of Apollo
	1	15	108	
Demetrius	1	52	30	Son of Philip V of Macedonia
Democritus of Abdera	1	15	79	Ca. 460–370 B.C.; Greek philosopher
	2	4	24	
	2	89	12	
	2	96	83	
Demosthenes	1	9	78	383–322 B.C.; Athenian orator, statesman
	1	117	36	
	2	5	39	
	2	25	79	
	2	56	17	

	Book	Dial.	Line	
Empedocles	2	115	31	Ca. 495–435 B.C.; Greek philosopher
England	2	125	144	
Ennius, Quintus	1	50	15	239–169 B.C.; early Roman poet
	1	78	45	
	1	95	72	
	1	112	32	
	2	82	37	
	2	107	10	
	2	125	73	
Epaminondas	1	7	21	Ca. 420–362 B.C.; Theban general
	1	15	88	
	1	23	52	
Ephesus	2	55	35	
	2	125	42	
Epicurean	1	69	173	
Epicurean triumph	1	19	25	
Epicurus	1	12	79	341–270 B.C.; Greek hedonistic philosopher
	1	18	79	
	1	18	94	
	2	10	63	
	2	40	16	
	2	53	46	
	2	114	95	
Epirus	2	125	107	
Eriphyle	2	13	89	Wife of Amphiaraus
Erotimus	2	12	45	King of the Arabs
Esquiline hill	1	96	150	In Rome
Eteocles	1	84	12	Son of Oedipus; brother of Polyneices
	1	102	23	
Ethiopia	1	60	21	
	2	125	43	
Etruscans	1	28	15	
	2	125	127	
Eudemus	2	125	12	Pupil of Aristotle
Eumenes	2	68	23	King of Pergamum
Euphrates river	2	125	112	
Euripides	2	Pref.	32	Ca. 480–406 B.C.; Attic tragedian

	Book	Dial.	Line	
	2	5	39	
	2	121	50	
Europe	1	22	65	
Eurydice	1	52	25	Queen of Ptolemy IV
Eusebius of Caesarea	1	43	109	Ca. A.D. 263–339; Greek Church historian
	2	57	42	
Eustochium	1	21	107	Daughter of St. Paula
Evander (1)	1	73	16	King of Palanteum who welcomed Aeneas
	2	63	19	
	2	83	147	
Evander (2)	2	53	57	Father of Pallas in Virgil, *Aeneid* viii
Evangelus	2	36	17	Critic of Virgil in Macrobius, *Saturn.*
Fabii	2	56	10	
Fabius Maximus, Q. Cunctator	1	35	23	Roman commander against Hannibal; relieved Tarentum 209 B.C.
	2	24	46	
	2	71	6	
(Fabius Maximus), sons of	2	24	46	
Fabius Pictor, Quintus (?)	2	83	149	Oldest Roman historian
Fabricius Luscinus, Gaius	1	18	21	Fl. 3d c.; Roman hero
	1	37	163	
	2	9	106	
	2	56	10	
Faustina	1	75	10	Wife of Emperor Marcus Aurelius
	2	12	110	
Fear	1	Pref.	236	
Fidenae	1	30	101	
Fidenates, King of the	1	41	61	
Flaccus, Valerius	2	125	77	Fl. ca. 80 B.C.; Roman historian
Flamininus, L. Quinctius	2	38	57	Consul 192 B.C.; Roman naval commander
Flaminius, Gaius	2	70	9	Roman general; vanquished by Hannibal at Lake Trasimenus 217 B.C.
	2	117	145	

	Book	Dial.	Line	
Gaius Marius. *See* Marius				
Galba	1	96	82	(Servius Sulpicius Galba) Roman emperor, A.D. 68–69
	1	110	19	
Galeazzo II Visconti	1	37	204	1320–1378
Gallienus	1	96	89	(Publius Licinius Egnatius Gallienus) Roman emperor, A.D. 255–268
	1	96	231	
	2	39	50	
Gallio	1	Pref.	129	Older brother of Seneca the Philosopher
	2	125	75	
Gallus	1	96	88	(Gaius Vibius Trebonianus Gallus) Roman emperor, A.D. 251–253
	2	125	78	
Ganges river	1	22	24	
Gaul	1	69	52	
	1	99	12	
	2	53	63	
	2	125	49	
Gauls	1	103	11	
	1	105	26	
	2	88	57	
	2	132	63	
Gelon of Sicily	2	81	78	D. 478 B.C.; brother of Hieron
Genoa	2	68	24	
Germanicus	1	64	41	(Nero Claudius Germanicus Julius Caesar) 15 B.C.–A.D. 19; nephew of Tiberius
	1	114	56	
	2	22	23	
	2	24	50	
Germany	1	69	52	
	1	88	25	
	1	114	38	
	1	114	83	
	2	91	39	
	2	125	135	
glandariae	1	64	78	
Gordian II	1	43	44	(Marcus Antonius Gordianus Sempronianus Romanus

	Book	Dial.	Line	
				Africanus) Roman emperor, A.D. 238
Gordiani	1	96	87	
Gospels	2	36	17	
Gracchi, the	1	65	20	
	1	95	14	
Gratian	1	96	91	(Flavius Gratianus Augustus) Roman emperor in the West, A.D. 375–383
	1	97	44	
Grecian Rome	1	22	62	
Greece	1	12	75	
	1	78	41	
	1	88	18	
	2	9	79	
	2	21	78	
	2	39	46	
	2	121	50	
	2	125	43	
Greek	1	29	44	
Greek authors	1	22	76	
	1	118	15	
histories	2	73	70	
language	1	43	39	
	1	64	82	
lords	1	69	64	
philosophers	1	40	39	
trickery	1	37	227	
Greeks	1	9	77	
	1	15	58	
	1	15	89	
	1	19	118	
	1	24	70	
	1	40	41	
	1	44	74	
	1	69	126	
	1	72	22	
	1	85	58	
	1	98	30	
	1	112	52	
	2	75	73	
	2	115	35	
gryphs	2	Pref.	56	

	Book	Dial.	Line	
	2	128	14	
Herodotus	1	23	8	Ca. 484–425 B.C.; Greek historian
	1	103	23	
Hiero of Sicily	2	81	78	Tyrant of Syracuse, 478–467 B.C.
Hiero II of Syracuse	2	78	9	D. 215 B.C.
Hilarion	2	63	22	
Hipparchus	1	95	12	Athenian tyrant; killed by Harmodius and Aristogiton 514 B.C.
Hippo	2	68	28	
Hippocrates	2	4	26	Ca. 460–370 B.C.; Greek physician
Hippolytus	1	72	23	Son of Theseus
	2	42	40	
Hirrius, Gaius	1	63	50	
Historia Augusta	2	60	34	
	1	96	97	Antonius Pius 1, 4–5
	1	96	212	Hadrian 8, 3
	1	96	118	Hadrian 17, 1
	2	83	155	Hadrian 20, 8
	2	121	56	Hadrian 24, 8–13
	1	25	14	Marcus Aurelius 4, 9
	1	68	46	Marcus Aurelius 19, 8–9
	2	60	29	Sev. Alex. 17, 1–2
	1	96	39	Sev. Alex. 33, 3
	1	97	40	Sev. Alex. 53–54
	1	96	186	Verus 5, 1–6
Holy Roman Emperor	1	96	59	
	1	96	227	
	2	96	125	
Homer	1	15	79	Fl. before 700 B.C.; first European poet on record
	1	32	79	
	1	117	49	
	2	25	76	
	2	35	26	
	2	36	16	
	2	96	83	
	2	101	20	
	2	121	50	
	1	21	49	*Iliad*

Book	Dial.	Line
1	69	52
1	75	21
1	95	67
1	96	81
1	97	35
1	99	12
1	101	23
1	104	19
1	104	33
1	106	55
1	107	76
1	108	30
1	112	101
1	114	15
2	1	81
2	9	173
2	30	21
2	33	47
2	53	63
2	56	11
2	61	9
2	63	19
2	64	48
2	73	9
2	75	6
2	77	4
2	77	84
2	80	15
2	81	85
2	82	28
2	83	24
2	84	69
2	86	20
2	113	35
2	118	107
2	118	148
2	121	33
2	123	12
2	131	22
2	131	76

Julius Caesar, father of. *See*
   Gaius Caesar

	Book	Dial.	Line	
Julius Solinus	1	37	154	Ca. 3d c. A.D.; compiled epitome of Pliny, *Nat. hist.*
Jupiter	1	69	60	Chief of Roman gods; identified with Greek Zeus
	2	90	268	
Jupiter, planet	1	52	21	
	2	114	221	
Jupiter, Temple of	1	42	59	In Rome
	1	118	23	
Justin	1	84	16	(Marcus Junianus Justinus) 2d or 3d c. A.D.; author of Latin abridgement of *Universal History* by Trogus Pompeius
Juvenal	2	31	33	(Decimus Junius Juvenalis) Fl. A.D. 98–128; Roman satirist
	2	103	51	
	2	125	77	
	1	64	24	*Sat.* 1, 142–143
	1	19	117	*Sat.* 3, 86, 100
	1	19	60	*Sat.* 5, 158
	1	47	49	*Sat.* 6, 76–77
	1	65	18	*Sat.* 6, 167–168
	1	106	40	*Sat.* 6, 290–293
	1	67	10	*Sat.* 6, 448–450
	1	67	16	*Sat.* 6, 456
	1	46	95	*Sat.* 7, 135–136
	2	5	142	*Sat.* 7, 194–196
	1	81	7	*Sat.* 7, 240–241
	2	83	93	*Sat.* 10, 2–4
	1	38	19	*Sat.* 10, 25–27
	2	116	29	
	1	95	24	*Sat.* 10, 112–113
	1	66	14	*Sat.* 10, 297–298
	2	21	18	
	2	93	93	*Sat.* 10, 350
	2	119	152	
	2	17	32	*Sat.* 10, 350–353
	2	54	42	*Sat.* 12, 22–24
	2	13	158	*Sat.* 13, 134
	2	13	252	*Sat.* 14, 140
	2	13	36	*Sat.* 14, 176–178
	1	48	43	*Sat.* 16

	Book	Dial.	Line	
Mars	1	31	80	Roman god of war
	1	69	60	
Mars, Temple of	1	118	22	In Rome
Mars, planet	2	114	212	
Marseilles	1	99	17	
	2	77	54	
	2	96	122	
Marsi	2	5	62	
Martial	1	64	60	(Marcus Valerius Martialis) Ca. A.D. 40–104; Roman poet
	1	64	60	*Epig.* 14, 73
	1	64	65	*Epig.* 14, 76
[Martin of Braga]	1	Pref.	123	Archbishop of Braga A.D. 572; putative author of *De remediis fortuitorum. See also* Seneca the Philosopher
Mary, Queen of Heaven	1	118	42	
Massilia, Battle of	2	77	54	49 B.C. *See* Marseilles
Massilians	2	132	71	
Massinissa	1	51	3	Ca. 238–149 B.C.; king of Numidia
	1	110	54	
	2	20	27	
	2	110	21	
Mausolus	2	88	17	Ca. 376–353 B.C.; Persian satrap of Caria
	2	132	45	
Maximi	1	95	87	
Maximin	2	5	97	(Gaius Julius Verus Maximinus Thrax) Roman emperor, A.D. 235–238
	2	39	51	
Maximini	1	97	43	
Maximiniani	1	96	87	
Maximus Petronius	2	5	88	(Flavius Ancius Petronius Maximus) Roman emperor in the West, A.D. 455
Medea	1	52	35	Wife of Jason
Medes	1	58	39	
	2	39	61	
	2	132	78	

	Book	Dial.	Line	
Medes, kingdom of the	1	78	52	
Menelaus	2	20	30	King of Sparta; brother of Agamemnon; husband of Helen, whom Paris carried off to Troy
	2	21	73	
Menenius Agrippa	2	9	92	D. 493 B.C.; Roman consul 503 B.C.
	2	74	22	
	2	75	32	
Menoeceus	1	73	15	Son of Creon, king of Thebes
Mercury	2	28	30	Roman god of trade
Mercury, planet	2	114	212	
Messalina	1	72	39	Executed A.D. 48; adulterous wife of Emperor Claudius
	2	21	86	
Metapontus	2	125	66	
Metaurus river	2	132	64	
Metella	2	21	76	Fourth wife of Sulla
Metelli	2	56	10	
Metellus Macedonicus	1	94	8	D. 115 B.C.; Roman general; subdued Greece 146 B.C
	1	104	32	
	1	108	20	
	2	38	68	
	2	67	39	
	2	120	110	
	2	131	67	
Metrodorus	1	12	80	Acquaintance of Epicurus in Cicero, De fin. 2, 3
Micipsa	1	78	35	149–118 B.C.; king of Numidia
	1	79	18	
Milan	2	68	27	
	2	69	11	
	2	125	51	
Milo of Croton	1	5	21	Celebrated Greek athlete crowned at 62d Olympiad 532 B.C.
	1	5	60	
	1	29	50	
	2	2	21	

	Book	Dial.	Line	
Miltiades	1	94	8	Athenian commander at Marathon 490 B.C.
	2	77	61	
Minerva, statue of	2	88	5	By Phidias
Minos	2	21	74	King of Crete, husband of Pasiphaë
	2	80	12	
Miseno bridge	1	96	175	In Rome
Misenum	2	125	140	
Mithridates VI Eupator	2	44	17	Ca. 131–63 B.C.; king of Pontus; defeated by Pompey
	2	94	41	
	2	116	31	
Moses	2	55	31	
	2	102	67	
	2	103	75	
Mummius, Lucius	1	35	26	Roman conqueror of Corinth 146 B.C.
	1	42	11	
	1	42	84	
	2	38	69	
Munatius Plancus	1	118	31	
Muses, the nine	1	37	155	
	1	38	145	
Mycenaean brothers	1	84	12	I.e., Atreus and Thyestes
Myrrhine ware	1	38	122	
Nabis of Sparta	1	95	11	Assassinated 192 B.C.
	2	39	54	
	2	81	73	
Nabis, Wife of	2	39	55	
Nabuchodonosor	1	41	51	605–562 B.C.; king of Chaldaea
Naples	1	63	44	
	2	91	36	
	2	125	70	
Nar river	2	90	16	
Neptune	1	87	2	Roman god of waters
	2	54	42	
Nero	1	15	29	(Lucius Domitius Ahenobarbus Claudius Drusus) Roman emperor, A.D. 54–68

	Book	Dial.	Line	
				daughter of Aemilius Paulus Macedonicus
Persepolis	2	69	5	
Perseus	1	14	22	Last king of Macedonia
	1	112	127	
	2	6	70	
Persia	1	33	79	
	2	39	52	
	2	125	42	
	2	125	152	
	2	132	76	
Persian kingdom	2	69	5	
Persian kings	2	9	168	
	2	106	14	
Persians	1	7	21	
	1	14	21	
	1	20	22	
	2	132	61	
Persis	2	125	108	
Persius	2	125	79	(Aulus Persius Flaccus) A.D. 34–62; Roman satirist
	2	13	140	*Sat.* 6, 75–76
Pertinax	1	96	78	(Publius Helvius Pertinax) Roman emperor, A.D. 193
	1	97	43	
	1	110	19	
	2	5	95	
Pescennius Niger	2	56	13	Roman general; defeated at Issus A.D. 194
Peter, the Apostle	2	3	17	
	2	7	46	
Petrarch	2	88	29	*Africa* 7, 292
	1	21	5	*Fam.* 3, 10, 5
	2	88	29	*Fam.* 7, 7, 5–6
	2	88	29	*Met.* 2, 14, 273
	2	83	232	*Secretum* 3
	2	88	29	
Petronilla	2	3	21	Daughter of St. Peter
Phaedra	2	21	74	Wife of Theseus
	2	42	40	
Phalaris	1	95	10	Ca. 570–554 B.C.; tyrant of Agrigentum in Sicily
	2	15	66	

	Book	Dial.	Line	
	1	92	4	*Nat. hist.* 2, 68, 173–175
	1	54	31	*Nat. hist.* 3, 20, 138
	1	22	25	*Nat. hist.* 7, 2, 25
	1	101	29	*Nat. hist.* 7, 24–25
	2	77	50	*Nat. hist.* 7, 28, 104–106
	1	23	28	*Nat. hist.* 7, 32, 119
	1	90	49	
	1	23	28	*Nat. hist.* 7, 52, 180
	1	90	49	
	1	26	22	*Nat. hist.* 8, 80, 215
	1	63	42	*Nat. hist.* 9, 80
	1	63	50	*Nat. hist.* 9, 81
	1	64	15	*Nat. hist.* 10, 72, 141
	1	57	27	*Nat. hist.* 14, 5, 44
	1	18	67	*Nat. hist.* 14, 7, 58
	1	30	52	*Nat. hist.* 36, 2, 5–7
	1	30	88	*Nat. hist.* 36, 24, 116–120
	1	39	12	*Nat. hist.* 37, 4, 8–10
	1	38	141	*Nat. hist.* 37, 12, 47
	1	37	41	*Nat. hist.* 37, 21, 81–82
	1	41	54	*Nat. hist.* 37, 32, 108
	1	37	220	*Nat. hist.* 37, 40, 124
	1	37	149	*Nat. hist.* 37, 54, 139
	1	38	39	*Nat. hist.* 37, 75, 107
	1	37	231	*Nat. hist.* 37, 76, 198
Plotinus	2	114	139	Ca. A.D. 205–270; Neoplatonist philosopher
	2	119	66	
	2	121	48	
Plutarch	1	81	17	Ca. A.D. 46–120; Greek biographer, moral philosopher
Poliorcetes, Demetrius	1	99	11	D. 283 B.C.; king of Macedon
Polyclitus	1	41	88	Fl. 450–440 B.C.; Greek sculptor
Polycrates	1	37	173	D. 522 B.C.; tyrant of Samos
Polydorus	2	13	145	Priam's youngest son
Polyneices	1	84	12	Son of Oedipus; brother of Eteocles
	1	102	23	
Pompeii	2	91	36	
Pompeius Strabo	2	5	113	Conqueror of Asculum, 89 B.C.

	Book	Dial.	Line	
Pompey the Great	1	Pref.	203	(Pompeius, Gnaeus) 106–48 B.C.; Roman general; rival of Julius Caesar
	1	35	41	
	1	37	90	
	1	38	124	
	1	42	83	
	1	63	46	
	1	75	21	
	1	93	11	
	1	97	52	
	1	104	33	
	1	108	14	
	1	112	101	
	2	5	114	
	2	24	46	
	2	38	4	
	2	56	11	
	2	70	9	
	2	73	50	
	2	75	6	
	2	80	15	
	2	91	36	
	2	114	313	
	2	114	371	
	2	121	33	
	2	125	109	
	2	132	32	
Pons Sublicius	2	77	38	Sublicius bridge in Rome
Pontius	1	101	87	Samnite general
Pontus	1	69	53	
	2	125	71	
Pope, Roman	1	107		
	2	13	213	
Poppaea Sabina	1	38	143	D. A.D. 65; second wife of Emperor Nero
Posidonius	2	114	372	Ca. 135–51 B.C.; Greek Stoic philosopher
Pothinus	1	93	11	Signs death warrant of Pompey in Lucan
Praeneste	1	35	26	Fortress of Palestrina
Priam	1	72	61	King of Troy; father of Paris and Hector

	Book	Dial.	Line	
	2	63	20	
Rhadamanthys of Knossos	2	126	38	
Rhea Silvia	1	78	49	Daughter of Numitor; mother of Romulus, Remus
Rhine river	1	88	28	
Rhine valley	2	91	43	
Rhodes	2	9	44	
	2	91	30	
Robert of Anjou	2	68	24	A.D. 1309–1343; king of Naples
Roc	2	Pref.	270	Legendary bird
Roman	1	72	26	
Roman brothers	1	84	13	I.e., Romulus and Remus
emperors	1	30	16	
	1	96	125	
	2	Pref.	259	
	2	88	58	
	2	132	55	
Empire	2	22	22	
	2	39	51	
	2	125	109	
	2	131	28	
histories	2	57	57	
Imperium	1	96	283	
kings	1	72	30	
	2	5	69	
law	2	61	2	
legions	2	57	47	
Nights	1	26	45	
Romans	1	9	77	
	1	14	55	
	1	30	9	
	1	32	53	
	1	37	150	
	1	40	37	
	1	69	126	
	1	85	38	
	1	100	19	
	1	103	12	
	2	32	48	
	2	43	6	
	2	58	70	
	2	73	21	

	Book	Dial.	Line
	2	78	19
	2	80	14
	2	90	266
	2	128	15
	2	132	62
Rome	1	14	26
	1	14	56
	1	15	138
	1	15	152
	1	16	108
	1	22	34
	1	28	16
	1	30	60
	1	35	15
	1	35	49
	1	37	44
	1	38	123
	1	40	35
	1	47	50
	1	50	23
	1	52	33
	1	58	46
	1	60	10
	1	62	19
	1	64	14
	1	64	48
	1	64	83
	1	64	100
	1	78	51
	1	88	21
	1	89	16
	1	95	14
	1	96	150
	1	96	188
	1	102	24
	1	103	38
	1	106	12
	1	107	24
	1	112	106
	1	114	11
	1	114	50
	1	114	83
	1	118	40

	Book	Dial.	Line	
Seneca Rhetor	1	46	81	Ca. 55 B.C.–A.D. 37; father of Seneca the Philosopher
	1	46	81	*Controv.* 3, Pref. 11
	2	25	82	*Controv.* 7, 4, 6
Senecas	2	125	75	
Senones	1	35	22	
Septimius Severus	1	15	150	(Lucius Septimius Severus) Roman emperor, A.D. 193–211
	1	118	20	
	2	4	32	
	2	5	94	
	2	21	82	
	2	22	24	
	2	24	49	
	2	44	18	
	2	84	54	
	2	125	142	
Serapion	2	7	90	Egyptian hermit
Serenus Sammonicus	1	43	42	Friend of Emperor Gordian I
Seres	1	20	22	
Sergius Orata	1	63	31	
	2	56	33	
Sergius, Marcus	2	77	50	Grandfather of Catiline
Seriphos island	1	15	47	
Serranus, Atilius Regulus	1	18	23	Consul, 170 B.C.
	1	21	32	
Servius Tullius	2	5	73	Sixth king of Rome, 578–534 B.C.
	2	9	165	
	2	55	28	
	2	80	14	
Seven Sages of Greece	1	12	76	
Severian Baths	1	118	21	In Rome
Severus Alexander	1	85	47	(Marcus Alexianus Bassianus Aurelius Severus Alexander) Roman emperor, A.D. 222–235
	1	96	39	
	1	96	85	
	1	97	40	
	2	60	25	
	2	75	75	

	Book	Dial.	Line	
Suetonius	1	2	21	(Gaius Suetonius Tranquillus) Ca. A.D. 70–160; Roman historian, jurist
	2	61	9	1, Jul. Caesar 4, 1–2
	1	107	77	1, Jul. Caesar 13
	2	118	172	1, Jul. Caesar 20, 4
	2	113	35	1, Jul. Caesar 45
	1	24	99	1, Jul. Caesar 53
	1	97	35	1, Jul. Caesar 69
	2	81	85	1, Jul. Caesar 78, 1–2
	2	33	53	1, Jul. Caesar 84, 2
	2	113	36	1, Jul. Caesar 87
	2	123	12	
	1	118	54	2, Aug. 28, 3
	1	118	22	2, Aug. 29
	1	20	17	2, Aug. 73
	1	18	39	2, Aug. 76
	1	18	62	2, Aug. 77
	1	21	51	2, Aug. 78
	2	86	13	2, Aug. 78, 2
	1	101	120	3, Tib. 61
	1	114	60	4, Calig. 6, 1–2
	1	96	128	4, Calig. 19, 1–3
	1	96	181	6, Nero 30, 3
	1	96	156	6, Nero 31, 1–2
	1	96	181	6, Nero 31, 3
	1	96	153	6, Nero 39, 2
	1	54	16	6, Nero 48, 3
	1	22	43	8, Vesp. 8
	2	88	86	8, Vesp. 12
	2	119	76	8, Vesp. 24
	1	23	20	8, Dom. 11
	2	90	280	8, Dom. 15, 2
	1	2	21	8, Dom. 18, 2
Sulla, Lucius Cornelius	1	29	28	138–78 B.C.; Roman general
	1	106	25	
	1	108	29	
	2	21	76	
	2	38	73	
	2	125	136	
Sulmo	2	125	71	
Sultan of Egypt	1	60	19	

	Book	Dial.	Line	
	1	51	29	*Andria* 67–68
	2	44	50	*Andria* 903
	2	29	14	*Eun.* 57–58
	1	96	54	*Eun. 245*
	2	50	4	*Heauton Timor.* 77
Terentia	2	18	31	Wife of Cicero
Tereus	2	Pref.	216	Legendary king of Thrace
Teutones	2	132	65	
Thais	2	69	6	
Thales of Miletus	2	14	45	Founder of first Greek school of philosophy; one of Seven Sages
Thamar	1	72	25	
"The wicked brothers"	1	84	13	I.e., Eteocles and Polyneices, sons of Oedipus and Jocasta; "Theban brothers"
	1	102	23	
Thebes	1	15	59	
	1	15	82	
	2	69	4	
Themistocles	1	8	40	Ca. 525–460 B.C.; Athenian naval commander; defeated Persians at Salamis 480 B.C.
	1	15	45	
	1	23	51	
	1	67	34	
	1	94	8	
	2	125	150	
Theodorus of Cyrene	2	15	66	Second half of 5th c. B.C.; Greek mathematician
	2	114	371	
	2	132	116	
Theodosius	1	75	23	(Flavius Theodosius) Roman emperor, A.D. 379–395
	2	114	339	
	2	125	144	
Theodotus	2	114	371	
Theophrastus	2	4	24	Ca. 371–287 B.C.; Greek philosopher; succeeded Aristotle as head of Peripatetic school
	2	9	59	

	Book	Dial.	Line	
Theramenes	2	116	39	D. 404 B.C.; tyrant of Athens
Thermopylae	1	103	20	Scene of battle of Spartans under Leonidas and Persians under Xerxes 480 B.C.
	2	73	70	
Thersites	2	35	26	Rancorous, misshapen Greek in Homer, *Iliad*
Theseus	1	52	29	Legendary king of Athens; Attic hero
	1	72	48	
	1	94	9	
	2	21	74	
	2	125	150	
Thessalonice	1	52	28	Wife of Cassander of Macedonia; mother of Antipater
Thessaly	1	31	76	
	1	37	124	
	1	69	52	
	2	70	10	
	2	73	50	
	2	125	14	
Thetis	1	73	27	Mother of Archilles
Thirty tyrants	2	39	46	Athens
Thyestes	1	84	12	Brother of Atreus
Tiber river	2	62	21	
	2	77	42	
	2	90	16	
Tiberius	1	30	101	(Tiberius Claudius Nero Caesar) Roman emperor, A.D. 14–37
	1	49	30	
	1	58	11	
	1	64	41	
	1	79	15	
	1	85	40	
	1	96	138	
	1	96	277	
	1	101	120	
	1	114	50	
	2	125	139	
	2	131	23	

Book	Dial.	Line	
1	99	31	
1	115	22	
1	117	49	
2	5	41	
2	9	136	
2	17	18	
2	36	17	
2	48	77	
2	53	10	
2	73	72	
2	86	15	
2	90	284	
2	121	52	
2	116	19	Aeneid 1, 91
2	120	15	Aeneid 1, 387
2	132	14	Aeneid 2, 646
2	55	26	Aeneid 2, 679–686
2	13	146	Aeneid 3, 54–55
2	13	84	Aeneid 3, 56–57
1	113	13	Aeneid 4, 175
1	112	118	Aeneid 4, 462–463
1	74	13	Aeneid 4, 569–570
2	18	39	Aeneid 4, 570
1	1	58	Aeneid 5, 227
1	2	89	Aeneid 5, 344
1	87	13	Aeneid 5, 848-849
1	109	91	Aeneid 6, 3–4
1	Pref.	221	Aeneid 6, 103–105
2	132	136	Aeneid 6, 362–371
2	118	26	Aeneid 6, 434–437
2	92	27	Aeneid 6, 481–482
2	73	72	Aeneid 6, 494–512
2	126	36	Aeneid 6, 566–569
2	81	34	Aeneid 6, 608–627
1	31	44	Aeneid 6, 652–655
2	93	51	Aeneid 6, 674
2	Pref.	401	Aeneid 6, 733
1	15	18	Aeneid 6, 784
2	130	39	Aeneid 6, 806–807
2	88	96	Aeneid 6, 815–816
1	32	50	Aeneid 6, 861–887
1	114	77	Aeneid 6, 884
1	85	60	Aeneid 7, 266

WORKS BY PETRARCH
REFERRED TO IN
THE COMMENTARY

ABBREVIATIONS

DP   *Dramatis personae:* The Argument of the Book
INT   Introduction
PW   Petrarch on His Work
TMR To the Modern Reader

(The abbreviations of Petrarch's works are listed in the Bibliography, I, ii.)

INDEX

	Book/Section	Dial.	Note
3, 87–90	1	14	5
3, 156–164	1	Pref.	11
3, 156–171	1	Pref.	11
3, 174–185	2	28	13
3, 282–287	2	Pref.	10
3, 524–536	1	81	3
4, 83	1	89	4
	1	89	5
4, 100–126	2	1	12
5	2	128	4
5, 385–485	1	14	5
5, 418–420	2	Pref.	85
5, 487	1	2	25
5, 680	1	69	5
	2	97	15
5, 988–992	1	51	2
6, 397–503	1	105	7
6, 765	2	54	6
6, 877–879	1	17	3
	1	107	9
6, 889	1	23	11
6, 900–902	2	95	14
6, 901–906	1	90	16
7	1	91	1
7, 1–8	1	103	5
7, 115–610	1	105	7
7, 292	2	88	6
7, 297	1	2	25
7, 329	1	Pref.	44
7, 329–330	1	14	13
7, 435	1	89	5
7, 972–1138	2	73	20
7, 1058	2	69	10
8	2	128	4
8, 105–107	2	90	35
8, 110–199	2	73	20
8, 139	2	90	35
8, 807–808	2	Pref.	85
8, 808	1	2	25
9	2	96	13
9, 1–428	1	78	6
9, 200–210	2	96	14

		Book/ Section	Dial.	Note
9, 456–457		PW		2
		2	21	23
9, 481–490		1	14	5
Buc. carm.	1, 99–100	2	93	20
	2	1	68	3
	3, 12–14	1	22	15
	3, 69–72	1	68	3
	4, 38–39	1	29	18
	4, 44–49	1	23	17
	5	1	89	4
	8, 49–50	1	Pref.	1
	9	1	57	1
	9, 37–38	1	16	4
	9, 39	1	89	2
	10, 1	1	52	12
	10, 72–80	2	Pref.	10
	10, 89	1	69	19
	10, 273–274	2	97	15
	10, 308–310	1	23	12
	10, 371–372	1	68	3
	11, 23	1	15	3
	11, 48	2	7	22
	11, 102	1	33	4
	12, 137–138	2	73	8
	12, 151	1	37	31
	12, 159	1	Pref.	44
	12, 160	1	11	22
Canzone *Quel c'ha nostra*		1	Pref.	1
Canzone *Quel c'ha nostra* 49		1	Pref.	47
75		1	Pref.	46
Collatio 1–17		2	90	35
10		PW		5
23		1	16	4
24		1	Pref.	39
33		2	90	35
Contra eum		1	Pref.	39
		1	11	22
		1	21	14

	Book/ Section	Dial.	Note
4, 347–350	1	69	30
4, 381	2	83	28
Contra quendam	1	14	13
	1	85	2
	1	91	1
	1	95	14
	1	108	2
	2	63	5
Coronation oration (1341)	[1	35	9]
	1	44	6
	1	44	20
	1	46	18
De ocio	DP		18
	1	Pref.	56
	1	1	4
	1	10	6
	1	11	1
	1	11	10
	1	13	14
	1	15	23
	1	15	49
	1	17	7
	1	22	7
	1	43	11
	1	44	21
	1	45	2
	1	46	14
	1	58	11
	1	69	13
	1	88	8
	1	89	5
	1	92	3
	1	106	6
	1	108	7
	1	108	13
	1	109	9
	2	Pref.	85
	2	Pref.	91
	2	3	7
	2	8	5

	Book/ Section	Dial.	Note
	2	12	16
	2	13	12
	2	13	36
	2	34	3
	2	49	1
	2	66	4
	2	68	7
	2	73	12
	2	77	2
	2	83	37
	2	87	6
	2	90	27
	2	91	10
	2	92	1
	2	93	7
	2	93	27
	2	93	29
	2	96	7
	2	99	3
	2	104	9
	2	108	1
	2	109	1
	2	111	5
	2	132	15
De sui ipsius	1	Pref.	16
	1	9	2
	1	9	5
	1	13	12
	1	15	23
	1	16	4
	1	41	15
	1	44	7
	1	44	8
	1	44	10
	1	45	2
	1	46	7
	1	46	10
	1	46	23
	1	64	7
	1	69	30
	1	69	32
	1	108	15

	Book/Section	Dial.	Note
	1	112	6
	2	Pref.	14
	2	Pref.	29
	2	Pref.	56
	2	41	3
	2	63	5
	2	83	29
	2	93	19
	2	97	13
De vir. ill.	1	12	19
	1	94	11
De vir. ill. 1, 3	2	6	12
5	1	78	5
5, 1	1	72	6
6	2	77	12
8, 19–32	1	105	7
8, 21–22	1	105	7
8, 39–43	2	71	3
8, 51–59	2	71	2
15	1	49	1
	2	90	35
15, 3	1	14	3
15, 11	2	18	14
15, 14–15	1	104	7
15, 17–23	1	18	11
15, 21	2	43	9
15, 30	1	49	1
15, 33–34	1	108	9
16	2	90	35
16, 20	2	96	13
	2	96	21
16, 25	2	1	14
16, 33	1	11	22
17	2	90	35
17, 30–35	1	83	1
17, 35	1	83	2
17, 36–42	1	63	17
17, 44	1	10	19
17, 45–46	1	68	7
18, 24–32	2	71	2
18, 26	1	60	6
19, 52	2	114	24

	Book/Section	Dial.	Note
21, 1, 2–3	2	90	35
21, 1, 6	2	1	12
21, 6, 47	1	78	4
21, 7–9	1	105	7
21, 8, 27	2	54	6
21, 12, 41–44	1	51	2
21, 12, 45–46	2	67	30
21, 2, 15; γ 74–75	1	51	1
22, 1	1	12	15
	1	110	16
22, 4	1	12	19
22, 5	1	7	6
	1	57	7
33	2	93	57
Jul. Caesar 20	2	35	2
De vita sol.	INT		40
	1	89	5
	2	13	4
	2	67	28
	2	88	9
De vita sol. Pref.	1	Pref.	55
	2	68	4
1	DP		14
	1	Pref.	2
	1	Pref.	29
	1	1	18
	1	2	25
	1	3	4
	1	8	7
	1	16	3
	1	18	13
	1	21	6
	1	23	34
	1	27	10
	1	29	5
	1	29	18
	1	44	5
1	1	44	19
	1	58	11
	1	89	5
	1	119	3
	2	9	4

	Book/Section	Dial.	Note
	2	10	1
	2	10	6
	2	10	11
	2	10	14
	2	13	8
	2	13	25
	2	13	59
	2	15	10
	2	17	4
	2	18	14
	2	21	23
	2	29	8
	2	29	9
	2	40	6
	2	53	9
	2	53	10
	2	57	6
	2	79	18
	2	83	28
	2	90	19
	2	93	32
	2	95	9
1	2	98	2
	2	102	9
	2	114	21
	2	117	5
	2	122	2
	2	125	7
2	TMR		2
	TMR		3
	1	Pref.	41
	1	Pref.	59
	1	1	10
	1	2	25
	1	12	30
	1	18	2
	1	18	3
	1	21	6
	1	29	7
	1	37	16
	1	43	18
	1	46	6

Book/Section	Dial.	Note
1	46	19
1	65	1
1	65	11
1	69	37
1	89	5
1	112	23
2	Pref.	16
2	5	4
2	7	6
2	7	13
2	7	17
2	8	3
2	10	18
2	21	13
2	21	26
2	40	8
2	63	5
2	63	6
2	67	30
2	73	12
2	75	20
2	77	4
2	88	11
2	88	14
2	93	59
2	94	2
2	96	2
2	96	10
2	96	12
2	96	14
2	96	24
2	104	10
2	114	22
2	114	32
2	114	33
2	117	17
2	117	42
2	119	12
2	122	3
Epigram, *Turris Parmensis*	1	Pref.	1

	Book/ Section	Dial.	Note
	2	90	21
Fam.	1	14	4
Fam. 1, 1	2	118	20
1, 1, 1–2	2	92	1
1, 1, 21–22	1	88	3
1, 1, 24	1	17	8
1, 1, 26	DP		12
	1	48	3
1, 1, 30	2	96	13
1, 1, 41	2	92	1
1, 1, 43	1	52	12
1, 2	1	117	1
1, 2, 1	1	11	20
	2	25	14
1, 2, 5	1	51	3
	2	52	1
1, 2, 6	2	5	9
1, 2, 16–18	1	12	22
1, 2, 17	1	12	18
1, 2, 20	1	11	20
	2	25	14
1, 2, 24	2	1	14
1, 2, 25	1	92	11
1, 2, 26	2	1	12
1, 2, 27	1	51	3
1, 2, 29	1	11	20
	2	25	14
1, 3, 2	1	1	12
1, 3, 6–7	1	2	25
1, 3, 7	1	9	6
	2	13	19
	2	41	3
	2	45	6
1, 3, 8	1	44	10
1, 3, 10	1	2	9
1, 3, 11	1	1	11
	1	11	15
1, 4, 10	2	97	15
1, 6, 2	2	54	6
1, 6, 9	1	19	12
1, 6, 13	1	1	12

	Book/Section	Dial.	Note
1, 6, 14	1	1	11
1, 7, 2	1	99	15
1, 7, 5	2	5	9
	2	90	7
1, 7, 6	1	9	12
1, 7, 12	1	43	16
1, 7, 13	2	13	4
	2	114	33
1, 7, 14	2	119	20
1, 7, 15–18	2	83	34
1, 8, 2–5	1	29	18
	1	119	3
1, 8, 9	1	41	8
	2	99	2
1, 8, 10	1	109	12
1, 8, 10–16	1	10	8
1, 8, 20	2	81	27
	2	102	10
1, 9	1	9	18
1, 9, 1	INT		45
1, 9, 10	1	16	4
1, 10, 1	2	10	12
1, 10, 4	1	2	25
	1	5	2
1, 12	1	44	8
2, 1, 6	2	Pref.	93
2, 1, 12	2	66	9
2, 1, 26	2	125	7
2, 1, 27	2	8	7
2, 1, 33	1	110	16
2, 1, 36	1	Pref.	58
2, 2, 2	2	132	4
2, 2, 3	1	108	13
2, 2, 6	1	11	1
2, 2, 14	1	11	1
	1	40	15
2, 2, 20	1	Pref.	4
	1	11	18
	1	40	15
2, 3, 3	1	11	1
	2	77	4
	2	95	7

	Book/Section	Dial.	Note
2, 3, 9–13	2	67	10
2, 3, 10	1	114	3
	2	67	10
	2	67	21
	2	77	2
2, 3, 13	2	67	8
2, 3, 17	2	84	13
	2	114	6
2, 3, 18	2	95	7
2, 3, 25	1	27	2
2, 3, 28	1	115	5
2, 4, 9	2	104	9
2, 4, 9	2	7	5
	2	55	3
2, 4, 11	1	2	11
	2	114	1
2, 4, 12	1	108	2
2, 4, 13	1	11	18
2, 4, 13–14	1	19	18
2, 4, 14	2	13	19
	2	45	6
2, 4, 17	1	Pref.	53
2, 4, 19	1	21	8
	2	5	4
	2	25	6
	2	88	7
2, 4, 20	1	11	15
2, 4, 21	1	11	22
2, 4, 28	1	Pref.	16
	2	114	27
2, 4, 32	2	84	13
	2	95	11
	2	121	3
2, 5, 2	1	1	8
2, 5, 16	1	114	3
2, 6, 4	2	53	6
2, 6, 9	2	96	21
2, 7, 3	1	89	4
	1	89	5
2, 7, 5	2	83	29
	2	83	40
2, 7, 12	1	104	5

	Book/ Section	Dial.	Note
2, 7, 16	2	117	4
2, 8	2	84	13
2, 8, 3	2	54	10
2, 8, 7–8	2	90	28
	2	117	5
	2	117	11
2, 9, 2	1	69	2
	2	73	12
2, 9, 5	2	Pref.	93
2, 9, 7	1	89	4
	1	89	5
2, 9, 11	1	10	8
2, 9, 13	2	90	7
2, 9, 14	2	125	7
2, 10	1	115	3
2, 10, 2	2	13	44
2, 10, 3	2	130	4
2, 10, 4	1	115	3
2, 10, 5	2	104	11
2, 12	2	90	27
2, 12, 9	2	117	28
2, 13	2	90	27
2, 15, 2	1	72	6
3, 1, 2	2	78	4
3, 1, 5	1	2	25
3, 1, 14	1	5	2
3, 1, 15	2	73	12
3, 2, 4	1	69	17
	2	9	4
3, 3, 6	1	10	19
3, 6, 1	1	2	11
	1	90	18
	2	13	4
	2	114	2
3, 6, 2–3	1	109	12
3, 7, 3	2	9	20
3, 7, 4	1	Pref.	41
	1	2	25
	1	17	7
3, 7, 6	2	93	57
3, 9, 4	2	96	2
3, 10, 5	1	20	1

	Book/ Section	Dial.	Note
	1	21	6
3, 10, 6	2	119	7
3, 10, 10	2	96	21
3, 10, 11	2	67	30
3, 10, 14	1	70	4
	2	114	22
3, 10, 17	2	7	16
3, 11, 5	2	5	9
3, 12, 9	2	117	28
3, 13	2	84	1
	2	84	6
3, 13, 11	INT		10
	DP		19
3, 14, 7	1	2	25
3, 15, 1	2	13	41
3, 16	INT		45
	INT		46
	2	56	10
	2	67	31
	2	84	13
3, 16, 1	2	Pref.	91
	2	13	19
	2	45	6
	2	67	31
3, 16, 2	INT		29
	2	1	14
	2	56	10
	2	67	31
3, 16, 12	1	17	8
3, 18	1	Pref.	41
	1	43	2
3, 18, 2	1	Pref.	41
3, 18, 13	1	43	9
3, 19, 1–7	1	109	17
3, 19, 11	1	109	17
3, 20, 8	1	108	7
3, 20, 9	1	108	7
3, 20, 10	1	2	25
3, 21	1	72	4
3, 21, 5	1	72	4
3, 22, 6	1	23	5
4, 1	2	79	18

	Book/Section	Dial.	Note
4, 1, 27–29	1	40	4
	1	42	2
	2	29	7
4, 1, 28	2	6	8
4, 1, 29	1	40	4
	2	96	1
4, 1, 30–31	1	40	4
4, 1, 32	2	29	7
	2	38	2
4, 1, 34	2	Pref.	85
4, 2, lemma	2	94	2
4, 2, 2	2	81	5
4, 2, 3	2	103	3
4, 2, 4	1	Pref.	5
4, 2, 5	2	117	24
4, 2, 8–10	1	85	10
	2	81	22
4, 2γ, 5	2	119	19
	2	125	7
4, 3, 13	2	25	10
4, 5	2	21	23
4, 7, 5	2	5	9
4, 7, 12	1	16	6
4, 8	2	90	27
4, 9	1	Pref.	1
4, 10, 3	1	46	13
4, 12, 13	2	1	14
4, 12, 15	1	17	8
4, 12, 21	1	Pref.	58
4, 12, 22	2	9	29
4, 12, 27	2	81	10
4, 12, 28	1	10	20
	1	89	2
	1	116	1
4, 12, 30	1	17	8
	2	1	14
	2	75	16
4, 12, 39	2	117	6
	2	119	12
4, 14	2	29	13
4, 14, 19	1	64	7
4, 15	1	46	23

	Book/ Section	Dial.	Note
4, 15, 19	1	46	3
	1	46	24
4, 16, 10	2	7	21
4, 17, 1	2	9	4
4, 17, 3	1	69	2
	2	10	18
5, 1, 3	1	81	3
5, 2, 5	1	35	6
5, 3, 4	1	Pref.	41
5, 3, 6	1	35	9
5, 3, 8–16	2	114	59
5, 3, 19	1	Pref.	44
5, 5	1	87	1
5, 5, 1	2	54	10
5, 5, 2	2	54	9
5, 5, 7	1	88	8
5, 5, 21	1	88	8
	2	54	12
5, 6	2	114	59
5, 8, 7	2	93	6
5, 9, 2	2	49	6
5, 10	1	Pref.	1
	2	68	15
5, 10, 9	2	Pref.	71
5, 11, 3	2	25	10
5, 11 and 12	2	25	10
5, 17, 6	1	40	10
5, 17, 9	1	2	25
5, 17, 3	1	Pref.	4
	1	1	11
	1	69	2
5, 17, 6	1	40	10
5, 17, 14	1	Pref.	53
	1	Pref.	56
5, 18, 1	1	2	10
	1	90	18
	1	109	12
5, 18, 5	DP		18
	1	2	9
5, 18, 6	2	117	6
6, 1, 4	2	13	29
6, 1, 9–12	1	105	4

	Book/ Section	Dial.	Note
6, 1, 12	2	13	36
	2	93	59
	2	105	1
6, 1, 16	2	13	35
6, 1, 22	1	43	2
6, 2	1	118	1
	2	129	6
6, 2, 1–4	1	13	5
6, 2, 4	1	Pref.	16
	1	109	12
6, 2, 6	1	77	7
6, 2, 7	1	72	6
	1	78	5
6, 2, 8	1	35	2
	2	77	12
6, 2, 9	1	72	8
6, 2, 11	2	57	6
	2	132	8
6, 2, 13	1	40	10
	2	114	24
6, 2, 16	1	Pref.	16
	1	14	6
6, 3	DP		19
	INT		45
	2	40	8
	2	83	1
	2	84	1
	2	84	6
6, 3, 3	2	50	1
6, 3, 4	1	11	19
	2	89	3
6, 3, 8–24	2	120	9
6, 3, 11	1	16	4
6, 3, 13	1	70	4
	2	120	14
6, 3, 14–15	2	101	6
6, 3, 15	2	101	5
6, 3, 21	2	96	21
6, 3, 23	1	16	6
6, 3, 26	2	96	21
6, 3, 33–34	1	16	4
6, 3, 35	1	75	6

	Book/Section	Dial.	Note
6, 3, 40	1	35	2
6, 3, 41	1	Pref.	29
	2	9	29
6, 3, 48–50	2	84	7
6, 3, 51	INT		45
6, 3, 54	1	1	18
6, 3, 62	2	67	22
6, 3, 69	1	89	4
	1	89	5
6, 4	DP		18
	1	29	18
	1	119	3
6, 4, 1	1	Pref.	52
6, 4, 1–5	1	44	17
6, 4, 3–4	1	Pref.	52
	1	29	17
6, 4, 4	1	Pref.	52
	2	13	19
6, 4, 5	2	21	23
6, 4, 7	TMR		3
6, 4, 8–13	1	29	18
6, 5	INT		43
	INT		45
	1	Pref.	46
6, 5, 1	INT		45
	2	Pref.	91
	2	Pref.	93
6, 5, 2	2	Pref.	91
	2	114	16
6, 5, 5	1	Pref.	20
6, 5, 6	1	43	20
	1	108	7
	1	108	13
6, 8, 1	1	2	11
	2	9	8
	2	55	3
6, 8, 4	2	93	57
6, 8, 6	2	63	5
	2	88	11
6, 8, 9	2	88	10
	2	88	11
7, 1	1	89	4

	Book/ Section	Dial.	Note
7, 1, 3	2	13	20
7, 2	1	10	8
7, 2, 3	1	10	8
7, 3, 1	1	18	2
7, 3, 2	1	55	1
7, 3, 10	2	9	4
7, 5	1	11	19
	1	89	4
7, 6, 3	1	1	11
	1	90	1
7, 6, 4	1	2	25
7, 7	1	89	4
7, 7, 5–6	2	88	6
7, 8	INT		45
7, 9, 4	1	11	19
7, 10, 4	2	92	16
7, 11, 3	1	110	1
7, 12, 5	2	53	6
7, 12, 6–7	1	69	5
7, 12, 16	1	Pref.	61
7, 12, 18	2	90	7
7, 13, 12	2	13	20
7, 14, 1–2	1	Pref.	61
7, 14, 2	1	69	3
7, 15	2	93	38
7, 15, 5	1	85	7
	2	75	20
7, 15, 49–51	1	43	14
7, 17, 3–8	2	43	4
7, 17, 5	1	11	19
7, 17, 8	2	82	10
7, 17, 13–15	2	41	3
7, 18, 9	1	17	7
8, 1	1	76	1
8, 1, 2	1	108	7
8, 1, 8	1	17	7
	1	29	9
	1	108	13
8, 1, 10	1	Pref.	53
	1	87	1
	2	49	1
	2	77	2

	Book/ Section	Dial.	Note
8, 1, 18	1	27	2
8, 1, 19	2	12	6
	2	97	8
8, 1, 21	2	34	3
8, 1, 31	2	49	1
	2	77	2
8, 1, 33	1	89	5
	2	Pref.	85
	2	Pref.	89
8, 1, 36	1	Pref.	39
	1	90	5
	2	13	19
8, 1, 37	1	2	26
8, 1, 38	1	17	8
	2	127	13
8, 2, 1	1	108	13
8, 3, 18	1	40	15
	1	69	17
8, 4, 1–8	1	2	25
8, 4, 17	1	Pref.	52
8, 4, 21	2	92	1
8, 4, 24	1	2	25
8, 4, 27	2	13	20
8, 4, 31	2	114	24
8, 5, 2	2	117	25
8, 7	1	89	5
	2	92	1
8, 7, 7	2	118	4
8, 7, 10	1	30	15
	2	Pref.	85
8, 7, 20	1	15	49
8, 7, 21	2	9	29
8, 7, 23–26	1	58	11
8, 8	2	83	1
	2	92	1
8, 8, 4	2	67	31
8, 9, 8	2	93	4
8, 9, 27	2	92	1
8, 10, 12	1	115	3
	2	28	17
8, 13, 13	2	84	13
8, γ 1, 2–5 n, 300–301	2	Pref.	93

	Book/ Section	Dial.	Note
9	2	35	2
9, 1, 1	1	69	2
9, 1, 2	2	1	14
	2	25	3
	2	25	15
	2	114	16
9, 1, 6	1	Pref.	53
9, 3, 3	2	9	29
9, 3–5	2	83	33
9, 4, 5	1	57	15
9, 4, 6	2	68	4
9, 4, 7	1	69	14
9, 4, 11	2	97	15
9, 5	1	Pref.	1
	1	81	3
	1	107	5
9, 5, 18	2	87	3
9, 5, 25	1	96	51
9, 5, 26	1	107	5
9, 5, 28	1	81	3
9, 5, 39	1	47	2
9, 5, 44	2	35	2
9, 5, 47	1	72	4
9, 5, 48	1	52	7
9, 5–6	1	1	4
9, 11, 4–5	1	51	1
9, 11, 8	2	88	11
9, 11, 9	2	125	7
9, 13, 3	1	16	4
9, 13, 10	2	67	14
9, 13, 11	2	67	8
9, 13, 13	2	15	14
9, 13, 18	1	21	8
	2	5	4
9, 13, 24–25	1	88	3
9, 13, 25	2	90	7
9, 14, 6	1	108	7
9, 15, 2 (orig. version)	2	76	2
9, 16, 1	1	Pref.	41
	2	14	5
10, 1, 12	2	5	4

	Book/Section	Dial.	Note
	2	88	7
10, 1, 12–13	1	21	7
10, 1, 16	1	35	2
	2	43	13
	2	67	8
	2	77	12
10, 2, 1	2	95	14
10, 2, 4	2	92	1
10, 3	1	20	10
10, 3, 8–9	1	15	23
10, 3, 13	1	11	18
	2	87	3
10, 3, 16	1	29	6
10, 3, 17	1	15	29
10, 3, 21	1	16	3
10, 3, 22	2	125	7
10, 3, 30–35	2	29	6
10, 3, 32	2	29	10
10, 3, 36	1	84	8
10, 3, 37	2	60	1
10, 3, 43	2	12	14
10, 3, 46	2	77	20
10, 3, 48	1	Pref.	52
	2	53	10
10, 3, 49–53	2	53	10
	2	93	20
10, 4, 9	2	13	51
10, 4, 31	2	125	7
10, 5, 2	2	117	24
	2	125	7
10, 5, 3	2	66	4
10, 5, 8	1	13	12
10, 5, 10	1	12	2
10, 5, 14	1	72	11
	1	72	13
10, 5, 18	1	27	4
10, 5, 18–21	2	119	12
10, 5, 29	2	110	8
10, 6, 1	1	11	20
11, 1, 2	2	114	16
11, 1, 3	2	57	17
11, 1, 10	2	13	4

	Book/Section	Dial.	Note
	1	52	12
	2	Pref.	85
12, 2, 7	1	110	16
12, 2, 9	1	Pref.	39
	1	37	16
12, 2, 10	1	108	2
12, 2, 12	1	5	2
	2	93	57
12, 2, 21	2	90	53
12, 2, 34	1	119	3
12, 2, 35	2	94	2
12, 3	1	81	8
12, 3, 4	1	40	15
	1	69	17
12, 3, 5	1	90	7
12, 3, 5–7	2	5	4
12, 3, 10	1	Pref.	16
12, 3, 13	1	57	14
	2	119	25
12, 3, 16	1	95	14
12, 3, 17	2	81	12
12, 3, 18	1	80	5
12, 3, 19	2	83	34
12, 4, 2	1	10	19
12, 4, 8	2	53	6
	2	96	13
12, 5, 2–3	2	102	9
12, 5, 4	1	69	5
12, 5, 7	1	64	6
12, 7, 2	2	84	13
12, 7, 6	2	101	5
12, 7, 7	2	125	5
12, 8	1	44	14
12, 11, 2	2	3	6
12, 11, 6	2	125	7
12, 11, 14	1	2	25
12, 11, 1	1	72	6
12, 14, 2	1	Pref.	61
	2	75	8
12, 14, 6	1	108	13
13, 1, 13	1	46	13
13, 1, 15	1	89	4

	Book/ Section	Dial.	Note
14, 6, 15–16	1	89	5
14, 7	2	7	16
15, 1, 4	1	117	6
15, 1, 8	1	92	11
15, 2	2	90	27
15, 3, 5	2	121	3
15, 3, 8	2	90	7
15, 4	1	100	1
	2	90	27
15, 4, 2–5	2	95	3
15, 4, 3	1	21	6
15, 4, 4	2	125	10
15, 4, 8	1	112	23
15, 4, 10	2	67	22
15, 4, 15	2	93	59
15, 5, 8	1	116	1
	2	114	11
15, 5, 9	2	125	7
15, 6, 4	2	126	22
15, 7	1	100	1
15, 7, 10	1	81	3
15, 7, 15	2	125	7
15, 7, 21	1	2	11
	1	115	5
15, 7, 22	1	2	26
15, 8, 3	2	Pref.	91
	2	85	8
15, 8, 19	2	1	14
	2	25	15
15, 9, 17–27	2	90	46
15, 9, 23	1	88	8
15, 9, 26	1	35	2
15, 11, 2	2	88	17
15, 12, 2	1	51	4
	1	90	23
15, 14, 4	1	12	2
15, 14, 7	2	117	24
15, 14, 8	2	93	59
15, 14, 27	1	92	11
15, 14, 29	2	117	24
16, 1, 20	2	90	53
16, 2	2	92	1

	Book/ Section	Dial.	Note
16, 2, 4	2	6	11
16, 2, 5	1	16	6
16, 3, 3	1	18	2
	2	Pref.	85
16, 3, 4	1	10	5
	1	11	1
16, 4	2	84	15
16, 4, 8	2	93	31
16, 4, 11	2	117	17
16, 4, 17–20	1	27	2
16, 5, 4	2	119	12
16, 6	1	Pref.	6
	1	Pref.	53
	2	40	8
16, 6, 1	2	67	31
16, 6, 2	DP		12
	1	48	3
16, 6, 5	2	66	4
16, 6, 13	1	89	5
	2	117	12
6, 6, 14	2	13	4
	2	114	33
16, 6, 14–17	2	114	30
16, 6, 15	1	109	12
16, 8, 6	1	51	4
16, 9, 9	2	125	7
16, 11, 12–13	1	40	10
16, 12, 7	2	7	16
	2	67	26
16, 13	2	25	12
16, 14, 11	1	Pref.	16
17, 1, 2	1	43	20
17, 1, 3	1	45	2
17, 1, 3–4	1	15	29
17, 1, 7	2	117	17
17, 1, 11–16	2	117	17
17, 1, 36	1	45	2
17, 1, 37	1	5	1
17, 2	2	43	1
17, 3	INT		45
	1	100	1
	2	64	6

	Book/ Section	Dial.	Note
	2	74	4
17, 3, 3	DP		18
	2	Pref.	82
17, 3, 3–4	2	Pref.	82
17, 3, 3–14	1	Pref.	41
17, 3, 5–6	2	118	26
17, 3, 6	1	Pref.	53
	2	84	13
17, 3, 6–7	2	119	20
17, 3, 8	2	117	24
17, 3, 9	1	Pref.	40
	1	90	5
	2	88	17
17, 3, 13	2	9	3
17, 3, 16	1	97	12
17, 3, 17	1	116	1
17, 3, 19–20	1	30	15
	1	38	10
17, 3, 22	1	Pref.	4
17, 3, 23	DP		7
17, 3, 25–27	2	83	19
17, 3, 27	1	Pref.	44
17, 3, 27–28	1	58	11
17, 3, 31	1	Pref.	39
17, 3, 33	1	Pref.	44
	1	14	8
	1	14	14
	2	5	16
17, 3, 40	2	77	20
17, 3, 42	1	1	4
	1	16	4
	2	69	7
17, 3, 44	2	39	14
17, 3, 46–47	1	15	40
17, 3, 48	1	Pref.	6
	1	46	31
17, 4	1	100	1
17, 4, 11	2	125	7
17, 4, 13	1	Pref.	56
	2	77	4
	2	95	7
17, 4, 13–14	1	Pref.	53

	Book/Section	Dial.	Note
18, 14, 4	1	109	12
18, 15	1	Pref.	61
18, 16	1	100	1
	2	Pref.	91
	2	1	14
18, 16, 4	2	107	12
18, 16, 7	1	17	8
	2	1	14
18, 16, 11	1	109	17
18, 16, 13	1	Pref.	39
18, 16, 17	1	48	12
18, 16, 30	1	81	3
19, 3	1	106	10
19, 3, 16	1	16	3
19, 3, 20	2	13	19
19, 5, 3–4	2	8	9
19, 5, 4	1	2	25
19, 7, 2	1	15	3
19, 9	1	100	1
19, 9, 4	DP		7
19, 9, 4	INT		45
	1	Pref.	39
	2	Pref.	91
[19, 9, 4, n. 21]	2	Pref.	91
19, 9, 10	1	48	12
19, 10, 5	1	Pref.	61
	1	109	13
	2	58	8
19, 11	1	46	23
19, 11, 1	1	69	3
	2	51	5
19, 11, 2	1	Pref.	61
19, 11, 9	1	69	3
19, 12, 2	2	41	2
19, 12, 5	2	104	7
19, 13, 1	2	6	15
19, 16, 1	1	1	22
19, 16, 2	2	87	3
19, 16, 12	1	2	25
19, 16, 20	1	21	2
19, 17, 1	1	2	25
	2	13	20

	Book/Section	Dial.	Note
19, 17, 3–4	1	43	20
19, 17, 10	2	41	3
19, 18, 20	1	7	6
	1	57	7
19, 18, 44	1	Pref.	52
	2	53	9
20, 1	1	115	3
	2	130	4
20, 1, 1	1	115	3
20, 1, 3	1	115	3
	1	115	4
	2	117	6
20, 1, 6	1	40	6
	2	10	6
20, 1, 8–9	1	58	3
20, 1, 10–11	2	10	9
20, 1, 15	1	Pref.	61
	2	Pref.	85
20, 1, 21	2	13	24
20, 1, 24	1	35	3
20, 1, 27	2	13	26
20, 2, 1	1	Pref.	21
20, 2–3	1	10	20
20, 3, 3	1	50	9
20, 4, 8	2	101	6
20, 4, 17	1	1	11
	1	90	2
20, 4, 19	2	75	20
20, 4, 27–28	1	21	14
20, 4, 28	1	43	7
	1	89	2
	1	115	2
20, 4, 33	1	11	1
20, 4, 34	2	18	7
20, 6, 6	1	12	28
20, 8, 11	1	14	6
20, 8, 15–16	1	2	25
20, 8, 16	2	Pref.	14
20, 8, 19	1	Pref.	20
20, 8, 20	1	Pref.	29
	1	69	12
20, 8, 22	1	Pref.	20

	Book/ Section	Dial.	Note
20, 12, 2	1	116	1
20, 12, 3	1	Pref.	60
21, 2, 9	1	Pref.	47
21, 4, 2	2	83	29
21, 5, 1	1	Pref.	47
21, 5, 5	1	10	8
21, 7, 4	1	Pref.	47
21, 8, 6	1	69	19
21, 8, 12	2	25	15
	2	28	9
21, 8, 13	2	132	11
21, 8, 14	2	94	6
21, 8, 24	1	72	6
21, 9	2	84	13
21, 9, 5	2	66	4
	2	84	13
21, 9, 6	2	28	9
21, 9, 7	DP		12
	1	48	3
21, 9, 7–11	1	Pref.	56
	1	21	8
21, 9, 8	1	Pref.	41
	1	Pref.	53
	2	84	13
	2	95	11
21, 9, 10–11	2	5	4
21, 9, 12	2	39	14
21, 9, 13	1	2	11
	1	19	18
	1	69	12
	1	89	2
	2	18	14
	2	64	2
21, 9, 14	2	125	7
21, 9, 15	2	55	3
21, 9, 18	2	35	2
	2	77	4
21, 9, 19	2	Pref.	85
21, 9, 20	1	27	2
21, 10, 7	1	11	18
21, 10, 10–11	2	93	27
21, 10, 12	2	13	41

	Book/ Section	Dial.	Note
21, 10, 24	1	Pref.	56
21, 11, 8	1	Pref.	47
	1	57	15
21, 12, 1	1	16	4
	1	72	6
21, 12, 5	2	7	16
21, 12, 5–6	2	117	5
21, 12, 12	1	Pref.	4
	1	11	1
21, 12, 21	DP		19
	1	Pref.	61
21, 12, 23	1	Pref.	13
	2	109	1
21, 12, 27–28	2	83	38
21, 12, 28	2	101	5
21, 13, 1	1	19	19
21, 13, 2	1	Pref.	41
21, 14, 1	1	14	8
21, 15, 5	2	28	18
21, 15, 12	1	29	18
	1	119	3
22, 1	1	65	1
22, 1, 8	1	91	1
22, 2, 6	2	Pref.	65
22, 2, 16–21	1	29	18
	1	119	3
22, 2, 27	1	29	18
22, 4	2	53	8
22, 4, 1	2	117	6
22, 5, 11	2	115	8
22, 7	2	43	1
22, 7, 5	1	21	2
22, 7, 11	1	69	3
22, 7, 13–14	2	126	2
22, 7, 16	1	Pref.	4
22, 7, 17	1	Pref.	41
22, 8, 6	1	23	2
22, 10	DP		18
	2	92	1
	2	118	20
22, 12	1	33	4
22, 12, 4	2	9	29

	Book/ Section	Dial.	Note
	2	101	5
	2	101	6
22, 12, 5	1	2	11
	2	9	2
	2	9	11
	2	55	3
	2	78	4
22, 12, 15–29	2	92	1
22, 12, 16–17	1	52	11
22, 12, 20	2	Pref.	85
22, 12, 27	2	126	39
22, 13	1	37	32
22, 13, 7	2	Pref.	91
22, 14	1	14	5
	1	37	32
	1	48	12
	2	90	27
22, 14, 7	1	92	11
22, 14, 25	2	77	20
22, 14, 59	2	13	19
22, 14, 64	2	55	10
22, 15	2	92	1
23, 1	2	125	7
23, 2	1	37	32
23, 2, 4	2	5	9
23, 2, 7	2	125	7
23, 2, 12	2	15	1
23, 2, 26	1	97	7
23, 2, 28	1	Pref.	53
23, 2, 32	1	62	2
23, 2, 42	1	2	25
	2	40	10
23, 2, 43	1	5	2
23, 4, 3	1	93	9
	2	90	7
23, 4, 22–24	1	43	11
23, 5	2	119	14
23, 5, 1	1	40	6
23, 5, 4	2	119	12
23, 5, 7	2	117	34
23, 5, 13	1	70	4
23, 5, 15	1	Pref.	44

	Book/Section	Dial.	Note
23, 12, 31	2	21	23
23, 12, 33–36	2	24	9
23, 12, 34	1	90	18
	2	88	17
23, 12, 37	DP		19
23, 15, 2	INT		10
23, 16, 4	2	9	4
23, 17, 6	1	42	18
23, 18, 2	1	Pref.	19
23, 18, 6	1	19	18
23, 19	INT		94
23, 19, 11–13	1	29	18
	1	119	3
23, 19, 13	1	44	3
23, 21, 8	2	83	2
24, 1	1	1	12
	2	83	1
	2	83	2
24, 1, 4	1	2	21
24, 1, 5	2	15	1
24, 1, 12	2	26	5
24, 1, 27	1	1	9
	2	117	6
24, 1, 30	1	Pref.	35
	2	120	10
24, 3–12	2	118	20
24, 4	1	44	14
24, 4, 1	1	51	4
24, 4, 8	1	46	2
24, 4, 12	1	44	16
24, 5, 5–9	1	Pref.	15
24, 5, 6	1	Pref.	41
	1	Pref.	53
	2	1	14
24, 5, 7	2	1	14
	2	25	15
24, 5, 11	2	121	3
24, 5, 15–19	1	52	12
24, 5, 17	1	46	25
24, 6	1	44	8
24, 6, 2	1	44	16
24, 6, 4	1	16	2

	Book/ Section	Dial.	Note
1, 14, 1–14	2	92	1
1, 14, 99–103	2	111	6
2, 1, 54–56	1	35	9
2, 9	2	85	1
2, 10, 67–68	1	64	6
2, 10, 244–249	2	96	13
2, 14, 273	2	88	6
2, 15	1	35	9
2, 15, 128	1	64	6
2, 18, 30–38	1	44	13
3, 5	2	Pref.	10
3, 5, 78–98	2	Pref.	9
3, 6, 1–6	2	93	38
3, 19	1	Pref.	44
	2	125	7
3, 19, 14–16	2	67	22
3, 23, 28–29	2	93	6
3, 27	1	16	3
3, 27, 70–74	1	Pref.	1
3, 33, 1–9	2	96	2
Misc. 18	1	23	32
Paris oration (1361)	INT		Item 4
	1	17	3
	1	37	32
	1	38	22
	2	90	18
	2	94	2
	2	121	3
Philologia	2	83	40
Ps. poen. 1, 7	2	9	11
4	2	93	20
5	1	2	20
5, 6	1	33	1
Rer. mem. libri	1	12	18
	1	88	8
Rer. mem. libri 1, 1, 7	1	23	23
1, 1, 9	1	23	24
1, 2	1	21	6
1, 10	2	68	7
1, 13, 1	2	86	2

	Book/ Section	Dial.	Note
3, 33, 1	1	Pref.	29
3, 33, 5–6	2	66	6
3, 35, 3	1	2	9
3, 39, 6–7	1	110	16
3, 42, 4	1	Pref.	52
	1	29	18
3, 45	2	104	11
3, 47, 3	2	83	34
3, 51	1	18	2
3, 62, 1–5	1	17	7
3, 62, 8	2	117	25
3, 64, 3	1	5	1
3, 65, 1	2	14	6
3, 66, 2–6	2	55	3
3, 69, 4	1	68	2
3, 69, 30	1	68	2
3, 71, 29	2	75	20
3, 71, 32–33	2	19	9
3, 71, 34–35	2	66	9
3, 72	1	69	30
3, 72, 5	2	66	4
3, 77, 8	2	67	11
3, 77, 12	1	Pref.	52
	1	29	18
	2	53	9
3, 80, 7	2	Pref.	2
3, 83	1	18	2
3, 84, 2	1	Pref.	60
	2	93	59
	2	105	1
3, 91, 3	2	55	3
3, 93, 11	1	44	6
3, 93, 12	1	44	2
	1	44	9
3, 94	1	96	51
3, 94–95	1	107	5
3, 95	1	107	5
3, 96	1	69	2
	2	68	3
3, 96, 17	2	93	4
3, 99, 2	1	12	2
4, 3	1	106	4

	Book/ Section	Dial.	Note
	1	69	2
136–138	1	107	4
136, 10	2	90	9
137, 9–11	2	55	11
138, 76–79	1	46	2
141, 7	1	30	15
142, 35–36	1	46	2
176, 7–8	2	40	8
187, 1–4	2	25	10
231, 12–14	1	16	6
232	1	41	4
	2	107	15
232, 12	2	33	4
238	1	Pref.	1
240, 6	1	30	15
244, 14	1	90	7
246, 70–72	2	122	3
252, 1–2	1	Pref.	60
260, 9–10	1	72	6
262, 9–11	1	72	6
264	2	88	1
	2	122	3
264, 99–108	1	69	17
274	2	Pref.	85
306, 4	2	117	24
325, 46–60	2	1	14
349, 11	2	117	24
355, 1–4	2	83	2
360, 91–92	1	68	7
360, 93–94	1	76	1
360, 100	1	72	6
361	2	83	11
366, 1–3	1	40	8
Secretum	1	11	18
	2	5	16
	2	109	1
Secretum, Prohem.	DP		7
	1	117	11
1	DP		11
	1	Pref.	7
	1	Pref.	37

Book/Section	Dial.	Note
1	Pref.	60
1	1	4
1	1	11
1	11	11
1	11	15
1	12	30
1	19	18
1	23	11
1	44	11
1	58	11
1	69	12
1	87	1
1	90	12
1	90	19
1	109	12
1	109	16
2	Pref.	85
2	6	11
2	8	9
2	13	4
2	13	19
2	45	6
2	64	3
2	70	8
2	77	4
2	83	34
2	84	13
2	90	23
2	93	31
2	93	58
2	95	7
2	95	8
2	95	13
2	109	1
2	114	1
2	114	32
2	117	9
2	119	18
DP		9
INT		45
PW		1
1	Pref.	38

2

Book/ Section	Dial.	Note
1	Pref.	41
1	Pref.	61
1	2	9
1	2	22
1	2	25
1	5	2
1	5	10
1	10	8
1	10	16
1	11	1
1	11	22
1	13	6
1	14	8
1	14	14
1	17	3
1	27	2
1	43	18
1	44	5
1	44	7
1	58	11
1	69	30
1	69	31
1	117	11
2	Pref.	14
2	Pref.	91
2	7	16
2	8	9
2	9	4
2	13	20
2	21	21
2	33	4
2	35	2
2	75	8
2	79	18
2	84	15
2	93	2
2	93	4
2	93	6
2	93	59
2	93	60
2	95	13
2	98	2

	Book/ Section	Dial.	Note
	2	102	9
	2	104	13
	2	111	3
	2	111	6
	2	117	24
	2	121	3
	2	122	2
3	INT		45
	1	Pref.	55
	1	1	15
	1	2	12
	1	5	8
	1	11	20
	1	15	40
	1	16	3
	1	27	4
	1	44	5
	1	44	20
	1	46	30
	1	46	31
	1	69	5
	1	69	14
	1	69	16
	1	69	39
	1	69	41
	1	72	4
	1	92	2
	1	92	4
	1	92	5
	1	92	11
	1	94	11
	1	110	4
	1	117	1
	2	1	5
	2	18	14
	2	67	24
	1	67	26
	2	73	12
	2	83	1
	2	83	27
	2	83	31
	2	83	34

	Book/ Section	Dial.	Note
	2	83	40
	2	88	1
	2	88	6
	2	90	35
	2	90	46
	2	91	18
	2	96	21
	2	97	15
	2	101	2
	2	117	28
	2	120	9
	2	120	16
	2	120	17
Sen. 1, 1	2	25	15
1, 3	2	90	28
	2	117	17
	2	120	9
1, 5	1	Pref.	60
	1	23	24
	1	43	3
	1	46	13
	2	49	6
	2	105	1
	2	117	28
	2	119	7
	2	119	12
1, 6	2	40	8
1, 7	1	40	8
	2	5	28
	2	38	4
	2	76	2
	2	114	24
	2	118	4
	2	119	14
2, 1	1	30	10
	1	37	16
	1	49	1
	1	57	15
	2	90	7
	2	94	2
2, 2	1	2	25
	1	69	12

	Book/Section	Dial.	Note
	1	40	10
4, 4	1	Pref.	44
4, 5	1	Pref.	61
	1	44	8
	1	81	3
	2	75	8
5, 2	INT		4
	1	11	18
	1	11	22
	1	19	16
	1	19	18
	1	29	17
	1	29	18
	1	40	15
	1	44	3
	1	44	5
	1	44	8
	1	46	5
	1	48	12
	1	49	2
	1	69	12
	1	69	17
	1	85	10
	2	35	1
	2	79	12
	2	84	13
	2	90	55
	2	96	2
	2	111	8
5, 4	INT		Item 6
	1	11	19
	1	12	28
	1	16	6
5, 5	2	48	21
6, 2	2	88	17
6, 4	1	Pref.	53
6, 6	1	114	13
	2	117	25
6, 7	1	5	2
	2	Pref.	68
	2	13	13
	2	13	14

	Book/Section	Dial.	Note
	2	13	44
6, 8	1	Pref.	7
	1	2	25
	1	11	1
	2	6	11
	2	13	36
	2	114	48
7, 1	1	1	9
	1	21	8
	1	107	6
	1	112	23
	2	13	41
	2	56	10
	2	57	6
	2	88	7
	2	90	28
	2	100	4
	2	114	61
	2	125	7
7, 2	1	2	19
7, 3	1	114	3
8, 1	1	58	11
	2	17	4
	2	90	28
	2	93	59
	2	110	8
	2	114	24
	2	117	39
8, 2	1	Pref.	4
	1	2	19
	2	83	1
	2	83	29
	2	98	9
	2	101	2
	2	118	7
	2	118	19
8, 3	INT		Item 8
	INT		14
	INT		45
	INT		46
	PW		4
	PW		11

	Book/ Section	Dial.	Note
	1	Pref.	39
	1	11	1
	1	43	20
	1	69	2
	1	89	5
	1	103	4
	1	114	3
	2	Pref.	91
	2	Pref.	93
	2	3	3
	2	5	28
	2	6	11
	2	51	11
	2	67	31
	2	77	4
	2	83	21
	2	84	1
	2	104	9
8, 5	1	Pref.	52
	1	Pref.	55
	1	69	2
	1	119	2
	2	49	1
	2	77	2
8, 6	1	10	8
	1	58	5
	1	121	2
	2	6	8
8, 7	INT		Item 9
	INT		41
	1	Pref.	3
	1	Pref.	6
	1	Pref.	53
	1	2	25
	1	10	8
	1	10	19
	1	98	1
	2	Pref.	91
	2	1	14
	2	7	16
	2	10	18
	2	25	15

	Book/Section	Dial.	Note
	2	114	16
9, 1	1	10	20
	1	108	13
	1	116	1
	2	66	4
	2	92	1
9, 2	1	1	11
	1	43	20
	1	89	5
	1	90	2
	2	55	12
	2	77	2
	2	79	12
	2	90	27
9, 3	2	Pref.	91
9, 11	2	Pref.	85
10, 1	1	2	14
	1	90	16
	2	93	33
	2	96	1
	2	126	19
10, 2	INT		43
	1	15	49
	1	35	6
	1	35	9
	1	37	32
	1	43	12
	1	88	8
	2	21	23
	2	91	10
	2	92	1
	2	94	2
10, 4	DP		19
	1	Pref.	56
	1	Pref.	61
	1	11	1
	1	35	9
	2	5	4
	2	48	11
	2	49	8
	2	68	7
	2	77	2

Book/Section	Dial.	Note
	2	93	61
	2	114	6
	2	120	9
11, 4	2	51	13
11, 5	1	23	29
	1	23	32
	1	72	4
11, 7	1	12	30
11, 11	1	29	7
	1	43	20
	1	69	2
	2	12	16
	2	13	41
	2	39	4
	2	83	17
	2	119	12
11, 16	1	114	3
	1	115	3
11, 17	2	77	7
	2	120	11
12	1	2	25
	2	83	28
12, 1	1	Pref.	56
	1	1	12
	1	2	25
	1	11	18
	1	16	3
	1	16	4
	1	18	3
	1	18	8
	1	19	18
	1	37	20
	1	44	8
	1	57	11
	1	57	12
	2	Pref.	84
	2	10	14
	2	68	3
	2	69	7
	2	83	1
	2	83	7
	2	83	28

	Book/ Section	Dial.	Note
	2	83	38
	2	84	8
	2	85	1
	2	117	5
	2	120	11
	2	122	3
12, 2	1	Pref.	44
	1	11	19
	1	37	20
	1	46	23
	2	83	1
	2	85	1
	2	117	17
12, 13	1	35	9
13, 1	1	108	13
	2	51	13
13, 2	1	10	8
	1	16	6
	1	19	18
	1	37	16
	1	69	3
13, 5	1	46	7
	2	117	28
13, 9	2	2	92
13, 13	1	Pref.	56
	1	1	12
	1	13	6
	2	38	10
13, 14	1	30	15
	1	89	2
	1	115	3
	2	13	12
	2	13	19
	2	45	6
13, 15	1	37	20
13, 16	1	37	20
	2	38	4
	2	118	4
14, 1	1	Pref.	30
	1	Pref.	49
	1	Pref.	56
	1	23	34

	Book/ Section	Dial.	Note
	1	36	2
	1	50	9
	1	85	6
	1	92	11
	1	95	1
	1	95	11
	1	95	14
	1	101	2
	1	101	4
	2	6	11
	2	58	8
	2	66	4
	2	79	18
	2	82	9
	2	119	7
15, 3	1	Pref.	5
	1	13	14
	1	18	5
	1	18	14
	1	23	6
	1	23	11
	1	40	10
	1	42	6
	1	43	11
	1	57	14
	1	58	11
	1	65	1
	1	73	8
	2	Pref.	88
	2	9	4
	2	13	4
	2	17	4
	2	21	18
	2	34	3
	2	49	6
	2	53	6
	2	53	10
	2	90	15
	2	93	7
	2	108	1
	2	111	5
	2	113	2

	Book/Section	Dial.	Note
	2	114	33
	2	119	25
15, 6	1	46	6
	1	46	7
	2	117	28
15, 10	2	92	1
15, 11	1	69	32
15, 12	1	47	9
	2	68	2
	2	75	13
	2	129	6
16, 1	1	43	18
16, 3	1	12	2
	2	88	14
16, 4	1	Pref.	49
	1	Pref.	61
	1	37	16
	2	53	14
	2	77	2
16, 5	2	96	23
16, 7	2	88	13
16, 8	1	69	13
	2	13	12
16, 9	DP		14
	INT		Item 1
	1	29	18
	2	Pref.	89
	2	84	15
	2	88	17
	2	90	16
	2	93	1
	2	93	31
	2	93	59
	2	97	15
17, 2	1	Pref.	52
	1	Pref.	61
	1	11	15
	1	17	7
	1	18	3
	1	37	32
	1	46	20
	1	89	2

		Book/ Section	Dial.	Note
		1	89	5
		1	90	18
		1	100	1
		2	83	1
		2	83	38
		2	88	14
		2	117	5
		2	117	17
17, 3		INT		38
(Griseldis)		INT		83
		TMR		3
		1	1	3
		1	27	4
		2	92	1
17, 4		INT		8
18, 1		1	Pref.	1
(Posteritati)		1	19	12
		1	46	20
		1	117	1
		2	93	44
		2	105	1
		2	110	8
SN		1	107	4
		1	118	3
SN	1	1	16	3
	2	1	89	4
	3	1	89	4
	4	1	Pref.	44
		1	16	4
		1	16	7
		1	17	8
		1	85	11
		1	89	4
		2	66	4
		2	117	8
	6	PW		3
		1	52	8
		1	114	13
		1	115	3
		2	Pref.	68
		2	117	8
	8	2	119	12

		Book/Section	Dial.	Note
	2, 162–163	1	Pref.	47
	3, 42	1	64	6
	3, 58	1	23	4
	3, 77–78	2	96	14
	App.	1	75	6
Tr. mort.	1, 82–84	1	15	40
	1, 129	2	14	5
	2, 22–24	2	119	12
Tr. pud.	107–111	2	94	6
	118–125	2	67	26
	130–135	1	72	6
		1	72	8
	187–189	1	2	27
Tr. temp.		1	117	1
Tr. temp.	40–45	1	2	11
	55–60	1	Pref.	55
	136–138	2	49	6
Var. 7		1	17	8
		2	1	14
		2	71	7
9		2	84	13
15		1	1	12
17		1	89	5
		2	77	2
18		2	85	1
19		1	Pref.	1
		1	69	2
		2	93	4
24		2	76	2
25		2	25	15
		2	93	8
28		1	Pref.	1
29		1	69	2
		1	69	3
		2	96	13
32		1	Pref.	56
		1	16	4
		1	69	2
		2	12	3
		2	38	11
		2	48	1
		2	48	9

	Book/Section	Dial.	Note
	2	48	11
	2	51	11
	2	75	19
	2	87	3
	2	91	13
	2	93	4
	2	93	59
33	2	118	32
38	1	89	4
40	1	89	4
42	1	89	4
	2	40	8
43	1	5	1
44	1	37	20
48	1	89	4
50	DP		23
	1	122	1
53	1	14	8
	1	14	14
	2	5	16
55	1	2	25
	2	99	2
56	1	14	13
	2	Pref.	91
	2	12	14
	2	87	3
60	DP		18
	1	14	8
	1	14	14
	2	5	16
61	DP		23
	1	Pref.	4
	1	108	15
63	2	1	14
	2	13	19
	2	25	15
	2	114	16
64	1	2	25
	1	122	3
	1	122	4
Venice oration	1	89	5
(1354)	2	Pref.	85

WORKS BY ANCIENT
AND MEDIEVAL AUTHORS
REFERRED TO IN
THE COMMENTARY

ABBREVIATIONS

DP   *Dramatis personae*: The Argument of the Book
INT   Introduction
PW   Petrarch on His Work
TMR   To the Modern Reader

(The title abbreviations of individual works are listed in the Bibliography, II.)

INDEX

	Book/Section	Dial.	Note
2, 6 1107a	1	5	2
3, 3 1112a 28	2	Pref.	91
3, 9	1	Pref.	23
	2	64	2
3, 10–12	2	108	5
4, 3 1124b 9–10	1	93	6
4, 5	2	107	11
5, 1 1129a 18	1	11	19
6, 13	2	114	38
6, 13 1144b	2	114	38
7, 1	1	72	14
7, 5	2	110	4
8	1	22	2
	1	50	7
8, 1 1156b 6	2	Pref.	3
8, 3	1	50	9
9, 1, 3	2	64	2
9, 9 1169b 18	2	31	3
10, 6–8	1	108	13
10, 7 1177b 31–35	1	109	11
10, 9	2	108	5
Eudemus	2	119	7
	2	125	3
Hist. anim. 4, 10 536b	1	31	1
Magna mor. 2, 8–9 1206b–1207b	1	37	34
Metaph. 1, 5 985b–986a	2	97	9
3, 4 1000b	1	18	15
5, 8	1	37	3
8, 2–3	1	37	3
13, 3 1078a 32	1	66	2
Meteor.	2	90	38
1, 2	2	Pref.	4
2, 8 366b 2–5	2	91	6
2, 9	1	116	2
1, 5 188a 19	1	11	19
	2	Pref.	58
1, 7 190b 1–4	1	37	3
Oeconomica 1, 6 1345a 12–17	1	21	15
Phys. 1, 9 192a	1	37	3
2, 2 194a	1	56	4
2, 4 196a	2	Pref.	91
4, 14 223b	2	93	19

	Book/Section	Dial.	Note
7, 6, 8	2	5	29
7, 7, 11	1	49	1
7, 17	DP		11
	2	3	3
	2	3	4
7, 21	1	Pref.	48
8, 1	1	13	12
8, 2, 3	1	41	15
8, 5, 10	2	7	16
8, 5, 10–12	DP		2
	1	1	19
	1	90	16
	2	109	4
	2	109	9
8, 7	1	11	11
8, 8–9	2	109	1
8, 9	2	93	59
8, 12	1	40	4
9, 6, 14	1	23	18
9, 7, 15	1	23	20
9, 7, 17	1	23	18
10, 2	2	103	15
10, 8	1	8	2
10, 8, 15	1	40	4
10, 14	1	8	7
10, 14, 21	1	89	1
10, 14, 22	1	89	1
10, 14, 23–24	2	3	3
10, 28	1	Pref.	48
10, 32	1	22	16
10, 33, 49	1	23	29
10, 33, 49–50	1	23	21
10, 33, 50	1	23	19
10, 33, 59	1	23	18
10, 34, 53	1	37	9
11, 2	2	3	3
11, 13	1	39	6
11, 13, 15	2	83	15
11, 3, 15–26	2	83	2
11, 13, 33	2	83	2
11, 15, 18–20	2	117	6
11, 15, 20	2	15	8

	Book/ Section	Dial.	Note
5, 9	2	5	28
5, 10	2	15	7
5, 14	DP		19
	2	104	13
5, 18	2	13	36
	2	43	11
5, 24	1	85	7
5, 26	2	114	61
7, 14	2	28	13
7, 25	1	69	30
8	2	39	4
8, 1	1	46	7
	2	117	16
	2	117	28
8, 4	DP		16
8, 4–9	1	69	30
8, 8	2	117	17
8, 12	1	25	1
	1	78	5
8, 12, 14	1	69	30
8, 12, 19	1	69	30
8, 13	1	23	34
8, 14	2	39	4
8, 15	2	Pref.	4
8, 23	1	13	14
	1	13	15
8, 24	DP		23
	2	39	5
9	2	39	4
9, 2	2	93	31
9, 8	1	Pref.	2
9, 10	1	69	30
	2	119	13
9, 11	2	119	12
10	2	39	4
10, 1	2	7	7
	2	42	7
	2	117	25
10, 9–11	1	69	30
10, 18	1	109	12
10, 30	1	15	23
10, 30, 22–26	1	69	30

	Book/ Section	Dial.	Note
14, 8	DP		11
	2	Pref.	90
	2	93	59
	2	94	1
14, 9	2	Pref.	90
14, 13	1	1	11
	1	10	8
	1	12	31
	1	13	6
	1	13	9
	2	111	12
14, 15	2	107	5
14, 19	1	Pref.	41
	1	Pref.	61
	2	74	2
	2	75	8
	2	109	7
15–18	2	83	7
15, 1–22	2	45	8
15, 5	2	45	2
15, 7	1	10	19
16, 3	2	129	4
16, 8	2	Pref.	13
16, 10	2	129	4
16, 17	2	129	4
16, 37	2	45	4
16, 42	2	45	4
17, 15	2	13	25
17, 16	1	Pref.	59
18, 2	2	129	4
18, 21–22	2	129	4
18, 25	1	12	18
18, 39	1	13	14
18, 42–43	1	43	8
18, 48	2	93	40
19	1	58	11
19, 1	1	18	14
19, 3	1	2	29
	1	10	19
19, 4	DP		2
	1	Pref.	41
	1	58	11

	Book/ Section	Dial.	Note
	2	28	8
	2	114	33
	2	118	30
19, 5	1	2	14
	1	33	1
19, 13	2	2	12
	2	74	6
	2	66	2
19, 14	1	65	1
19, 15	2	7	12
19, 17	1	10	19
20, 19	1	114	13
21, 3	DP		11
	2	Pref.	90
21, 4	1	62	5
	2	Pref.	52
21, 4, 4	2	67	26
21, 13	DP		11
21, 14	1	90	5
	2	93	52
	2	129	5
22, 1	2	74	2
22, 4	2	93	22
22, 22	1	58	11
	2	Pref.	1
	2	111	6
22, 24	1	40	6
	2	2	6
	2	90	10
	2	93	10
	2	93	13
	2	93	25
	2	93	41
	2	93	53
	2	111	6
De div. quaest. 31, 1	1	Pref.	2
58, 2	1	1	15
	2	83	7
83, 38	2	90	49
De doct. 1, 4, 4	INT		39
	1	10	19
1, 22, 20	1	10	18

	Book/Section	Dial.	Note
2, 21–23	2	114	37
2, 29	2	114	37
3, 8, 12	1	44	17
4, 5, 7	1	9	18
4, 6, 9	1	44	17
4, 8, 22	1	44	17
De gen. ad litt. 1, 2	2	93	22
3, 10	2	Pref.	60
3, 20	2	93	9
4, 28, 45	1	15	3
6	2	93	31
6, 12	2	93	9
7, 22	2	93	9
12, 4–8	2	93	31
16, 59	1	66	2
De gen. contra Manich. 1, 2, 4	2	90	49
1, 23, 39	2	83	7
2, 56	2	90	14
De lib. arb. 1, 6, 15	1	44	5
1, 13, 27	2	84	13
2, 3, 8	1	11	10
2, 16, 24	1	43	4
2, 16, 43 and 45	2	2	12
2, 19	1	Pref.	7
3, 17, 48	2	13	36
	2	105	1
3, 48	1	38	12
	1	105	4
9, 19	2	34	3
De magistro 8, 21	1	44	17
10, 32	1	23	8
11, 8	1	15	29
14, 46	1	15	29
De musica 1, 4, 6	1	23	3
1, 9, 15	2	2	12
6	2	97	12
6, 4, 7	2	2	6
6, 5	2	2	7
6, 12, 41	1	37	9
De op. mon.	2	9	18
De ord. 1, 6, 18	1	11	19
	2	93	14

	Book/Section	Dial.	Note
70, 2, 4	1	1	15
83, 11	1	Pref.	53
99	1	23	30
104, 25	2	106	4
115, 6	2	7	16
118, 1	2	117	25
125, 10	2	93	52
135, 8	1	13	12
145, 5	1	86	3
Ench. 1, 2	2	42	7
2, 2	1	13	12
Ep. 118, 3, 22	1	12	31
In ev. Ioan.	2	90	10
	2	93	31
	2	96	7
Prof. fidei 28	1	12	12
Quaest. Simpl. 58, 2	2	126	12
Retract. 1, 1	2	Pref.	91
Serm. 23a	1	Pref.	48
	1	2	31
103	2	67	20
393	2	126	12
Solil.	DP		7
1, 1, 1	1	15	29
1, 5, 9	2	34	3
1, 6, 12–13	2	96	1
	2	96	7
1, 15, 27	2	13	41
Aulus Gellius *Noct. Att.*	1	78	5
	2	98	2
1, 5, 2–3	1	62	7
1, 11, 16	2	103	3
1, 14	2	93	57
1, 15, 18	1	9	2
1, 17, 1–3	2	19	9
1, 17, 4–6	2	19	8
2, 7, 20	1	69	12
2, 18, 9	1	14	3
2, 18, 9–10	1	14	3
3, 3, 14	2	9	22
3, 10, 11	1	16	4
3, 15	1	23	14

	Book/Section	Dial.	Note
3, 15, 3	1	29	9
3, 16, 13	1	12	28
6, 1	2	6	13
6, 3, 8	2	7	21
6, 18, 11	2	98	2
7, 1, 4	1	11	19
7, 2, 12–14	2	95	8
7, 3	1	21	6
7, 4	1	14	4
7, 13, 1–4	1	26	7
8, 3	1	21	6
8, 15	1	16	4
9, 4, 6	2	Pref.	14
9, 4, 11	2	Pref.	13
9, 4, 44	2	Pref.	13
9, 4, 46	2	Pref.	14
9, 13	2	43	11
10, 5	1	38	12
10, 11	2	83	44
10, 17	2	96	14
10, 18	2	88	5
10, 26, 8	1	57	15
10, 28	1	1	15
11, 13, 10	2	103	3
11, 18, 6–8	2	61	1
12, 3	2	27	2
12, 9	1	7	7
13, 3	2	15	7
13, 4	2	6	13
13, 9, 1–3	2	7	21
13, 10, 1	2	62	1
13, 18	1	110	16
14, 1	1	112	1
	2	114	37
14, 3, 11	1	69	30
15, 4	2	5	23
15, 6, 2	2	7	21
15, 17, 1–2	1	23	25
15, 19	2	104	11
15, 20	1	1	15
15, 20, 9	2	Pref.	10
16, 19	2	23	6

	Book/Section	Dial.	Note
17, 14	2	57	117
17, 14, 4	1	95	11
	2	54	12
18, 2, 1–6	1	26	7
18, 13, 1–4	1	26	7
19, 11	1	69	32
Aurelius Victor. *Caes.* 4, 14	1	64	20
12, 1	2	131	1
13, 10	2	131	1
16, 7	2	75	20
20, 25–26	2	84	14
38, 1–4	2	55	2
Epit. 1, 19	1	118	12
4, 9	1	64	20
11, 11–12	1	52	7
	2	21	15
11, 15	2	131	2
12, 1 and 8	2	131	2
13, 12	2	131	2
39, 6	2	79	7
41, 8	1	43	14
41, 11–12	1	52	7
48	2	114	61
Aurelius Victor. *See also* Pseudo-Aurelius Victor			
Ausonius, Decimus Magnus.			
Lud. sept. sap.	1	12	18
52–53	2	73	12
55–58	1	17	7
69–70	2	14	6
73–130	1	17	7
124–125	2	18	14
136–139	2	73	12
180–181	2	14	6
—Petrarch's ms.	1	23	4
Avicenna. On the Form.	1	111	8
Bartholomaeus Anglicus. *De prop. rer.*	2	Pref.	18
2	2	Pref.	61
2, 1	1	40	6
3, 1	1	40	6
4, 1	2	Pref.	4
5, 12	1	40	6

	Book/ Section	Dial.	Note
10, 1	2	90	9
11, 30	2	117	6
12, 12	1	44	4
Eccli. 1, 7, 40	2	95	13
1, 16	1	13	12
2, 6	1	63	2
2, 11	1	63	3
2, 13	2	42	7
	2	119	23
3, 9	2	6	6
3, 19–20	2	55	12
7, 1	1	11	3
7, 3–7	1	23	3
7, 40	2	95	13
8, 8	1	104	9
10, 8	2	79	24
10, 9	2	90	15
10, 9–10	2	13	14
	2	105	5
10, 10	2	13	48
10, 12–15	2	111	6
10, 14–15	2	77	7
10, 15	2	105	1
11, 19–20	2	105	3
11, 30	1	17	7
	1	108	13
12, 12	1	44	4
13, 32	2	91	17
14, 4	2	105	4
14, 8–9	2	106	1
17, 31	2	90	15
18, 6	2	83	38
18, 8	1	1	8
21, 11	2	41	3
27, 21–23	1	52	13
28, 1	1	101	9
28, 3–4	1	101	8
28, 6	1	101	15
33, 14–15	1	11	19
33, 15	1	1	11
37, 32–34	1	18	17
39, 35	2	90	43

	Book/ Section	Dial.	Note
41, 13	2	132	20
42, 12–14	1	65	1
51, 31	2	119	19
Eph. 3, 16–17	1	15	29
5, 24	1	65	1
6, 2	2	6	6
6, 5	2	119	11
6, 5–6	2	7	7
i Esdr. 4, 6	1	69	40
Esth. 1, 1	1	69	40
2, 1–16	1	69	40
Ex. 3, 1	2	103	16
3, 2	2	55	8
4, 10–16	2	102	11
8	2	90	9
8, 16	2	90	10
8, 19	2	90	12
8, 20–24	2	90	12
8, 21	2	90	12
8, 24	2	90	11
14, 15	2	103	16
20, 2	1	85	3
20, 12	2	6	6
20, 17	2	17	7
21, 17	2	24	6
Ez. 18, 20	2	6	7
Gal. 5, 17	2	3	2
5, 24	2	67	12
6, 14	2	67	12
Gen. 1, 1–27	2	93	22
1, 3	2	93	22
1, 26	2	93	9
	2	93	22
	2	93	31
	2	93	33
	2	122	1
1, 26–30	2	90	17
1, 31	2	90	11
2, 7	2	55	12
2, 9–10	1	16	6
3	1	65	1
3, 17	1	56	4

	Book/Section	Dial.	Note
9, 6	1	39	6
11, 11–14	2	117	14
12, 12–19	2	57	9
12, 31	2	119	12
14, 6	2	93	31
14, 30	2	119	12
15, 5	DP		22
16, 11	2	119	12
i Joan. 5, 6	2	13	41
5, 16–17	2	126	4
5, 21	1	41	18
Job 1–2	2	84	18
1–42	2	84	18
1, 1–3	1	59	7
1, 3	1	60	8
1, 13–15	1	59	7
1, 21	2	11	2
2, 1–10	2	90	9
2, 7–10	2	84	18
4, 6	1	Pref.	41
4, 19	2	63	2
5, 6	2	Pref.	10
	2	119	25
5, 7	2	84	13
	2	118	10
7, 1	DP		12
	1	48	3
	1	48	11
	2	84	13
7, 12	2	67	12
7, 14	1	21	4
	2	86	7
8, 9	2	90	15
9, 21	2	13	25
10, 9	2	90	15
14, 1	1	58	11
	2	93	1
14, 2	1	2	2
	2	13	25
	2	17	4
	2	90	15
14, 22	2	64	6

	Book/Section	Dial.	Note
	2	91	16
Marc. 1, 40–41	2	126	19
2, 7	2	126	2
2, 7–8	2	126	13
3, 1	1	2	20
3, 5	1	14	13
3, 22–30	2	90	9
6, 17	2	128	4
7, 10	2	6	6
	2	24	6
10, 14	2	119	19
Matth. 1, 17	2	83	7
3, 12	2	93	40
3, 17	1	85	11
4, 6	2	95	6
5, 44	2	42	9
6, 13	1	13	13
6, 19–20	1	36	2
	2	13	12
6, 25	2	58	9
6, 25–26	1	64	24
7, 12	1	101	7
	2	21	4
7, 24–27	2	127	4
8, 2–3	2	126	19
10, 25	2	90	9
10, 28	2	132	6
10, 36	1	33	1
11, 1–10	2	57	9
11, 12	2	28	10
11, 29	2	112	6
12, 10	1	2	20
12, 22–30	2	90	9
12, 42	2	88	15
13, 2–9	2	13	39
13, 31–32	1	64	24
14, 3	2	128	4
14, 42	2	88	15
15, 4	2	6	6
	2	24	6
15, 14	1	14	13
	1	64	23

	Book/ Section	Dial.	Note
	1	58	11
	2	12	4
	2	113	2
15, 21	2	95	4
16, 18	1	23	11
17, 22	2	93	59
18, 21	1	9	21
19, 2	2	95	6
19, 11	2	84	13
19, 19	2	84	13
20, 20	2	24	6
21, 19	1	65	4
22, 1	1	11	2
27, 9	1	22	15
27, 15	2	19	2
28, 20	2	13	9
Ps. 2, 4	1	46	9
	2	87	3
2, 9	2	58	5
5, 6	2	114	25
6, 5	2	117	6
8, 4	2	93	20
8, 8	2	93	20
9, 21	1	38	10
H10, 7	2	90	43
	2	119	11
H10, 15	2	126	23
11, 3	2	103	13
11, 9	1	24	6
18, 13	2	13	25
23, 1	1	90	5
26, 10	2	127	5
30, 16	1	90	23
	2	76	2
33, 22	2	117	34
35, 10	1	16	6
	1	40	8
36, 3–5	2	58	8
36, 5	2	12	17
	2	58	8
38, 2	2	103	7
38, 5	2	83	29

	Book/ Section	Dial.	Note
38, 7	2	13	35
38, 13	2	67	22
39, 3	2	93	20
41, 4	2	93	4
41, 16	2	Pref.	38
45, 3–7	2	69	6
45, 5	2	90	52
48, 13	2	110	4
48, 19	1	56	1
50, 7	2	6	4
54, 6	2	119	11
54, 23	2	58	9
57, 12	2	39	3
61, 11	2	13	37
61, 12	2	Pref.	91
	2	39	18
65, 5	2	58	6
67, 9	2	69	6
72, 7	1	56	2
73, 28	1	109	12
74, 9	1	90	5
75, 6	1	53	2
	1	53	3
75, 7	1	31	14
77, 30	1	58	11
77, 30–31	1	23	11
77, 59	2	69	6
78, 2	2	132	6
81, 5	2	69	6
81, 6	2	93	27
84, 9	2	81	27
85, 5	2	119	23
88, 11	1	49	1
	2	77	8
88, 12	1	90	5
89, 10	1	1	7
	2	119	11
90, 3–5	2	14	8
90, 12	2	95	6
93, 10	2	40	4
93, 11	2	87	3
99, 3	2	13	25

	Book/ Section	Dial.	Note
101, 12	2	90	15
101, 25	2	123	4
102, 5	2	83	16
102, 8–9	2	107	10
102, 10–11	2	13	25
102, 12	2	13	25
	2	126	2
102, 13–14	2	13	25
102, 15	1	1	5
	2	13	25
102, 17	2	13	25
103, 10	2	93	20
104, 4	2	71	5
104, 31	2	90	9
	2	90	11
104, 34	2	90	11
106, 23–27	1	107	2
110, 10	1	13	12
111, 7	2	130	7
114, 5	2	58	6
115, 15	2	117	34
	2	132	6
117, 26	1	85	11
118, 28	2	109	9
126, 5	2	93	20
137, 8	2	119	24
138, 8	2	53	10
138, 15	2	103	14
138, 16	1	12	5
	2	109	8
141, 8	2	64	6
	2	119	11
144, 9	2	13	25
144, 14	2	13	25
144, 16	2	12	12
144, 18	2	13	25
	2	119	24
	2	126	2
145, 7	2	66	8
i Reg. 1, 1–7	2	22	2
1, 10–13	2	22	2
1, 19–20	2	22	2

	Book/ Section	Dial.	Note
2, 10	2	90	40
12, 14	2	103	14
21, 13	2	103	14
24, 15	2	90	11
25	2	128	9
26, 20	2	90	11
ii Reg. 6, 14–23	1	24	3
10, 4	2	21	23
11	2	128	9
12, 15–23	2	48	7
13	1	72	6
iii Reg. 10, 1–10	2	88	11
11, 3	1	12	13
11, 4–8	1	12	14
iv Reg. 1, 2–3	2	90	9
1 and 2	2	55	8
16, 3–4	2	90	33
Rom. 2, 4	2	117	39
5, 3–4	2	84	13
7, 19	1	27	4
7, 24	2	64	6
9, 20–21	2	114	19
10, 17	1	Pref.	59
11, 34	1	46	11
13, 1	2	39	18
13, 11	2	109	9
13, 13	1	19	12
20–21	2	114	19
Sap. 2, 1	2	98	2
3, 6	1	84	7
4, 7	2	112	6
7, 4–6	2	11	2
8, 21	2	23	5
	2	104	13
9, 15	2	117	24
11, 21	1	Pref.	64
11, 25	2	13	24
14, 7	2	95	6
15, 7	2	90	15
15, 14	2	111	9
19, 10	2	90	11
i Thess. 4, 4–5	1	42	19

	Book/Section	Dial.	Note
5, 3	2	119	11
ii Thess. 2, 1–11	1	114	13
i Tim. 2, 2	2	119	11
2, 5	2	93	31
2, 10	2	42	7
2, 11–15	1	65	1
3, 6	1	10	9
6, 7	2	11	2
6, 8	2	58	9
6, 9–10	2	13	36
6, 10	1	105	1
	1	105	4
	2	13	36
6, 17–18	2	13	36
6, 17–19	2	13	58
Tit. 2, 9–10	2	7	7
2, 12	1	57	2
Tob. 4, 16	1	101	7
	2	21	4
13, 6	2	119	11
Zach. 10, 5	1	31	14
13, 9	1	84	7
	2	55	5
Bible. *Vetus Latina*	1	11	19
Boccaccio, Giovanni. *Corbaccio*	1	65	15
	1	76	3
Decameron	2	116	6
1, Intro.	1	23	11
	2	92	1
1, 4–5	1	23	11
2, 9	2	Pref.	39
4, Pref.	2	35	2
4, 7	2	81	8
5, 1	1	23	11
6, 5	1	40	10
7, 10	1	85	10
10, 8	2	131	1
10, 10 (Griselda)	INT		83
	1	Pref.	2
	1	65	11
	2	48	10
	2	83	38

	Book/ Section	Dial.	Note
1 M4 3	1	Pref.	39
1 M4 17–18	2	18	14
1 M7	DP		11
1 P1 1–15	2	5	24
1 P1 1–25	2	5	24
1 P1 16	1	8	1
1 P2	2	77	3
1 P2 1	DP		19
1 P3	1	11	18
1 P3 1–3	1	40	6
1 P3 31–34	1	117	6
1 P3 37–39	1	108	13
1 P3 43–46	1	Pref.	61
1 P3 44	2	117	17
1 P4	1	12	28
1 P4 14–18	1	44	5
1 P4 43–46	1	Pref.	61
1 P4 141–143	2	7	3
1 P5	2	119	20
1 P5 20–24	1	8	2
1 P5 34–41	2	93	59
1 P5 38	2	93	60
1 P5 40	DP		19
1 P5 42	1	49	1
1 P6 21–24	2	93	59
1 P6 23–24	DP		19
1 P6 35	2	117	6
1 P6 40	2	73	7
1 P6 40–42	2	93	30
1 P6 56	DP		19
2, 1–3	DP		5
	2	9	2
2 M3	2	117	8
2 M7	2	119	19
2 M7 15–22	1	15	40
2 M8	2	67	15
2 P1 3–4	2	93	59
2 P1 19–25	DP		19
2 P1 35–37	1	Pref.	8
2 P1 58–62	2	38	4
2 P1 59–62	1	Pref.	44
2 P2 1–33	2	9	2

	Book/ Section	Dial.	Note
3 P8	1	6	1
3 P8 15–17	2	2	10
3 P8 17	1	1	21
3 P8 17–19	1	2	8
	1	40	6
3 P8 17–31	1	2	8
	1	117	11
3 P8 22–26	1	2	8
	2	96	13
3 P10 80–94	2	93	27
3 P12 20–24	1	44	5
3 P12 65	DP		18
4, 1, 1	1	Pref.	49
4, 6, 111	2	Pref.	58
4 M3 34	1	Pref.	61
4 M6 19–29	2	Pref.	84
4 M7 19	1	Pref.	11
4 M7 29–30	1	40	6
4 M7 32–33	1	11	22
4 P2 71–73	1	40	6
4 P3 5–31	2	93	27
4 P3 50–69	2	31	5
4 P4 135–136	2	65	6
4 P5 22–24	1	44	6
4 P5 41	1	2	14
4 P6	1	44	5
	2	39	7
4 P6 25	1	Pref.	61
4 P6 25–51	1	39	6
4 P6 90–101	1	44	5
4 P6 115–119	2	93	59
4 P6 133	1	11	1
4 P6 189–195	1	11	1
	1	44	5
4 P7	1	69	12
4 P7 38–55	1	Pref.	53
4 P7 40	1	Pref.	22
4 P7 44	2	28	9
5 M5	2	93	46
5 M5 10–15	1	40	6
5 P1 24–30	2	Pref.	91
5 P1 38–53	2	Pref.	91

	Book/ Section	Dial.	Note
	2	105	1
	2	106	4
Prol. 321–322	2	13	55
Canon's Yeoman's Prol. & T.	1	111	1
Prol. 645	1	5	2
Knight's T.	2	Pref.	10
1773–1781	1	96	47
Knight's T. 2065–2068	2	Pref.	10
Man of Law's Prol. 18–32	2	15	1
	2	83	2
T. 422–427	1	23	11
1133–1134	2	15	8
Melibee 1085	2	19	2
1087	1	65	4
Merchant's T. 1441–1450	2	18	13
Monk's T. 2015–2094	1	65	1
	2	19	5
2253–2254	2	94	6
2325–2326	2	94	6
Nun's Priest's T. 3205	1	23	11
3279–3280	1	11	19
Pardoner's Prol.	2	105	1
Prol. 329–334	2	13	36
T. 743	2	13	58
Parson's T.	DP		19
	2	93	59
	2	105	1
	2	109	7
432–434	1	31	14
483	2	106	4
489–490	2	106	4
631	2	19	2
685–688	2	109	4
690–691	2	109	1
692–704	2	98	3
705	2	109	9
724–725	2	93	59
935–942	2	18	13
Physician's T. 93–102	1	29	17
115–116	2	106	4
Sir Thopas' T.	INT		92
830	2	28	9

	Book/ Section	Dial.	Note
Summoner's Prol. 1665–1708	1	54	11
Wife of Bath's Prol. 278–280	2	19	2
727–732	2	19	10
778–781	2	18	12
T. 1109–1162	1	16	1
Gentilesse	2	5	19
House of Fame 2, 898–909	1	92	4
2, 926–934	2	39	4
Legend of Good Women F 165–166	1	5	2
F 1773	2	28	9
Parliament of Fowls 1	1	90	7
18–25	2	114	63
57–70	1	92	4
343	1	112	20
Romaunt of the Rose	2	83	2
369–394	2	15	8
369–398	2	83	2
1585–1588	1	Pref.	41
6525–6528	1	5	2
Troilus and Criseyde	1	30	15
1, 400–420, *Cant. Troili*	1	69	2
1, 637	1	11	19
	2	58	2
1, 708–709	2	21	20
2, 771–805	2	26	2
4, 1–7	1	Pref.	44
4, 1368–1359	2	15	5
5, 897–899	1	12	14
5, 1835–1841	1	1	5
6, 600–601	2	28	9
Chauliac, Guy. *See* Guy de Chauliac			
Christine de Pizan. *Livre des Trois Vertus* (1405)	2	19	2
3, 4	1	76	3
Chrysippus. *On Providence*	1	11	19
Cicero, Marcus Tullius,			
the Orator. *Acad.*	1	69	30
1, 4, 16	1	12	19
1, 12, 45–46	DP		14
2, 1, 2	1	8	11
2, 39, 123	2	68	13
2, 44, 136	2	7	5
Ad Att.	2	66	6

	Book/Section	Dial.	Note
21, 6	2	27	4
21, 76	1	50	8
24, 90	1	50	14
27, 102–104	2	48	5
27, 104	2	8	7
De div. 1, 1, 1	1	112	9
1, 3, 5	1	80	6
1, 6, 10	1	Pref.	6
1, 15, 26	1	112	19
1, 25, 53	2	86	4
	2	125	3
1, 28, 59	1	118	9
1, 29, 60–61	2	87	1
1, 34, 76	1	61	3
1, 36, 79	1	28	6
1, 38	2	40	2
1, 45, 102	1	112	21
1, 46, 103	1	112	23
1, 50, 112	2	91	1
1, 53, 120	1	112	15
2	1	112	12
2, 8, 20	1	112	19
2, 9, 24	2	Pref.	91
2, 13, 30	1	112	6
2, 19, 44–45	1	116	2
2, 23, 50	1	37	16
2, 24, 51	1	112	13
2, 31, 66	1	28	6
2, 32, 69	1	61	3
2, 37, 78–79	1	112	19
2, 40, 83	1	112	23
2, 40, 84	1	112	22
2, 42, 87–2, 47, 99	2	114	37
2, 47, 99	1	112	17
2, 52, 107–108	1	112	7
2, 58, 119–120	2	87	1
2, 62, 128	2	87	1
2, 67–68	2	87	1
2, 71, 146	1	112	5
	2	84	10
2, 129	2	86	7
2, 134	2	86	7

	Book/Section	Dial.	Note
	2	114	28
3, 22, 76	1	17	7
5	2	28	1
5, 3, 7	1	69	30
5, 6, 16	2	Pref.	65
5, 16, 44	2	73	12
5, 21, 58	1	1	22
5, 22, 61	1	Pref.	52
5, 23	1	122	1
5, 23, 67	1	Pref.	2
	1	Pref.	53
5, 28, 78	2	114	28
5, 29, 86	2	117	25
5, 30, 92	2	89	3
6, 16	2	Pref.	65
De inv.	1	9	18
1, 1	1	9	18
1, 5, 7	1	46	23
1, 6, 8	1	46	23
1, 7	1	21	7
1, 19, 27	1	10	20
1, 25, 36	1	115	1
1, 26, 37	1	58	1
2, 18	1	90	18
2, 22	1	40	15
2, 43, 125	2	114	44
2, 49, 145	2	15	7
2, 53	1	Pref.	1
	1	Pref.	5
2, 53, 159	1	Pref.	27
2, 53–54	1	Pref.	27
2, 53, 159–54, 165	1	Pref.	2
2, 53, 160	1	Pref.	2
2, 55, 166	1	94	11
De leg. 1, 9	1	40	6
	2	93	51
1, 9, 26	1	40	6
1, 12, 33	1	50	1
1, 19, 51	1	7	7
1, 22, 59	2	73	12
1, 22, 61	2	67	15
2, 13, 32	1	112	9

	Book/Section	Dial.	Note
2, 14, 32	1	23	34
2, 15, 38–39	1	23	34
2, 17, 43	1	11	18
3	1	23	34
3, 1, 16	1	69	30
3, 40	2	75	17
De nat. deor.	2	Pref.	1
1, 1, 1	1	Pref.	49
1, 8, 18	1	46	10
1, 17	1	27	4
1, 20, 54–55	2	7	16
1, 35, 97	1	61	4
2	2	93	18
	2	93	53
2, 2, 4	2	93	19
2, 12, 32	1	69	30
2, 20–22	1	86	8
2, 20, 51	1	92	4
2, 38, 97-2, 41, 105	2	93	19
2, 43, 110	2	93	38
2, 53	2	93	20
2, 56	2	93	20
2, 56, 140	1	Pref.	61
	1	40	6
	2	99	3
2, 56–58	2	93	51
2, 59, 147–150	2	93	11
2, 59, 148	2	93	13
2, 60, 152	1	10	19
2, 62, 154	2	67	15
2, 62, 155	1	86	8
2, 140–146	2	93	51
3, 22, 56	1	13	14
3, 30, 74	2	62	1
De off.	2	118	26
1, 1, 1	1	80	6
1, 5, 15	1	122	1
	2	71	5
	2	109	5
1, 12, 38	2	54	6
1, 13, 41	2	61	2
1, 14, 42-17, 58	1	93	2

	Book/ Section	Dial.	Note
1, 15, 49	1	19	9
1, 17, 53–58	2	27	2
1, 20	1	122	1
1, 20, 68	2	13	13
	2	13	54
	2	13	58
	2	105	7
1, 24, 84	1	98	4
1, 26, 90	1	30	12
	1	38	10
	2	75	20
1, 27, 93–94	2	9	7
1, 27, 94	1	1	18
1, 28, 97	1	95	14
1, 31, 112	2	98	5
	2	118	24
1, 36, 130	1	2	25
1, 39	1	14	4
1, 39, 139	1	34	1
2, 5, 16	1	114	4
	2	132	15
2, 6, 19	INT		46
	1	Pref.	39
	1	Pref.	43
	2	Pref.	91
	2	67	31
2, 7, 24	1	95	14
2, 7, 25	2	82	9
2, 10, 37	2	110	5
2, 12, 43	1	11	21
2, 13	1	1	15
2, 17, 59	1	2	25
2, 18, 64	1	19	7
2, 23, 80	2	81	15
2, 25, 89	1	56	9
3, 1, 1	1	21	6
3, 1, 3	2	48	21
3, 5, 22	2	74	3
	2	75	11
3, 10, 45	1	50	2
3, 14	2	62	1
3, 14, 58–60	2	62	4

	Book/ Section	Dial.	Note
3, 8–28	2	28	11
6, 2, 26	2	93	27
6, 14, 14	1	2	22
	2	80	4
	2	117	6
	2	119	12
6, 14, 15	2	118	26
6, 15, 15	1	2	22
	2	98	9
6, 16	1	92	4
6, 16, 16	1	92	2
	2	119	12
	2	125	7
6, 17, 17	2	114	37
6, 18	1	23	31
6, 18, 18–19	1	23	22
6, 18, 19	2	90	4
6, 18, 30	1	112	6
6, 19, 20	1	92	2
	2	68	13
6, 20, 21–22	2	67	15
6, 20, 22	1	92	2
6, 21, 23	1	92	5
6, 21, 23–22, 24	2	130	3
6, 22, 24	1	92	4
6, 23, 25	1	92	2
	2	10	2
	2	130	3
6, 24, 26	1	16	3
	1	29	6
6, 26, 29	1	2	22
De sen.	2	38	6
	2	83	46
1, 2	1	Pref.	42
1, 3	2	90	26
2, 4	2	83	46
	2	119	25
3, 8	1	15	16
5, 13	2	83	7
5, 31	2	120	14
7, 24	1	110	4
	2	123	2

	Book/Section	Dial.	Note
8, 26	1	23	24
	2	101	5
10, 31	2	120	14
11, 37	2	12	9
13, 44	1	69	30
14	2	108	5
14, 50	2	100	6
15, 51–16, 55	1	57	11
16, 56	2	93	57
19, 67	1	110	4
19, 67–69	2	48	5
	2	48	6
20, 73	2	118	26
20, 74	1	110	4
20, 75	1	14	4
	2	132	10
23, 84	2	48	5
Ep. fam. 1, 9, 16	2	67	9
4, 9, 2	2	7	16
4, 12, 2	1	114	3
7, 1	1	30	5
7, 28, 2	1	30	17
7, 30, 1	1	30	17
9, 22, 3	1	23	24
9, 22, 4	1	30	17
In Catil. 1, 1	2	28	17
2, 11, 25	1	18	3
3, 29	2	100	6
4, 21	2	5	11
In Verr. 2, 1, 15	1	2	14
3, 76, 176	2	10	9
Opt. gen. or. 6, 17	1	30	4
Orator 2, 8	2	88	2
18, 60	2	75	13
45, 153	1	27	1
Panegyric for Cato	2	98	8
Parad. Stoic. 1	2	7	5
4	2	34	3
5, 33–41	2	7	5
	2	8	9
5, 39	1	110	1
6, 42, 52	2	8	9

	Book/Section	Dial.	Note
Part. orat. 6, 21	1	11	19
22, 76	2	114	48
22, 77	2	84	13
23, 79	1	9	9
Philip.	1	9	20
2, 3, 5	2	61	6
9, 2, 4	1	41	13
9, 10	2	61	6
Piso	1	8	1
22	1	Pref.	44
29, 71	1	Pref.	52
Pro Archia 7, 15	2	100	10
10, 24	2	25	10
Pro Deiot. 11, 31	2	28	17
Pro Marcello 2, 7	2	Pref.	91
	2	1	14
3, 9	2	107	12
8, 26	1	94	11
Pro Ligario 12, 35	1	101	4
Pro Milone	1	48	9
	2	66	6
Pro Murena 61	2	34	3
Pro Roscio Comoedo	1	28	6
Pro Tullio frag. 21, 50	2	61	1
29	2	52	1
Rabir. perd. 29	2	5	11
"Rhetorics"	1	9	18
Top. 9, 40	2	62	1
15, 58	1	21	7
20, 76	2	100	5
Tusc. disp.	2	13	4
	2	64	1
1	2	51	8
	2	121	15
1, 2, 4	1	23	22
	1	23	23
1, 3, 6	1	44	6
	1	44	9
1, 4, 8	DP		14
1, 4, 9	1	37	4
1, 6, 12	1	52	1
1, 7, 13–14	DP		14

	Book/ Section	Dial.	Note
1, 10, 20	1	Pref.	61
	2	75	6
1, 10, 22	1	Pref.	2
	1	69	30
1, 11, 24	2	114	40
1, 15, 32–34	2	88	4
1, 16–17	2	83	35
1, 17, 40	1	92	3
1, 19, 44	1	2	22
1, 22, 52	2	73	12
1, 24	1	101	6
1, 26, 65	2	10	10
1, 27, 66–67	1	Pref.	2
1, 28, 68–70	1	86	8
1, 28, 69	1	40	6
1, 30, 72	1	2	22
1, 30, 73	2	117	24
	2	119	17
1, 30, 74	1	2	22
	2	98	8
	2	117	28
1, 31, 75	2	117	24
	2	119	12
1, 31, 76	1	1	12
1, 33, 80	2	75	6
1, 34, 84	2	44	3
1, 35, 85	1	108	7
	2	12	6
	2	120	14
	2	131	6
1, 36, 86	1	108	7
1, 36, 87	1	90	18
1, 36–41	2	83	35
1, 37, 89	2	125	30
1, 38	2	86	9
1, 38, 91–92	1	21	2
	2	117	14
1, 38, 92	1	21	2
1, 39, 93	2	120	4
1, 41, 97–99	2	48	5
1, 42, 100	2	117	11
	2	120	6

	Book/ Section	Dial.	Note
1, 42, 101	1	103	2
1, 42, 102	2	15	14
	2	48	9
	2	114	67
	2	132	23
1, 43, 104	2	125	34
	2	132	2
1, 45, 108	2	132	27
1, 45, 109	1	92	11
1, 46, 111	1	29	9
1, 48, 114	2	49	6
	2	119	12
1, 48, 114–115	2	49	7
1, 48, 115	2	119	7
1, 49, 118	1	57	14
	2	119	13
2	2	57	15
	2	64	2
	2	114	5
	2	114	33
2, 1, 3	1	40	15
2, 3, 9	DP		14
2, 4, 10	1	90	18
2, 4, 11	2	28	9
	2	117	17
2, 5, 13	2	114	63
2, 6, 16	2	117	17
2, 7, 17–18	2	114	14
2, 11, 27	1	23	34
2, 13, 32	1	Pref.	53
	2	84	13
2, 14	1	122	1
2, 14, 33	2	114	30
2, 16, 37–38	2	57	11
2, 17, 40	1	29	16
2, 18, 43	DP		12
	1	Pref.	41
	1	Pref.	53
	1	7	7
	2	84	13
2, 19, 44	2	114	3
2, 19, 44–45	2	8	7

	Book/Section	Dial.	Note
	2	114	14
2, 19, 45	2	84	2
2, 20–21	7	75	5
2, 21, 47	DP		7
2, 22	2	114	67
2, 22, 51	2	114	39
2, 22, 52	2	114	67
2, 22, 53	2	5	11
	2	114	67
2, 23, 54–55	2	114	44
	2	114	49
2, 23, 56	1	29	16
2, 24, 57	1	29	16
2, 24, 58	1	Pref.	61
	2	114	27
2, 25, 60	2	114	47
2, 25, 61	2	114	67
2, 26, 64	2	28	18
2, 47–48	2	75	8
3	2	93	60
3, 1, 2	1	11	1
3, 3, 5–6	2	117	11
3, 4, 7	2	93	59
3, 4, 7–8	DP		9
3, 5, 11	2	107	5
3, 6, 13	2	117	17
3, 7, 14	1	Pref.	53
3, 8, 16–18	1	Pref.	27
	1	122	1
3, 10, 22	1	2	25
	2	114	2
3, 10, 22–23	2	93	59
3, 11, 24	2	93	59
3, 11, 24–25	DP		11
	2	90	53
3, 11, 25	1	96	40
	2	93	6
3, 12, 26	2	79	4
	2	95	8
3, 12, 27	2	81	12
3, 14, 30	2	48	15
3, 15, 31	1	2	18

	Book/Section	Dial.	Note
3, 16, 34	2	38	4
	2	74	2
3, 20, 49	2	10	15
3, 23, 56	2	9	4
3, 24, 57	2	5	31
3, 25, 60	2	118	4
3, 25, 61	2	94	1
3, 26, 63	1	72	4
3, 27, 64	2	19	6
3, 27, 66	2	77	4
3, 33, 82	1	11	1
4	1	69	35
	2	15	12
4, 4, 8	2	90	53
4, 5, 10	2	75	8
4, 6, 13	2	90	53
	2	93	59
4, 7, 1	1	11	1
4, 7, 16	1	69	28
4, 8, 18	1	69	28
4, 9, 21	2	107	5
4, 10	1	Pref.	38
4, 11, 26	1	64	17
4, 12, 27	1	69	28
	1	70	1
4, 13, 28	1	Pref.	38
4, 13, 30–31	1	2	24
4, 15, 34	1	11	1
4, 17	1	29	17
4, 17, 40	2	38	11
4, 19, 43	2	58	17
4, 19, 44	2	56	5
4, 20, 46	1	2	25
4, 23, 52	2	107	3
4, 24, 53	1	Pref.	53
4, 24, 54	2	34	3
4, 27, 58	2	117	17
4, 29, 63	1	49	1
4, 31, 66	2	90	53
4, 32, 69	1	69	14
4, 33, 70	1	69	22
	1	69	29

	Book/Section	Dial.	Note
5, 43–46	2	114	1
Claudian. De bello Gild., 365	2	51	1
385	1	51	3
	1	92	9
De bello Goth. 610	1	96	20
De cons. Stil. 2, 414–420	1	64	7
In Ruf. 1, 22–23	1	107	8
Paneg. de tertio cons. Hon. Aug. 93–98	2	114	61
Phoenix	1	64	7
Cleanthes. Frag. 527	2	121	3
Clement. See Eusebius, Hist. eccl. 3, 23, 13			
Coluccio Salutati. De laboribus Herculis 3, 13, 2	2	125	20
4, 1, 1	2	125	20
Epistolario	INT		9
	2	55	9
	2	114	30
Columella, L. Junius Moderatus. Res rust. 1, Praef. 3–4	2	117	16
Cornelius Nepos. De exc. duc.	1	78	5
	2	39	14
1, 4–6	2	132	14
2, 3	1	103	2
2, 4–5	2	132	14
7	1	78	5
7, 1	1	7	7
	2	26	3
7, 10, 3–6	2	55	1
10	2	39	14
10, 2, 3	1	14	3
20	2	39	14
22, 1	1	98	4
23, 3–4	1	60	6
De lat. hist. [24], 1	2	5	11
2, 1, 3–4	2	5	11
Cronica volgare	2	96	25
Curtius Rufus, Quintus. Hist. Alex.	1	39	3
	2	1	12
	2	6	13
	2	88	11
2, 64	2	119	21
3, 5	2	90	35
3, 11, 24	1	14	3
3, 12, 16	2	1	12

	Book/ Section	Dial.	Note
4, 1, 19–26	2	5	17
4, 2, 3	1	15	26
4, 16, 8–15	2	83	18
5	1	104	7
5, 2, 13	2	1	12
5, 7, 1–9	2	69	2
5, 12, 20	2	18	14
5, 13	2	80	3
6, 5, 29	2	1	12
7, 2, 22–27	1	58	9
8, 1, 14–17	1	49	5
8, 1, 19–52	2	43	11
8, 2, 5	1	18	11
8, 4, 22–30	2	58	17
8, 5, 8–24	1	15	26
8, 8, 19–23	1	18	11
9, 1, 31–33	2	Pref.	9
9, 3, 23	1	31	4
10, 10, 14	1	108	9

	Book/ Section	Dial.	Note
7, 11–12	2	Pref.	61
7, 67–96	2	Pref.	91
7, 67–99	DP		5
7, 79–96	2	17	3
7, 117–125	2	109	1
8, 81 and 85	2	38	4
11, 97–111	1	56	4
11, 100	1	39	6
	1	56	4
12, 134	1	85	11
14	1	21	6
14, 48	2	83	44
14, 111	1	40	6
15, 67–68	2	77	7
15, 94–96	1	Pref.	44
17, 34–75	1	56	7
19, 52–57	1	35	6
24, 97–120	1	64	7
25, 18	2	83	44
25, 94–138	1	Pref.	52
26	2	115	8
27, 85–88	1	107	4
27, 85–105	1	35	6
27, 94–95	2	114	24
27, 110	1	35	6
32, 125–132	2	107	15
34, 121	2	Pref.	61
Purg. 1, 1–3	1	Pref.	9
1, 71–75	2	98	9
6, 1–9	2	16	1
	2	17	2
6, 124–151	2	71	6
6, 148–151	2	75	13
7, 28–29	2	129	2
9–27	2	105	1
9, 13–15	2	Pref.	48
9, 76–78	2	5	24
9, 79–108	2	88	4
10, 34–39	1	1	11
	1	24	3
10, 64–69	1	24	3
10, 98	1	24	3

	Book/Section	Dial.	Note
Mon. 1, 3, 2	1	39	6
2, 2, 3	1	39	6
2, 3, 4	1	16	5
2, 3, 9	1	72	14
2, 5, 15	2	74	3
2, 15, 17	2	118	24
3, 10, 1	2	114	24
3, 10, 7–12	1	96	3
3, 10, 10	1	85	9
3, 12, 4	1	96	5
Quest. de aqua 1, 4	1	37	3
Vita nuova 2, 8	1	72	14
De fructibus	DP		23
De imitatione Christi. See Thomas à Kempis			
De nugis curialium. See Walter Map			
Der Ackermann aus Boehmen. See Johannes von Tepl			
De vera sapientia	1	12	28
De vir. ill. (incerti auct.). *See* Pseudo-Aurelius Victor			
Dicta Catonis.	1	21	2
1, 14	1	11	15
See also Publius Syrus	1	23	8
Dietrich of Vrieburg	2	93	44
Dig. 1, 1, 10, 2	1	84	8
1, 4, 1	1	96	9
3, 39	1	65	8
4, 3, 1	2	62	1
24, 22, 1	1	65	8
28, 2, 14	1	110	8
37, 10, 1, 9	1	110	8
50, 16	1	65	7
Diodorus Siculus. *Bibl. hist.* 17, 70, 1	2	69	1
Diogenes Laertius. [*Lives*]	1	12	18
1, 34	1	112	6
2, 4	1	112	6
3, 4	1	29	11
7, 114	2	90	53
7, 116	2	90	53
Dittamondo. See Fazio degli Uberti			
Donatus. *See* Aelius Donatus			
Dondi, Giovanni. *See* Giovanni de' Dondi			
Durand, William. *See* William Durand			

	Book/ Section	Dial.	Note
1, 1, 10–11	1	72	6
1, 1, 6	2	9	26
1, 1, 7, 1–13	1	77	7
1, 1, 10	1	30	9
1, 1, 10–11	1	72	6
	2	81	14
1, 2–3	1	78	5
1, 3, 9	1	72	6
1, 4, 8	1	102	4
1, 7	1	105	7
1, 11	1	101	13
1, 12	2	80	3
1, 13	1	37	29
	1	60	1
1, 17, 24	1	72	8
1, 18, 29	2	90	55
1, 18, 33	1	98	4
1, 19	2	58	17
1, 22	1	63	10
1, 22, 12	1	22	13
1, 22, 13	1	83	1
1, 22, 15–20	1	63	17
1, 22, 21	1	10	19
	1	68	7
1, 28	1	63	10
1, 31	1	101	13
1, 31, 5	1	106	4
1, 31, 12–13	2	131	3
1, 32, 6–7	1	42	4
1, 35, 20	2	131	5
1, 36	1	78	4
1, 38, 3	2	132	12
1, 38, 7–18	2	132	12
1, 40, 30	1	37	24
1, 40, 40	1	37	24
1, 41	1	37	17
1, 45, 15	2	30	4
1, 46	2	5	23
	2	70	3
1, 46, 10	2	132	7
2, 13	1	37	22
	1	60	1

	Book/Section	Dial.	Note
	2	45	4
	2	45	8
	2	58	5
	2	90	13
	2	93	22
Ex. 8, 19	2	90	13
8, 21	2	90	9
	2	90	13
Job	1	Pref.	8
	1	Pref.	41
	1	44	21
Gower, John. *See* John Gower			
Gregory I, the Great. *Hom. in Ev.* 1, 7, 4	1	10	8
2, 24	1	Pref.	41
	2	84	13
37, 1	2	119	12
Moral.	2	105	1
5, 27, 46, 77	1	24	3
22, 1	1	122	1
Grosseteste. *See* Robert Grosseteste			
Guido of Arezzo. *Regulae rythmicae*	2	97	11
Micrologus 3	2	96	19
Guigo of Chastel. *Meditationes*	2	90	16
Guillaume de Blois. *Alda* 31–32, 47–48	1	85	12
Guillaume de Lorris and Jean de Meun.			
Roman de la Rose	DP		7
	1	Pref.	55
	1	16	6
	1	65	1
	2	83	2
169–290	2	105	1
339–406	1	2	21
363–381	2	15	8
727–776	1	24	2
907–984	2	105	1
3980–3990	1	Pref.	44
4293–4334	1	69	2
4422–4433	2	13	36
4803–4836	1	50	11
	1	110	10
4837–4864	1	Pref.	29
4839–4895	1	Pref.	29

	Book/ Section	Dial.	Note
5320–5352	2	13	6
	2	17	2
5842–5868	2	75	20
5918–5920	2	Pref.	91
5976–5977	1	112	20
6631–6632	DP		18
6774–6776	1	14	3
8687	1	65	15
9517–9586	2	105	1
9578	2	13	5
13823–13874	1	69	8
15976	1	64	7
16005–16148	1	20	8
16065–16148	1	111	1
16323–16700	1	65	1
16617–16700	1	65	1
	2	19	5
16747–16767	1	Pref.	64
16801–16832	1	92	4
16801–17100	2	114	36
16939–16945	1	23	31
16955–16957	1	2	3
17059–17100	2	114	37
17101–17526	2	7	16
	2	17	17
17570	2	73	12
17679–17702	2	114	36
17779–17874	2	73	12
18061–18089	1	69	8
18589–18606	2	13	5
18607–18896	1	16	1
18999–19054	1	40	6
20002–20026	1	1	21
20369–20404	1	16	6
20465–20578	1	16	6
21021–21059	1	24	3
21573	2	58	2
—Oxford ms.	1	Pref.	44
Guillaume de Machaut. *Le jugement du Roy de Behaigne*	2	96	25
Remede de Fortune	INT		Item 8
	2	58	15
Guy de Chauliac. *Chirurgia*	2	114	26

	Book/ Section	Dial.	Note
5, 4	1	96	14
6, 1	1	75	2
12, 1–6	2	75	20
13, 1	1	96	14
18, 4	2	24	9
19, 8–9	1	68	6
26, 7–8	1	96	14
Pesc. Niger	2	56	3
Sept. Severus 18, 8	2	21	15
18, 9–10	2	84	14
18, 9–11	2	44	2
19, 5	1	118	6
20, 2	2	24	9
20, 5–21, 8	1	16	2
21, 5	2	23	6
Severus Alex. 4, 1	1	85	6
9, 1–2	1	78	7
17, 1–2	2	60	6
19, 5	1	118	10
24, 3–5	1	118	10
28, 3–5	2	60	7
29, 5	2	75	20
33, 3	1	96	19
53–54	1	97	7
Tyr. trig. 30, 13–15	2	94	6
30, 26	2	18	14
Valerian 7	1	96	19
Verus 4–5	1	19	14
5, 1–6	1	96	38
6, 3–5	1	31	8
—Petrarch's ms.	1	16	2
	1	25	4
	1	71	5
	1	76	1
Homer. *Iliad*	1	69	8
	2	120	14
2, 23–25	1	21	10
2, 61–62	1	21	10
2, 209–269	2	35	2
3, 6	2	Pref.	12
3, 40	2	21	15
5, 638	2	9	26

	Book/ Section	Dial.	Note
322	1	30	17
372–373	1	46	19
408–410	2	52	5
453–467	2	97	11
476	2	115	4
	1	95	8
Carm. 1, 1, 3	1	Pref.	8
1, 3, 5–8	2	53	2
1, 4, 13–14	2	119	19
1, 12, 37	1	14	4
1, 22, 18	1	94	6
1, 35, 26–27	1	19	16
1, 37, 1	1	24	13
2, 2, 17	1	84	6
2, 4, 1	1	76	1
2, 9–12	1	17	3
	1	96	13
2, 9–16	2	116	2
2, 10, 5–8	1	2	25
2, 10, 9–12	1	17	3
2, 12	2	114	43
2, 14, 22–24	1	57	18
2, 16, 10	1	69	28
	2	93	60
2, 26–27	1	69	2
3, 1, 17–18	1	95	10
3, 1, 33–34	1	96	31
3, 2, 14	2	114	44
3, 2, 29–30	2	39	6
3, 3, 7–8	2	91	12
3, 5	1	14	4
3, 5, 1	2	90	41
3, 6, 45–48	1	115	3
3, 14, 25	1	2	18
3, 16, 9–11	2	13	24
3, 16, 17–18	2	13	31
3, 16, 42	2	13	32
3, 16, 42–43	2	12	13
3, 24	1	100	4
3, 24, 1–8	2	67	26
3, 24, 5–8	2	7	16
	2	67	24

	Book/ Section	Dial.	Note
2, 1, 50–55	1	78	5
2, 1, 69–71	1	80	5
2, 1, 76–82	1	28	5
2, 1, 194	2	89	3
2, 1, 237–241	1	39	3
2, 2, 26–40	1	100	3
2, 2, 61–63	1	19	1
2, 2, 68–69	1	15	33
2, 2, 76	1	11	22
Epod. 4, 6	1	43	15
7, 11–12	2	31	5
11, 7–8	1	16	2
Sat. 1, 1, 68–69	1	43	10
1, 1, 106–107	2	99	2
1, 2, 90–91	2	96	13
1, 2, 109–110	1	69	33
1, 3, 107–110	2	Pref.	20
1, 4, 43–44	1	46	19
1, 8, 26–28	1	26	6
1, 9, 59–60	2	12	14
2, 1, 52–53	2	Pref.	20
2, 3	2	34	3
2, 3, 239–242	1	28	3
2, 5	1	110	1
2, 5, 23–57	1	110	1
2, 7, 103–104	2	21	1
2, 8, 62–63	1	Pref.	8
Hrabanus Maurus. *De univ.* 7	1	6	5
7, 7	1	Pref.	11
8	1	64	8
	1	64	10
8, 1	1	31	1
8, 2	2	Pref.	36
	2	Pref.	38
	2	Pref.	41
8, 6	1	32	3
8, 7	2	90	9
19, 6	1	57	18
22, 6	1	64	24
Exp. in prov. Sal.	2	Pref.	38
	2	Pref.	41
Hugh of St. Victor. *De anima* 4, 13–16	2	82	11

	Book/Section	Dial.	Note
	2	119	11
1, 21	1	Pref.	5
	2	113	2
1, 27	2	122	1
2	2	105	1
2, 11	2	13	37
2, 12	2	13	25
2, 14	1	43	10
2, 21	2	110	3
2, 29, 8	1	107	9
2, 29, 10	1	107	8
2, 31	1	10	11
	2	77	7
Isidore of Seville. *De nat. rer.*	2	67	15
Diff. 2, 40, 159	DP		9
2, 50, 159	DP		11
Etym. 1, 6, 1–2	1	122	4
1, 29, 3	1	85	10
	2	99	3
1, 37, 4	1	1	5
1, 37, 23	1	12	14
2	2	6	9
2, 3, 1	1	9	5
2, 4, 4	1	10	20
2, 5, 1	2	114	44
2, 9, 1–8	1	9	11
2, 9, 28	1	9	11
2, 10, 2–3	1	40	15
2, 10, 6	1	40	15
2, 12, 6	2	90	7
2, 21, 5	1	1	11
	1	11	19
	1	18	3
2, 23, 1–2	1	9	12
2, 24, 2	1	11	1
2, 24, 6	1	Pref.	20
	1	Pref.	27
	1	Pref.	41
	1	Pref.	53
2, 24, 9	1	46	16
	2	117	28
2, 25, 7	1	2	3

	Book/Section	Dial.	Note
2, 26, 7	1	2	4
2, 26, 11–15	1	2	3
2, 29, 1–16	1	9	12
2, 31	1	11	19
2, 78	2	83	7
3, 4	1	Pref.	64
3, 4, 4	2	97	9
3, 15, 1	1	23	3
3, 16, 2–3	1	23	22
3, 19, 8	1	23	3
3, 21, 8	1	24	3
3, 24–71	2	114	37
3, 62–63	2	Pref.	4
3, 71, 8–9	1	15	3
3, 71, 18	1	15	3
4, 8, 11	2	114	21
5	2	6	10
5, 2, 2	2	6	9
5, 3–4	1	40	15
5, 6, 7, 1–3	1	44	15
7, 5	2	93	32
8, 6, 13	1	25	1
8, 9, 31	1	112	10
8, 11, 26	2	90	9
8, 11, 45–49	2	28	13
8, 11, 90	2	Pref.	91
	2	5	28
9, 2, 40	1	20	4
9, 3, 4	1	85	10
10, 9	1	38	12
	2	13	62
10, 46	2	114	44
10, 168	2	99	2
10, 172	2	99	2
11, 1, 4	2	99	3
11, 1, 5	1	40	6
11, 1, 12	2	93	9
11, 2	1	1	15
11, 2, 1	2	83	7
11, 2, 1–5	2	83	7
11, 3, 1–4	2	Pref.	53
11, 3, 7	2	Pref.	13

	Book/Section	Dial.	Note
11, 3, 33	1	Pref.	11
11, 7, 24	1	64	8
12, 1, 8	1	59	1
12, 1, 14	2	67	26
12, 2	1	5	9
12, 2, 5	1	31	1
12, 2, 17	2	Pref.	14
12, 2, 26	2	Pref.	10
12, 2, 29	2	Pref.	11
12, 3, 7	2	Pref.	36
12, 3, 9	2	Pref.	15
	2	Pref.	38
	2	Pref.	41
12, 3, 32	2	90	7
12, 3, 33	1	Pref.	11
12, 4, 10–11	2	Pref.	29
12, 5, 1	2	Pref.	34
12, 5, 10	2	Pref.	34
12, 5, 15	2	90	14
12, 6, 34	2	Pref.	55
12, 6, 50	1	20	5
12, 7, 22	1	64	7
12, 7, 24	1	64	7
12, 7, 39	1	112	20
12, 7, 46	1	64	10
12, 7, 48	1	62	5
12, 7, 61	2	Pref.	31
12, 8	2	90	11
13	2	90	38
13, 3, 1	1	21	7
13, 18, 4–5	2	90	7
14, 3, 7	2	Pref.	14
14, 6, 12	2	78	4
14, 6, 32	2	90	7
14, 8, 18	2	91	8
15, 1, 27	1	20	5
16, 13, 2	2	67	26
17, 1	1	57	6
17, 6, 3	1	58	6
17, 7, 34	1	57	18
18, 59–68	1	26	1
19, 19, 4	1	21	7

	Book/Section	Dial.	Note
3, 7	1	29	6
4, 17	1	Pref.	61
	1	57	14
Policrat. 1, 1	2	110	4
1, 6	1	23	31
	1	65	15
2, 1	2	Pref.	91
2, 16	2	84	16
2, 19	2	28	13
	2	114	37
2, 27	DP		12
	1	48	3
	2	98	9
	2	118	24
3, 2	2	73	12
3, 5	1	11	15
3, 7	DP		20
3, 8	DP		20
	1	16	7
	1	23	11
	1	48	3
	2	Pref.	91
3, 10	1	23	8
3, 15	2	81	6
4, 1	1	85	11
	2	39	18
4, 2	1	85	9
	1	96	3
4, 4	1	33	3
5	1	81	3
5, 4	1	Pref.	44
	1	16	7
5, 7	1	18	2
	1	18	5
	2	9	18
	2	90	35
	2	93	57
5, 10	2	19	9
6, 14	1	96	37
6, 26	2	19	8
7, 2	1	96	37
7, 6	1	78	5

	Book/Section	Dial.	Note
	1	81	3
7, 8	2	109	5
7, 15	DP		19
7, 17	1	85	11
7, 24	2	35	2
	2	81	21
7, 25	2	118	23
	2	118	28
8	1	96	51
	1	107	13
8, 8 and 10	1	26	7
8, 11	1	54	8
	1	64	21
	1	65	1
	1	65	15
	1	69	12
8, 12	1	14	2
	1	25	2
	1	28	9
8, 14	1	46	27
	1	81	3
	1	95	11
	2	54	12
	2	57	17
8, 17	1	85	8
	1	85	11
8, 19	1	23	28
8, 23	1	81	3
	1	95	10
	1	107	5
8, 24	1	32	2
John the Scot. *See* Scotus Erigena			
Joinville, Jehan. *See* Jehan Joinville			
Josephus Flavius. *Ant. Jud.* 6, 165–175	2	88	15
8, 6, 5–6	2	88	15
8, 165–175	2	88	15
9	1	69	30
11, 2	1	69	40
11, 6, 2	1	69	40
17, 168–170	2	121	12
18, 7, 195–204	1	112	19
19, 346–350	1	112	19

	Book/Section	Dial.	Note
39, 5, 6	2	12	6
42, 4, 14	2	12	6
Justinian Code 1, 14, 4	1	85	9
Juvenal. *Sat.* 1, 37–44	1	110	1
1, 90	1	27	1
1, 142–143	1	64	3
1, 161	1	29	6
3, 38–40	1	91	1
3, 86–91	1	19	15
3, 100–108	1	19	15
3, 29	2	Pref.	91
4, 23	1	19	12
5, 137–145	1	110	1
5, 157–158	1	19	10
6	1	65	1
6, 38–40	1	110	1
6, 115–132	1	72	10
6, 165	1	65	15
6, 167–168	1	65	4
6, 169	1	78	4
6, 268–269	1	65	11
6, 290–293	1	22	7
	1	106	6
6, 306	1	11	22
6, 443	2	117	14
6, 448–450	1	67	2
6, 456	1	67	3
7, 27–35	1	44	20
7, 50–52	1	44	2
7, 79–80	1	78	4
7, 86–87	2	9	22
7, 135–136	1	46	27
7, 139–140	1	43	13
	1	46	28
7, 194–196	2	5	27
7, 197–198	1	16	7
7, 202	1	65	15
7, 240–241	1	81	1
8	1	16	1
8, 245–253	2	5	11
8, 272–273	1	16	1
9, 9	2	99	2

	Book/Section	Dial.	Note
14, 319	2	10	15
15, 140–142	2	50	1
15, 142–147	1	40	6
15, 159–174	2	31	5
16, 1–2	1	48	9
16, 48	1	48	10

Kilwardby, Robert. *See* Robert Kilwardby

Lactantius, L. Caecilius Firmianus.

	Book/Section	Dial.	Note
De ave Phoenice [Phoenix]	1	64	7
De ira 11	1	13	14
De mort. pers. 18	1	114	21
	2	131	2
De opif. Dei 8	1	40	6
	2	93	46
10	1	40	6
	2	93	46
Div. inst. 1, 6	1	13	5
1, 7	2	39	5
1, 15	1	44	21
1, 15–18	2	39	4
2, 1	1	40	6
	2	93	46
	2	93	48
2, 2	1	40	9
2, 9	1	11	19
2, 11	2	99	3
2, 16	1	13	14
2, 18	1	40	6
	2	93	46
3, 3	1	11	1
3, 9	1	40	9
	2	93	46
3, 12	1	73	2
3, 13	2	117	17
3, 18	1	15	23
	2	118	33
3, 19	1	15	21
	2	49	6
	2	117	33
	2	119	7

	Book/Section	Dial.	Note
1, 4, 7	2	63	5
1, 7, 8–15	2	63	5
1, 15	1	41	13
1, 31, 8	1	34	2
	2	55	2
1, 33, 6	2	77	12
1, 34	2	5	13
1, 39, 1–3	2	55	6
1, 40–41	2	80	3
1, 40, 7	1	34	2
1, 41	2	5	14
1, 47–48	1	77	7
1, 56–59	1	72	6
1, 58	2	115	4
1, 59, 10	1	77	7
1, 59, 11–12	1	34	2
1, 60, 1–3	1	78	5
2, 1, 3	1	34	2
2, 7, 5–12	1	35	2
2, 10	2	77	12
2, 32, 5–12	2	75	11
2, 33	1	89	4
2, 41, 10	2	43	3
3	2	5	12
3, 44–59	1	72	8
3, 70, 7	2	13	59
4, 17	1	41	13
5, 6, 5	2	84	13
5, 19, 2	1	105	7
5, 32, 8–9	2	67	8
5, 54, 3	2	67	8
5, 55	1	112	23
6, 6, 3–7	2	71	3
6, 24, 9	1	Pref.	39
7, 2	1	28	2
7, 6, 1–5	1	96	41
8, 10, 10	2	72	3
8, 15, 7–8	2	21	25
8, 24	2	125	26
9, 1–15	1	101	13
9, 3, 4–13	1	101	13
9, 17	2	73	16

	Book/ Section	Dial.	Note
12, 7, 13	1	83	2
14, Perioch.	2	21	25
17, Perioch.	2	72	3
18, Frag.	1	21	6
Perioch.	1	14	4
21, 1, 2	1	103	3
21, 4, 5–7	2	63	6
	2	90	35
22, 2, 1–2	1	60	6
22, 2, 10–11	1	60	6
22, 4–7	1	83	1
22, 7, 13	1	23	13
22, 8, 2	2	93	59
22, 23, 2	2	72	1
22, 46, 8–9	1	63	17
22, 51	2	103	5
22, 57	2	21	25
22, 61, 13–15	2	69	12
23, 45, 2–4	1	68	7
24, 4	2	78	2
24, 34, 8–15	1	99	13
26, 19, 3–9	2	1	12
26, 36, 1	2	109	1
27, 12–14	2	73	4
28, 35, 5–9	1	51	1
28, 43, 6	1	29	15
29, 6–9	1	35	5
29, 14, 8–14	2	38	6
30, 12	2	128	4
30, 14, 11	2	110	7
30, 16–25	1	105	7
30, 17	1	72	7
30, 19, 11	2	125	18
30, 37, 3	1	60	3
30, 45, 6	1	108	9
30, 20, 19–20	1	102	2
30, 33	1	60	1
30, 354–11	2	73	20
32, 38	2	39	14
34, 4, 1–3	2	81	26
34, 4, 2	2	13	1
	2	81	26

	Book/Section	Dial.	Note
1, 11, 7	1	14	2
1, 11, 42	1	14	3
1, 18–19	1	15	26
1, 20, 13–15	1	Pref.	11
1, 23, 10	1	68	7
2, 1, 12	2	7	21
2, 2	1	69	32
2, 2, 15–17	1	69	32
2, 4, 11	1	52	7
2, 4, 26	2	90	22
2, 4, 29–30	1	64	4
2, 5, 4	2	23	2
2, 7, 3	1	16	4
2, 7, 4–5	1	95	11
2, 7, 6	2	85	8
2, 7, 11	2	54	12
	2	57	17
3, 11–13	1	28	9
3, 13, 1	1	62	5
3, 14, 11	1	28	3
3, 14, 13	1	28	9
3, 14, 14	1	28	3
3, 15, 1	1	63	9
3, 15, 3	1	63	15
3, 15, 6	1	63	12
3, 15, 10	1	63	13
5, 3, 12	1	21	2
5, 16, 7	2	120	2
5, 17, 5–6	1	81	3
6, 1 and 2	2	121	10
6, 1, 35	2	114	11
6, 1, 62	2	28	9
6, 2, 7–14	1	59	6
6, 4, 16	1	57	15
6, 6, 7	2	54	9
6, 8, 8–13	2	83	44
6, 16	2	119	2
7	1	26	7
7, 6, 13	1	57	15
9, 3–4	1	24	4

Maecenas, Gaius. *See* Gaius Maecenas
Malory, Thomas. *See* Thomas Malory

	Book/ Section	Dial.	Note
Map, Walter. *See* Walter Map			
Marbod of Rennes. *Liber decem capitulorum*	1	1	15
Marcus Aurelius. *Meditationes* 8, 33	2	13	58
Marcus Pacuvius. Frag. 45	2	33	5
Medea	2	95	8
Martial. *Epig.* 1, 61, 7	1	46	25
2, 69, 3	1	18	15
2, 89, 5	1	18	15
3, 2, 1	1	64	10
5, 13, 3	1	29	6
5, 76	2	116	7
9, 97, 3–4	1	29	6
13, 70	1	62	5
14, 73	1	64	8
14, 76	1	64	10
Martianus Capella. *De nupt.*	1	11	19
1, 6	1	112	9
2, 117	1	23	14
4, 347	1	2	3
4, 361–362	1	2	3
5	1	22	3
5, 508	1	46	22
5, 539	1	22	3
7, 736	1	24	3
8, 807	1	12	28
9, 923	1	23	14
Martin de Leon	2	99	3
Martin of Braga. *De ira* Praef.	2	33	4
De quat. virt. = *Formula vitae honestae*	1	Pref.	2
	1	Pref.	35
	2	113	6
See also Seneca, *De rem. fort.*			
Maternus Firmicus. *See* Firmicus Maternus			
Matthew of Vendôme. *Ars* 1, 15–16	2	93	55
1, 52, 44–50	1	37	16
1, 56, 1–2	1	20	8
1, 57, 18	2	Pref.	31
2, 5	1	20	8
Mirabilia mundi	1	118	1
Mirabilia urbis Romae	1	118	1
	2	132	8
Monumentum Ancyranum	1	79	1

	Book/Section	Dial.	Note
2, 351–359	2	53	13
2, 670	1	2	20
3, 26	1	69	15
3, 62–64	2	14	1
	2	15	1
3, 353–366	1	26	1
3, 367–380	1	27	12
3, 501–504	1	27	12
3, 687–746	1	69	8
Cons. 65–72	1	32	5
441–442	1	32	5
Ex ponto 1, 3, 61	1	11	22
2, 2, 31–32	2	35	2
2, 3, 55–56	1	Pref.	44
2, 7, 25	2	114	63
3, 3, 3	2	122	3
4, 3, 49	1	Pref.	8
4, 13, 15	2	35	2
Fasti 1, 493–494	2	67	20
3, 362	DP		11
4, 305–344	2	23	2
5, 304	2	99	2
6, 173–176	1	18	7
6, 455–460	2	21	25
6, 473	2	90	26
6, 771	2	15	8
Heroides 1	1	72	6
2, 85	1	17	7
4, 13–14	1	44	7
6, 21	1	69	3
19	1	69	8
Metam.	1	12	27
1	2	90	41
1, 1–75	1	18	15
1, 21–68	2	67	15
1, 84–86	2	93	48
1, 84–88	1	40	6
1, 85	2	93	20
1, 138–140	1	54	6
1, 141	2	13	21
1, 141–142	1	98	3
1, 145	1	84	1

	Book/Section	Dial.	Note
	2	Pref.	25
1, 146	1	84	1
1, 149–150	2	59	5
1, 170	2	90	41
1, 433	1	11	19
1, 568–779	1	62	1
1, 625	1	62	1
1, 722–724	1	62	1
2, 46	2	90	41
2, 328	1	10	1
2, 531–533	1	62	1
2, 534–632	1	65	15
2, 847–875	1	69	8
3, 135–137	1	17	7
3, 174–252	2	Pref.	10
3, 434	2	122	3
3, 466	1	43	20
4, 55–166	1	69	8
4, 171–189	1	69	8
5, 327	1	69	8
5, 549–550	1	112	20
5, 552–562	1	62	2
6	2	90	26
6, 1–145	1	7	4
6, 90	1	18	7
6, 103–122	1	69	8
6, 355–381	2	90	26
6, 424–674	2	Pref.	48
7, 19–21	DP		2
7, 62–65	2	90	7
7, 404–424	1	9	22
7, 694–865	1	69	8
7, 826	1	69	5
8	2	80	3
8, 8	2	80	3
8, 802	1	2	19
9, 163–165	2	84	13
9, 454–665	1	69	8
10, 40–44	1	24	5
10, 75	2	93	4
10, 488	2	126	2
11, 198	2	90	41

	Book/ Section	Dial.	Note
12, 82	2	4	5
12, 96	2	4	5
12, 188	2	120	14
12, 365	2	4	5
13, 384–398	2	107	15
13, 429–438	2	13	47
13, 730	2	90	7
14, 242–307	2	119	12
14, 283	2	119	12
14, 362	2	122	3
14, 466–482	1	98	4
14, 699–769	1	69	8
15, 158–175	1	15	23
15, 176–260	2	83	19
15, 178–236	2	17	5
15, 199–205	1	15	27
15, 232–233	2	83	11
15, 386	2	Pref.	32
15, 391–407	1	64	7
15, 497–546	1	72	4
15, 712	2	91	5
15, 871–879	1	117	2
Rem. am.	1	69	35
13–14	1	69	4
18	1	69	8
19	1	69	8
213–224	2	53	13
369–370	1	17	3
462	1	69	39
Tristia	1	117	2
1, 1, 83–84	1	98	4
2, 105–106	2	Pref.	10
3, 4, 25	1	92	7
4, 1, 57	2	114	63
4, 10, 115–130	1	117	2
O virgo princeps virginum	DP		23
Pacuvius. *See* Marcus Pacuvius			
Palladius, Rutilius Taurus Aemilianus. *Hist. Lausiaca*	1	57	15
28	2	21	26
83	2	7	17

	Book/Section	Dial.	Note
2, 99, 212–101, 220	2	Pref.	6
3, 5, 53	2	90	3
3, 8, 87	2	90	7
3, 11, 103	1	68	7
3, 12, 109	2	90	3
3, 20, 138	1	54	9
4, 12, 70	2	91	3
4, 12, 79	2	90	5
4, 30–31	2	88	5
5, 8, 45	2	90	33
6, 24, 89–91	2	78	7
6, 30, 121	2	55	11
6, 32–33	2	93	19
7, Praef. 1–5	2	111	6
7, 1	1	58	11
7, 1, 4	2	49	6
7, 1, 4–5	2	31	5
7, 1, 5	1	97	5
7, 2	2	93	52
7, 2, 15	2	5	11
7, 2, 25	1	22	6
7, 2, 26	2	Pref.	13
	2	Pref.	14
7, 14, 37	1	21	6
7, 14, 61	1	110	14
7, 16, 67	2	49	4
7, 16, 69	2	94	5
7, 19, 79	2	75	20
7, 20, 83	1	5	3
7, 24, 89	1	8	10
7, 24–25	1	101	6
7, 27, 100	1	7	6
	1	57	7
7, 27, 125	1	41	4
	2	107	15
7, 28, 104–106	2	77	13
7, 28, 106	2	69	12
	2	77	13
7, 29, 106	1	68	7
7, 30, 110	1	69	30
7, 31, 1	1	69	30
7, 32, 119	1	23	13

	Book/ Section	Dial.	Note
9, 79, 168	1	63	6
9, 79, 168–169	2	56	6
9, 79, 169	1	63	19
9, 80, 170	1	63	7
	1	63	12
9, 81, 171	1	63	13
9, 81, 172	1	63	15
	1	63	18
9, 82, 173	1	63	19
10, 2, 3–5	1	64	7
10, 2, 5	1	64	20
10, 16, 34–35	2	90	20
10, 23, 46	1	62	6
10, 30, 58	2	Pref.	13
10, 59, 118	1	64	11
10, 59, 119	1	64	13
10, 59, 120	1	64	15
10, 60, 121–123	1	64	6
10, 68	1	19	12
10, 68, 133	2	56	6
10, 72, 141	1	64	1
	1	64	2
10, 82, 169	2	Pref.	29
11, 18, 58	1	62	10
11, 22, 68	1	62	10
11, 35, 102	2	Pref.	34
11, 36, 109–110	2	Pref.	41
11, 36, 111	2	Pref.	15
13, 3	1	22	7
13, 5	1	22	8
	1	22	11
14, 5, 44	1	57	8
	1	57	11
14, 7, 58	1	18	11
14, 14, 91	1	18	2
14, 28, 147	2	24	9
15, 24, 88–89	1	38	22
25, 7, 20	1	40	11
25, 34–37	1	40	12
25, 36, 77	1	40	13
25, 88	2	84	11
25, 140	2	84	11

	Book/Section	Dial.	Note
26, 2, 5–7	1	30	7
26, 64–66	2	84	11
26, 100–104	2	84	11
27, 2, 9	2	48	21
28, 32, 122	2	96	13
29, 8, 24	2	116	7
32, 1, 3	2	Pref.	55
32, 1, 3–5	2	Pref.	56
32, 12–14	1	63	9
32, 13, 47	1	37	1
32, 43	1	63	9
32, 57	1	63	9
32, 135	1	63	9
33, 1	1	30	8
33, 7	1	28	7
33, 19	1	84	7
33, 49–53	1	42	12
33, 53	1	42	14
33, 148–149	1	37	25
34, 19, 49	1	41	19
34, 19, 54	1	41	19
34, 19, 55	1	41	19
35, 2, 6	1	41	7
35, 5, 15–16	1	41	3
35, 7, 19	1	78	6
35, 7, 20	1	40	11
	1	40	12
35, 8, 24	1	42	17
35, 36, 67–68	1	41	3
35, 36, 77	1	40	13
35, 36, 79–97	1	41	19
35, 36, 101–106	1	41	19
35, 43, 151	1	41	7
35, 44, 153	1	41	7
35, 45, 157	1	41	9
35, 46, 160	1	42	18
35, 151	1	41	7
36, 1, 1–3	1	30	8
36, 1, 3	1	21	17
36, 2, 5–7	1	30	7
36, 4, 15–19	1	41	19
36, 4, 18–19	2	88	4

	Book/Section	Dial.	Note
36, 4, 27–29	1	41	5
36, 4, 30–31	2	88	5
36, 24, 111–113	1	96	35
36, 24, 113–115	1	30	7
36, 24, 116–120	1	30	13
36, 70	2	5	14
37, 2, 3–5	1	37	30
37, 3, 6	1	37	26
37, 4, 8–10	1	39	2
	1	39	3
	1	41	5
37, 4, 59	2	67	26
37, 6, 12–16	1	37	21
37, 6, 14	1	19	5
37, 7, 18–20	1	38	21
37, 8, 21–22	1	38	20
37, 9, 23	1	38	15
37, 10, 29	1	38	16
	1	38	19
37, 12, 47	1	38	26
37, 12–16	1	37	18
37, 15, 55	1	37	11
37, 15, 59	2	Pref.	51
37, 15, 61	2	Pref.	52
37, 16, 62	1	37	12
37, 21, 81–82	1	37	8
37, 32, 108	1	41	11
37, 40, 124	1	37	33
	1	38	5
37, 41, 125	1	37	13
37, 54, 139	1	37	27
37, 75, 197	1	38	4
37, 76, 198	1	37	35
—Petrarch's ms.	1	39	2
Pliny the Younger. *Ep.* 1, 7, 3	2	75	5
2, 3, 8	2	88	13
4, 7	1	9	8
4, 11	2	21	25
4, 11, 3	1	Pref.	8
5, 20, 5	1	9	2
9, 23, 4	1	29	6

Pliny the Younger. *See also* Pseudo-Aurelius Victor

	Book/ Section	Dial.	Note
	Book/		
	Section	*Dial.*	*Note*
Pseudo-Areopagite. *De coel. hier.*	1	15	2
Pseudo-Aristotle. *De bona fortuna*	2	Pref.	91
Pseudo-Aurelius Victor. *De vir. ill.* 11	2	77	12
15	1	35	2
33	2	93	57
44, 1	1	106	4
	2	38	6
47	2	101	6
77	2	132	7
Pseudo-Callisthenes	1	18	11
	1	108	9
	2	90	35
89	1	Pref.	44
182	2	25	10
197	1	Pref.	44
Pseudo-Rufinus. *De schem. lex.* 15	2	97	15
Pseudo-Seneca. *See* Seneca-Ps.			
Publilius Syrus. *Sent.*	2	54	12
41	1	50	4
55	2	58	14
111	2	84	13
116	2	57	17
166	2	77	1
331	2	54	12
336	2	117	8
433	2	77	10
See also Dicta Catonis			
Quintilian. *Inst. orat.* 1, Praef., 9	1	9	8
1, 3, 5	2	114	63
1, 9, 5	1	29	12
1, 10, 14	1	23	24
2, 4, 24	2	119	12
2, 19	1	20	8
2, 20, 7	1	9	12
3, 8, 15–55	1	10	20
6, 21	2	7	21
9, 3, 81	1	11	19
10, 1, 32	2	88	13
10, 1, 130	1	7	1
10, 2, 12	1	7	1
11, 2, 11	1	8	10

	Book/Section	Dial.	Note
	2	13	43
10–12	1	100	4
	1	106	7
10–13	1	105	8
13, 1–2	1	96	31
15, 4	2	75	18
39, 5	2	43	3
52, 30–31	2	43	12
54, 6	1	29	14
Jug.	1	78	4
2, 3	1	16	4
	2	117	8
2, 3–4	2	83	36
9, 3–10, 8	1	79	3
41, 2–4	1	106	1
68, 1	2	93	59
85, 40	1	20	1
	2	84	13
	2	118	10
Sallust-Cicero Invectives	2	25	10

Salutati, Coluccio. *See* Coluccio Salutati

Scotus Erigena. *De div. nat.*	1	15	3
1, 7, 1	2	93	27
1, 56–57	1	37	3
3, 6	1	11	19
	2	93	14
3, 17	2	93	12
	2	93	27
4	2	93	22
5, 3	1	37	9
5, 36	1	11	19
	2	93	14
De praedest. 2	2	93	27
Super Hier. Coel. S. Dionysii	1	37	9

Seneca, Lucius Annaeus, the Philosopher.

Agamemnon	1	17	3
	1	52	11

Apocolocyntosis. See below Ludus de morte Claudii

De benef.	1	93	2
1, 3, 7	2	28	13
1, 10, 1	1	115	4

	Book/ Section	Dial.	Note
1, 10, 3	2	75	6
2, 11, 2	1	93	7
2, 27, 1–2	1	93	4
3, 18, 2	2	9	3
3, 20	2	7	11
3, 28, 2	1	8	1
4, 13, 1	2	109	1
4, 27, 3	2	96	13
4, 38, 2	1	11	22
5, 25, 2	1	96	57
6, 38, 4	1	110	1
7, 26, 4	2	109	1
De clem. 1, 1, 1	1	Pref.	52
1, 12, 4	1	95	14
1, 19, 2–3	1	96	45
1, 26, 3–4	2	31	5
1, 49, 4	1	25	1
2, 2, 2	1	95	14
De matrim. 45–88	1	65	1
56	1	65	15
61	2	18	7
62	2	19	10
63	2	21	14
65	2	19	14
74	2	128	4
De quatuor virtutibus. See Martin of Braga			
De rem. fort. See Seneca (Ps.)			
Dial. 1 De prov. 2, 9–12	2	118	15
4, 16	2	7	5
5, 1	2	117	31
5, 4	2	7	5
5, 4–6	2	7	16
5, 4–10	2	121	3
5, 9	2	7	16
2 De const. 4–5	1	Pref.	7
5, 6	2	55	3
6, 8	1	Pref.	61
7, 2	2	75	6
	2	97	4
15, 2	1	1	18
18, 5	2	19	10
19	2	109	1

	Book/ Section	Dial.	Note
3 De ira 1 1, 1–2	2	33	4
1, 20, 4	1	95	14
3 De ira 2 10, 5	2	89	3
11, 4	2	36	9
19	2	109	1
5 De ira 3 8, 6	2	107	9
17, 1	1	49	4
17, 2	1	49	5
22, 1	1	29	17
27, 1	1	101	3
37, 4	1	Pref.	56
39, 2	1	101	11
39, 42–43	1	101	14
6 Ad Marciam 2, 3–4	1	32	5
3, 1–2	2	48	11
10, 5	2	117	8
11	1	Pref.	12
16, 3	2	48	11
19, 2	1	110	1
21, 2	1	92	4
21, 6	2	117	6
22, 1	1	85	13
22, 3	2	49	6
23, 3–5	1	37	16
23, 4	1	107	9
26, 6	1	92	4
7 De vita beata	1	Pref.	35
1–5	1	10	1
15, 5	2	7	3
	2	7	16
	2	117	31
15, 6	2	118	4
19	1	10	1
	1	89	5
19, 1–5	2	67	18
22, 5	1	53	2
8 De otio 4, 1–2	2	67	18
5, 4	1	40	6
7	DP		16
9 De tranqu.	1	43	23
	2	93	60
2, 12	2	75	13

	Book/Section	Dial.	Note
2, 1	2	95	3
2, 2–4	1	43	3
3, 3	2	29	5
4	2	117	1
4, 9	2	117	7
5, 2	2	Pref.	93
5, 6	2	13	51
	2	13	53
5, 7–9	1	Pref.	10
6, 5	1	30	17
6, 6	1	29	17
7, 3	1	30	4
8, 3	1	55	1
8, 5	1	40	4
9, 6	1	50	11
9, 18	1	99	3
	2	55	3
9, 21	2	77	4
9, 21–22	2	10	6
9, 22	2	95	9
10, 1	1	122	2
11, 8–10	1	29	17
12, 6	2	133	2
12, 10	2	15	7
13, 4	1	11	1
14, 10	2	36	9
16, 9	1	11	1
	1	17	4
17, 9	2	9	4
18, 7	2	9	4
19, 9	1	107	9
21, 5	1	117	2
24, 2–4	2	67	9
24, 4–5	2	114	67
24, 6–8	2	117	7
	2	118	23
24, 13	2	25	11
24, 19–20	2	117	6
24, 19–21	2	117	7
25, 4	2	9	4
25, 5	1	29	17
	2	53	10

	Book/ Section	Dial.	Note
61, 2–4	2	117	38
61, 3	2	7	16
65, 16	1	2	22
65, 21	1	2	22
	2	117	26
65, 24	2	117	27
66	2	114	16
66, 2	1	2	28
66, 6	1	89	5
66, 17–20	2	114	28
66, 24–26	2	117	11
66, 39–43	2	117	39
66, 41	2	Pref.	91
	2	117	39
66, 49	1	Pref.	24
70, 16	2	117	1
	2	118	19
70, 16–18	2	117	1
70, 19	2	118	23
71, 5	2	114	28
71, 15–17	2	118	23
71, 16	1	Pref.	34
71, 37	1	Pref.	39
72, 5	2	114	28
74, 7	1	Pref.	8
74, 17	1	90	18
76, 2	2	9	3
76, 33–35	1	Pref.	58
77, 18	2	117	6
77, 21–23	2	120	14
78, 25	2	98	2
79, 12–18	1	117	2
79, 13	1	92	11
80, 4	2	81	4
81, 13	2	81	4
81, 17–21	2	28	19
82	2	117	42
82, 3	2	109	1
82, 5	2	114	27
82, 6	2	73	12
82, 9–11	2	117	33
82, 9–14	1	69	12

	Book/Section	Dial.	Note
82, 22	2	117	30
83, 13	1	Pref.	45
85, 8–10	2	75	5
86, 1	1	97	2
87	2	13	4
87, 1	2	11	3
87, 6–8	2	12	11
87, 19–21	2	12	5
87, 29	1	90	18
87, 36–67	1	90	18
88, 14–15	2	114	37
88, 36	2	21	23
88, 38	1	11	22
90, 46	2	24	7
91, 17	2	41	8
92, 16	1	90	18
	2	114	28
92, 29	1	50	7
92, 30	1	40	6
92, 34–35	2	132	6
	2	132	22
93, 2	2	117	40
94, 24	2	28	9
94, 26	2	21	6
94, 43	2	58	14
94, 52	1	50	7
94, 56	1	40	6
94, 73	1	107	9
95, 19	2	108	1
95, 31	2	31	5
95, 53	2	50	1
95, 72–73	1	42	10
96, 5	DP		12
	1	48	3
97, 1	1	115	4
98, 9	1	9	7
98, 13	1	42	10
99, 11	1	21	17
99, 22	2	7	16
	2	9	19
99, 25–28	2	93	4
103, 5	1	107	11

	Book/ Section	Dial.	Note
105	2	Pref.	91
	2	36	9
105, 1–6	2	36	9
105, 3	2	25	4
	2	35	1
	2	36	9
105, 4	2	36	10
	2	82	9
106, 11	1	26	5
107, 3–4	1	Pref.	56
	2	7	16
	2	114	43
	2	121	3
107, 6	2	120	4
107, 7	2	Pref.	91
107, 7–12	2	46	2
	2	67	27
	2	114	43
	2	117	39
	2	121	3
107, 8	2	93	14
107, 9–10	2	117	31
	2	121	3
107, 11	2	Pref.	91
111, 2	1	1	18
111, 32	2	15	8
113, 31	2	29	9
113, 32	2	25	6
115, 3–7	2	109	5
115, 6–7	2	1	5
	2	109	5
115, 16	2	13	17
116, 7	2	Pref.	84
119, 11–12	1	53	2
	1	85	1
	2	122	2
120, 7	2	77	12
120, 14	1	2	22
120, 17–18	2	117	7
123, 16	1	11	20
130, 10	2	117	6
Herc. fur.	1	24	5

	Book/Section	Dial.	Note
	2	115	4
89–90	1	11	22
Herc. Oet. 1099	2	117	7
Hippolytus	1	52	7
Ludus de morte Claudii (Apocolocyntosis) 2, 3	2	Pref.	66
Medea	1	52	8
650	1	11	22
1007–1008	1	11	22
Nat. quaest. 1, Praef.	1	92	3
1, 6, 5	2	93	44
1, 8	1	92	3
1, 11	1	92	3
1, 17, 4	1	Pref.	55
	2	73	12
1, 17, 9	2	9	18
2, 2, 6–23	2	90	38
2, 36, 1	2	7	11
2, 41–46	2	90	41
2, 59, 13	2	54	9
	2	90	33
3, Praef., 10	2	29	9
3, 28, 7–29, 2	2	55	11
4, Praef., 22	1	107	9
5, 1	2	90	38
6, 1, 1–2	2	91	6
6, 1, 1–2, 7	2	91	19
6, 1, 13	2	91	3
6, 2	2	75	5
6, 2, 9	2	90	55
6, 21, 1	2	91	3
6, 32, 3	1	1	18
7, 27	1	11	19
Phaedra 195–196	1	69	14
Phoenissae	2	98	8
Thyestes 133–135	1	115	3
344–349	2	81	5
519	1	49	1
Troades 434 (437)	2	119	19
Seneca (Ps.) De rem. fort.	1	Pref.	35
	2	9	30
2	2	8	1
	2	117	42

	Book/Section	Dial.	Note
	2	127	7
2, 3	2	117	10
	2	119	9
2, 5	2	117	9
2, 8	2	119	29
2, 9	2	121	16
	2	127	7
3, 1	2	77	5
3, 2	2	120	4
	2	125	34
4, 2	1	Pref.	35
	2	120	10
5, 1–4	2	132	5
6, 2	2	112	7
7	2	67	23
7, 2	1	Pref.	35
8, 2	2	125	6
8, 3–4	2	67	32
10	2	9	30
10, 9	2	9	5
11	2	13	64
12	2	96	27
12, 4	2	97	3
	2	103	6
13, 4–9	2	48	22
13, 10	2	49	2
16	2	18	14
16, 1	2	18	5
	2	18	17
16, 2	2	18	10
16, 4	1	74	2
	2	18	8
16, 8	2	67	32
Formula vitae honestae (De quattuor virtutibus cardinalibus) Martin of Braga	1	Pref.	35
Octavia	1	52	12
557–558	1	69	14
Seneca, Lucius Annaeus the Elder, "Rhetor"			
Controv. 1, Praef. 7	1	115	3
1, Praef. 9	1	9	5
1, 1, 3 and 5	1	Pref.	52
1, 6, 4	2	5	11

	Book/Section	Dial.	Note
6, 826–910	1	29	2
7, 464	2	98	2
7, 478	1	70	3
7, 503	1	70	6
	2	122	1
7, 718–722	1	88	4
8, 320	2	67	20
8, 739	2	107	15
10	1	73	2
10, 540–569	2	121	7
10, 703–705	2	70	7
12, 35	1	Pref.	8
12, 810–819	1	117	2
Suetonius Tranquillus. *De gramm.* 9	2	4	5
De poet.	2	5	9
Horace	1	110	8
	2	9	22
Lucan	1	78	4
Persius	1	78	4
Terence 1	2	7	18
Virgil 13	2	9	22
Virgil 32	1	32	5
De vita Caes. 1 Jul. Caesar 4, 1–2	2	61	4
7, 2	2	84	16
13	1	107	11
20, 4	2	118	31
37	1	27	13
44, 2–3	1	63	5
45	2	1	12
	2	113	5
45, 1	2	1	12
52, 1–2	1	69	7
53	1	18	12
	1	24	10
68, 4	2	77	17
	2	77	20
69	1	97	7
74, 1	2	61	4
78, 1–2	2	81	17
81, 3	2	86	7
82, 1–3	2	77	6
83	2	9	28

	Book/Section	Dial.	Note
	2	131	2
84, 2	2	33	5
87	2	113	5
	2	123	3
2 Aug.	1	75	1
1	2	4	5
2–3	2	5	20
5–6	2	63	5
27, 1	1	42	5
28	1	96	14
28, 1	2	78	2
	2	79	14
28, 2	2	129	4
28, 3	1	118	12
29	1	118	10
29, 3	2	91	2
44, 3	1	30	2
50	1	39	2
53, 1	1	85	4
58, 1–2	1	96	26
61, 1	1	108	11
62	2	128	4
62, 1–2	2	19	12
63	2	131	2
63–65	1	108	12
	2	21	15
65	1	79	1
65, 1	1	114	8
70, 2	1	26	2
	1	42	6
71	1	26	3
73	1	20	3
76, 1	1	18	5
77	1	18	10
78	1	21	11
78, 2	2	86	2
79, 2	2	1	12
	2	84	16
83	1	25	3
90	2	90	46
	2	91	2
99, 1	2	83	28

	Book/Section	Dial.	Note
101	1	79	5
	2	9	28
101, 3	2	117	36
3 Tib.	1	49	5
7, 3	1	114	8
23	2	9	28
27	1	85	4
40	1	30	14
43–44	1	58	3
45	1	58	2
61	1	101	19
69	2	90	46
	2	91	2
4 Calig. 4, 8	2	4	5
6, 1–2	1	114	18
8	2	4	5
11	1	23	26
19, 1–3	1	96	30
30, 1	1	95	14
34, 2	2	88	14
37, 1–3	1	96	32
52	1	20	7
54	1	23	26
5 Claud.	1	52	11
	1	75	3
1, 1–5	1	114	14
2, 1	2	21	18
3, 2	2	21	17
26, 1–2	2	21	18
27, 2	1	79	5
6 Nero 5, 26–27	1	75	3
6, 7–8	1	75	3
6, 33	1	75	3
20, 1	1	23	27
24	1	52	4
30, 3	1	96	37
31, 1	1	96	33
31, 1–2	1	96	35
31, 3	1	96	37
35	1	38	16
	1	52	10
39, 2	1	96	34

	Book/ Section	Dial.	Note
88r	1	64	14
89v	1	65	9
92r	1	68	4
93r	1	69	6
93v	1	69	11
97v	1	72	5
99r	1	73	6
100v	1	76	1
101v	1	77	4
102v	1	78	6
103r	1	79	4
104r	1	80	8
114v	1	92	8
122r	1	96	39
129r	1	102	3
140r	1	111	7
144r	1	114	6
145v	1	114	13
149r	1	118	11
158v	2	Pref.	54
164v	2	2	4
167v	2	5	8
174r	2	8	6
189r	2	15	9
190r	2	15	16
191r	2	17	10
195v	2	21	8
	2	21	9
196v	2	21	21
197v	2	22	2
	2	22	4
201v	2	25	13
207v	2	30	2
215v	2	39	13
221r	2	45	3
	2	45	5
222v	2	48	3
229r	2	53	3
	2	53	4
233r	2	76	1
239v–240r	2	64	9
244r	2	67	23

	Book/ Section	Dial.	Note
244v	2	67	29
252v	2	75	20
255v	2	79	4
257r	2	79	20
	2	79	23
258v	2	81	7
267r	2	84	3
	2	84	4
268v	2	85	4
	2	85	5
269r	2	86	5
271r	2	88	8
276r	2	90	27
286r	2	95	12
296r	2	104	4
310r	2	115	2
310r–310v	2	115	5
311r	2	116	4
311v	2	117	5
	2	117	8
316r	2	118	8
	2	118	10
318v–319r	2	118	34
319r	2	119	6
329v	2	125	11
330r	2	125	22
338r	2	129	4

		Book/Section	Dial.	Note
Ulrich Boner. *Der Edelstein*		2	128	3
Uta ms.		1	40	8
Valerius Maximus. *Facta et dicta mem.*		DP		18
		1	78	7
	1, 1	2	Pref.	47
	1, 1, 5	2	Pref.	47
	1, 1, 14	1	14	4
	1, 1, 20	2	93	59
	1, 6, 1	2	5	14
	1, 7, 5	1	78	8
	1, 7, 7	1	103	4
	1, 7, Ext. 5	2	9	26
	1, 8, Ext. 12–13	2	94	5

	Book/ Section	Dial.	Note
1, 8, Ext. 19	2	21	6
2, 1, 4	1	65	7
2, 4, 4	1	28	2
2, 6, 8	2	88	14
2, 6, 12	2	119	7
2, 7, 6	2	43	12
2, 9, 2	2	38	6
2, 10, 2	1	51	2
2, 10, 5	2	67	9
2, 10, 6	2	9	27
3, 1–2	2	114	67
3, 2, 1	2	77	12
3, 2, 11	2	77	18
3, 2, 22	2	77	17
3, 2, 23	2	77	20
3, 3, Ext. 2–3	1	117	6
	2	114	67
3, 3, Ext. 2–5	2	114	67
3, 3, Ext. 8	1	35	1
3, 4, 1	2	5	12
3, 4, 6	2	63	5
3, 5	1	16	2
	2	24	9
3, 5, 1–2	2	44	5
3, 8, Ext. 6	2	90	35
4, 1, Ext. 9	2	79	17
4, 1, 1	1	35	2
4, 1, 12	1	104	7
4, 1, 13	2	67	9
4, 1, 15, Ext. 1	2	59	6
	2	107	13
4, 1, 15, Ext. 2	2	107	14
4, 2	1	18	2
4, 2, 2	2	66	6
4, 3	1	18	2
4, 3, 5	2	93	57
4, 3, 7	1	42	9
4, 3, 11	1	18	2
4, 3, Ext. 4	2	88	11
4, 4	2	12	3
4, 4, 5	1	18	2
4, 4, 7	1	18	2

	Book/Section	Dial.	Note
4, 5, 6, Ext. 1	1	2	27
4, 6, Ext. 1	2	88	5
4, 7, Ext. 2	2	35	2
4, 8	1	42	9
5, 1, 10	1	104	7
	2	118	28
5, 2, Ext. 4	1	51	1
5, 3	2	67	6
5, 3, 2	2	66	6
	2	67	30
	2	125	29
5, 3, 4	1	58	10
	2	66	6
5, 3, Ext. 2	2	67	6
5, 3, Ext. 3	2	66	6
	2	67	6
	2	132	37
5, 6, 5	2	72	3
5, 6, Ext. 4	1	15	40
5, 8, 2 and 5	2	43	3
5, 9, 2	2	24	5
5, 10, 2	2	48	6
5, 10, Ext. 1–2	2	48	6
5, 10, Ext. 3	2	48	15
	2	117	8
6, 1	2	132	12
6, 1, 1	1	72	4
	1	72	6
6, 2, Ext. 3	2	15	3
6, 4, 4	2	67	9
6, 9, Ext. 6	2	81	12
7, 1, 1	1	108	7
7, 1, Ext. 1	2	66	9
7, 2	1	78	5
7, 2, Ext. 2	1	17	7
7, 2, Ext. 3	2	55	3
7, 2, Ext. 5	1	96	51
7, 2, Ext. 7	2	39	15
7, 2, Ext. 9	1	68	3
7, 2, Ext. 17	1	101	13
7, 2, Ext. 18	1	27	10
7, 4, Ext. 1	2	39	14

	Book/Section	Dial.	Note
7, 5, 2	2	38	6
7, 5, 2–5	2	38	6
7, 5, 6	2	38	6
7, 8, 5–6	1	110	13
7, 8, 6	2	62	7
8, 1, 13, damn. 4	2	90	55
8, 3, 3	1	62	8
8, 7	2	101	6
8, 7, 7	1	28	3
	1	28	9
8, 7, 7, Ext. 6	2	59	6
8, 7, Ext. 2	2	67	6
8, 7, Ext. 4	2	96	14
8, 7, Ext. 6	2	9	29
8, 7, Ext. 8	1	23	24
8, 7, Ext. 11	2	9	22
8, 7, Ext. 14, 4–5	2	101	5
8, 8, 2	1	25	2
	1	26	2
8, 10, 2	1	28	3
8, 13, 5	2	96	21
8, 13, 6	2	18	6
8, 14, 6	2	88	4
8, 14, Ext. 2–5	2	43	9
8, 15, 3	2	38	6
9, 1, 2	1	28	3
9, 1, 4, Ext. 1	1	14	4
	2	15	14
9, 1, 4, Ext. 9	2	15	14
9, 10, 2, Ext. 1	2	132	11
9, 11, 1	1	77	7
9, 11, 4	1	114	3
9, 12, Ext. 3	1	64	12
9, 12, Ext. 5	1	23	13
9, 12, 2	1	23	13
	1	83	2
9, 12, 8, Ext. 4	2	Pref.	10
9, 15, 1	2	24	9
10, 2	1	28	3

Varro, Marcus Terentius.
De ling. Lat. 5, 14, 8

	Book/Section	Dial.	Note
	1	47	6
6, 7, 76	1	112	21

	Book/Section	Dial.	Note
9, 85	1	28	8
10, 22	1	26	4
De re rust.	1	57	1
1, 1	1	57	12
2, 3, 7	1	57	15
2, 7, 9	1	57	15
3, 3, 10	2	56	6
3, 6	1	62	5
3, 17, 3	1	63	13
Menippean Satires	2	19	8
Frag. 348–369b	1	12	28
Vegetius (Flavius Vegetius Renatus). *De re. mil.*	1	99	8
Velleius Paterculus, Gaius. *Hist. Rom.* 1, 6, 2	2	39	14
2, 11, 1	1	106	5
2, 13, 2	2	67	9
2, 15, 3–4	2	67	9
2, 17, 1	1	106	5
2, 19	2	9	27
2, 65, 3	2	5	23
2, 78, 1	2	5	23
2, 128	2	5	11
Vincent of Beauvais. *De erud. fil. nob.* 17, 174	1	Pref.	35
41, 123	1	Pref.	35
Spec. hist. 8, 116	1	Pref.	35
8, 123	1	Pref.	35
Spec. nat. 8	1	111	2
16, 9	2	Pref.	14
29, 4	2	2	12
Virgil (Publius Vergilius Maro). *Aeneid*	1	81	24
	2	21	24
1, 91	2	116	5
1, 99	2	4	5
1, 103 and 105	2	54	9
1, 137	2	83	44
1, 142	1	2	22
1, 286–288	2	55	7
1, 327–330	2	109	5
1, 387	2	120	5
2	2	80	3
2, 197	2	4	5
2, 494	2	28	9
2, 604–606	2	96	1

	Book/ Section	Dial.	Note
2, 646	2	132	4
2, 679–686	2	55	6
2, 739	2	Pref.	10
3, 54–55	2	13	36
3, 56–57	2	9	20
	2	13	22
3, 420	2	90	7
3, 570–577	2	90	6
4, 83	2	53	6
4, 175	1	113	1
4, 462–463	1	112	20
4, 477	1	2	18
4, 514–515	2	90	19
4, 569–570	1	74	2
4, 570	2	18	8
4, 653	2	117	4
5, 59–60	1	44	21
5, 217	1	1	13
5, 344	1	2	28
5, 378–379	1	29	16
5, 680–684	2	58	3
5, 848–849	1	87	1
6	1	69	30
6, 3–4	1	109	13
6, 103–105	1	Pref.	58
6, 274–275	2	114	43
6, 278	1	21	2
6, 278–279	2	117	14
6, 286	1	81	4
6, 288	1	81	4
6, 318–330	2	132	30
6, 362–371	2	132	29
6, 417–423	1	Pref.	11
6, 425	1	4	2
6, 434–436	2	118	4
6, 434–439	2	118	34
6, 436–437	2	118	7
6, 481–482	2	92	4
6, 494–512	2	73	18
6, 522	1	21	2
6, 541–543	2	41	3
6, 566–569	2	126	9

	Book/Section	Dial.	Note
6, 570	2	18	8
6, 585–594	1	99	12
6, 608–627	2	81	9
6, 652–655	1	31	9
6, 674	2	93	16
6, 709	2	81	27
6, 724–751	1	2	22
6, 730–734	1	69	12
6, 733	DP		9
	DP		11
	2	93	59
6, 733–734	2	Pref.	90
6, 734	2	64	3
6, 784	1	15	8
6, 806–807	2	130	8
6, 815–816	2	88	20
6, 816	1	94	11
	2	88	20
6, 851–853	1	96	47
6, 860–886	1	32	5
6, 869–870	1	71	6
6, 882–883	1	32	5
7, 11, 12	2	17	6
7, 266	1	85	8
7, 277–279	2	11	5
7, 417	1	2	18
7, 646	1	11	20
7, 678	2	55	6
8, 333–334	2	Pref.	91
8, 334	INT		45
	1	16	4
	1	17	8
	2	Pref.	91
8, 478–495	2	81	18
8, 560	2	83	22
8, 592–593	2	53	11
8, 670	2	118	34
9, 311	1	37	16
9, 485	2	132	22
9, 503–504	1	Pref.	56
9, 641	2	41	3
10	1	73	2

	Book/ Section	Dial.	Note
10, 284	2	28	9
10, 467	2	120	2
10, 467–468	2	15	1
10, 474–500	1	73	2
10, 515–516	2	53	11
10, 544	2	55	6
10, 796–830	2	121	7
10, 896–908	2	81	18
11	2	17	6
11, 51, 52	2	120	5
11, 260	1	98	4
11, 677–689	2	121	7
12	2	17	6
Carmen saeculare 1–2	2	93	18
Culex 58–122	1	59	4
Ecl. 2, 70	2	97	15
3, 33	2	42	3
6, 5	2	80	3
8, 63	2	114	11
8, 108	1	69	5
	2	97	15
10, 8	2	13	59
Georg.	1	57	12
1, 5–6	2	93	17
1, 53–58	2	12	5
1, 155–159	2	Pref.	35
1, 186	2	Pref.	37
1, 336	2	109	1
1, 474–475	2	91	8
1, 475	2	91	10
2, 109	2	114	11
2, 473–474	1	57	4
2, 505–506	1	38	1
2, 526	2	Pref.	20
3, 9	INT		45
3, 72–283	1	31	13
3, 113–119	1	31	11
3, 258–263	1	69	8
3, 284	2	15	1
3, 350	2	90	5
3, 474	2	91	8
3, 478	1	59	6

	Book/Section	Dial.	Note
3, 500	1	59	6
3, 503	1	59	6
3, 505	1	59	6
3, 509	1	59	6
3, 528–530	2	86	3
3, 546	1	59	6
3, 548	1	59	6
4	1	62	10
4, 189–190	1	62	11
4, 246–247	1	7	3
4, 514–515	2	90	19
4, 564	2	91	5
Petrarch's Ambrosian Virgil	2	Pref.	80
	2	9	12
Vita di Cola di Rienzo 1, 18	1	103	7
1, 25	2	114	24
1, 36	1	103	9
	2	81	12
Vitruvius Pollio. De arch. 1, 1, 2	2	122	3
2, 8, 10–15	2	88	5
6, Praef., 1	2	9	9
6, Praef., 2	2	9	12
Voragine, Jacobus. See Jacobus de Voragine			
Walafrid Strabo. See Glossa ordinaria			
Walther von der Vogelweide. 1, 19, 13	2	Pref.	31
Walter Map. De nugis cur.	1	Pref.	44
1, 10	1	33	4
	2	28	9
2, 17	2	13	36
4, 3	1	65	1
4, 5	1	115	4
5, 1	2	25	10
William Durand. Rationale	1	40	9
William of Saint Thierry. Vita S. Bernardi	2	40	8
Xenophon. Apology	1	117	6

Tables and Maps

TABLE 1

THE WRITING OF THE *DR*

1354	*DR* begun, at the latest, shortly before June.	(Item 1)
?	Boccaccio: *De remediis ad utranque fortunam* to be published soon.	(Item 2)
1360	First version, *De remediis ad utranque fortunam,* complete: *et feci,* December 1. Dedicated to Azzo da Correggio, *DR* i, Preface.	(Item 3)
1361	Petrarch's oration in Paris, January 13, containing a reference to *constantia fortune ad utramque partem* and recalled in the *DR.*	(Item 4)
1362	March. Jan ze Středa refers to *liber ille qui loquitur utriusque fortune remedium.*	(Item 5)
1366	Second version, *De remediis utriusque Fortune,* nearly complete by September 1.	(Item 6)
	Completed, October 4. (Fossadolce explicit.)	(Item 7)
1367	*DR* finished "recently" and in the hands of others.	(Items 8, 9)

TABLE 2

PETRARCH'S ACTIVITIES, 1354–1366

Since Summer of 1353		Petrarch in Milan, ruled by Archbishop	Work on the *DR*.
1354	May	Giovanni Visconti.	
	June		Correspondence with Jean Birel (item 1).
	July 1	Cola di Rienzo reenters Rome as papal Senator.	Work on *De viris illustr.*
	October 5	Death of the Archbishop.	
	October 17	P.'s. commemorative oration.	
		Matteo, Galeazzo, and Bernabò Visconti become rulers of Milan. Cola di Rienzo killed in Rome. Emperor Charles IV enters Italy.	
	November	Charles IV in Mantua.	
	December	P. travels to Mantua at the Emperor's request. P. and Socrates exchange canonries. Robbers sack Vaucluse on Christmas day. P.'s books saved.	
1355	January 4	Charles IV enters Milan to be crowned king of Italy (January 6).	
	January 12	Charles IV leaves Milan. P. accompanies him to near Piacenza.	
	April 5	Charles IV crowned in Rome by Cardinal Pierre Bertrand de Columbario.	
	April 18	Doge Marin Falier be-	

		headed in Venice (*Fam.* xix, 9, 26).	
May	Chancellor Benintendi dei Ravagnani of Venice and a friend of P. in Milan.	
May 6	Charles IV returns to Pisa.	
May 24	Charles IV crowns Zanobi da Strada poet laureate to the dismay of P.'s friends (Wilkins [1951], chap. 3, 7).	
June 6–7	Cardinal Pierre Bertrand visits P. Charles IV flees Italy (*Fam.* xix, 12).	
First half of year	P. learns that "Cardinal Jean de Caraman had been speaking ill of him in Avignon, disparaging his writings, and calling him a companion of tyrants" (Wilkins [1961], p. 147).	P. replies with invective *Contra eum.* Writes *Var.* 50 and 61 (*Dramatis personae,* note 23); and replies with an *epistola metrica* to one received from Zanobi da Strada.
September	Death of Matteo Visconti.	Boccaccio sends ms. with parts of Varro's *De lingua Latina.*
1356 January–	Hostilities against the Visconti, who take into service P.'s friend Pandolfo Malatesta as military commander.	
May–		P. finishes *Fam.,* Books i–viii.
May 20–June 20	P.'s mission to the Emperor. P. in Basel; dangerous journey to Prague. Charles IV creates P. Count Palatine and Councilor.	

	August	Return to Milan.	Begins work on the third form of the *Canzoniere*.
	Autumn	Illness of Pandolfo Malatesta; daily visits to him (*Sen.* i, 6).	Continued revision of the *Canzoniere*.
	October 18	Basel earthquake.	
1357	December–January	Hostilities by the Marquis of Monferrato, who captures Pavia. Conflict between Pandolfo Malatesta and Bernabò Visconti. Pandolfo flees to Prague.	
	February	Sagremor de Pommiers delivers to P. the diploma as Count Palatine, with gold seal. P. refuses (*Fam.* xxi, 2).	
	April		P. plants trees in the garden of Sant' Ambrogio in Milan.
	Summer	Spent in Garegnano (*Fam.* xix, 17).	
	July	At London court of Edward III, Sagremor de Pommiers challenges Pandolfo Malatesta to single combat in defense of the honor of the Visconti. Pandolfo does not respond and returns to Italy.	P. sends a copy of *Contra med.* to Boccaccio.
	September	P. returns to Milan via Pagazzano, where Bernabò Visconti has a castle.	Work on the *Trionfi* i; the *Bucolicum carmen*; the third form of the *Canzoniere,* a copy of which P. was planning to send to Azzo da Correggio. Interpolation on Basel earthquake (1356) in *De ocio.* P. reaches Book x of the *Familiares.* Revision of dedicatory poem of *Epistolae metricae* to Barbato da Sulmona.

1358	March	Sagremor de Pommiers returns from Prague with the golden seal. P. accepts.	*Itinerarium syriacum* for Giovannolo da Mandello.
	April 6	Thirty-first anniversary of P.'s falling in love with Laura; tenth of her death.	P.'s last anniversary poem *Tennemi Amor* for Laura. Further revision of the *Trionfi*.
	June	Peace treaty between the Visconti and their enemies. Novara restored to the Visconti.	P.'s oration to the Novara assembly.
	July	P. as peacemaker between Socrates and Laelius (*Fam.* xx, 13).	P. finishes copying and annotating a Terence ms.
	September Later in the year	P. in Pagazzano.	Continued work on the *Trionfi*; finishes third form of the *Canzoniere*; revisions of *Bucolicum carmen* and *Secretum*
	Winter	P. in Venice and Padua, where he meets Leontius Pilatus.	
1359	February	Return to Milan.	
	March	Visit from Boccaccio. Boccaccio copies *Bucolicum carmen* and other writings. Boccaccio and P. discuss Dante (*Fam.* xxi, 15).	Refusal to release *Africa* to the public.
	Summer	P.'s huge Cicero volume injures his leg.	
	October	P. spends some days at Pagazzano. Troublesome servants dismissed. Alone, P. has to leave the great house by Sant' Ambrogio and moves into a smaller one at San Simpliciano, just outside the walls of Milan.	Further revision of *Bucolicum carmen*.

	November		Begins work on the fourth (Chigi) form of the *Canzoniere*.
1360	April–	P. in Padua and Venice; suffers from Ciceronian leg wound (*Var.* 25).	
	August	Niccolò Acciaiuoli visits the Visconti and P.	Continued work on *Trionfi*. Letter to Homer (*Fam.* xxiv, 12).
	May–October	Anglo-French treaty of Bretigny permitting King John's return to France. Marriage at Milan of Gian Galeazzo Visconti, aged 8, to Isabelle of France, aged 11. The plague threatens Milan (*Fam.* xxii, 2).	
	November	The plague reaches Milan.	First draft of
	December–	Mission to Paris.	the *DR* complete (item 3).
1361	January 13	Oration before King John II and Prince Charles of France (item 4).	
	February–	Return to Milan "over the icy Alps" (*Fam.* xxiii, 13, 10).	
	March	First of several invitations by Charles IV to P. to come to Prague. The plague in Milan.	Correspondence with Emperor Charles IV begins.
	Mid-June	P. goes to Padua.	
	July 9–10	Death of P.'s son, Giovanni, during the plague in Milan.	
	August	Death of Socrates, Philippe de Vitry, Zanobi da Strada. Invitation to Naples; Cardinal Talleyrand tenders Pope's invitation to become papal secretary.	Work on *De vita solitaria*; the *DR*; and the *Familiares*.
	End of year	Decision to go to Provence.	*Familiares* nearly finished; begins collection of *Seniles*.
1362	January–March	P. starts for Provence; remains in Milan. Invitation	

		to Prague renewed (item 5).	
	May	Return to Padua.	Letter to Senate of Venice offering his books as nucleus of a *bibliotheca publica* in return for a residence. Completion of the fourth (Chigi) form of the *Canzoniere*.
		The plague reaches Padua.	
	Autumn	Residence in Venice, Palazzo Molin, Riva degli Schiavoni. Visits to Padua. Death of Pope Innocent VI and Azzo da Correggio. Pope Urban V.	
1363	April	Boccaccio spends three months with P. Leontius Pilatus visits also. Death of Nelli, Laelius, Barbato da Sulmona.	
	Before October 8	P. to Pavia with Galeazzo Visconti, via Padua.	
	December	P. meets Philippe de Mézières, Chancelor of King Peter I of Cyprus and future translator into French of P.'s Latin version of Boccaccio's *Griselda* story. Philip the Bold becomes Duke of Burgundy. Cretan rebellion against Venice. The plague in Venice.	
1364	January 15	Venice resolves to put down the Cretan rebellion.	
	Spring	P. visits Bologna to greet Cardinal Androin de la Roche, papal legate, and the Casentino to see Robert di Battifolle. Charles V, King of France.	*Sen.* vi, 1, to Luchino dal Verme urging acceptance of the command of the Venetian forces against Crete. Work on the Triumph of Fame; *Sen.* vi, 2, to Luchino dal Verme.
	Summer	Luchino's victory celebration in Venice. Visit of	Work on *Bucolicum carmen*, Ecl. x.

		Bartolomeo Carbone dei Papazurri, newly elected Archbishop of Patras.	
	Autumn	P. suffering from *scabies* (*DR* ii, 85, *De scabie*). P. takes the baths at Abano.	Revisions of *De vita sol.* complete.
1365	March	Venice.	
	Summer– December	Pavia; visit to Milan; death of Leontius Pilatus.	
1366	January– February	In Venice, in P.'s house, his daughter gives birth to grandson, Francesco, her second child.	
		Du Guesclin helps Henry of Trastamera against Peter the Cruel of Castile.	Letter to Pope Urban V urging him to return to Rome (*Sen.* vii, 1, Venice, June 29).
	June		P. sends copy of *De vita sol.* to Philippe de Cabassoles.
	July–December	Pavia.	
	October 4		Autograph of *DR*, revised version, complete (item 7).
	End of October		Giovanni Malpaghini finishes copying the *Familiares*; starts Vat. lat. 3195, the fifth and final version of the *Canzoniere*.
	December	Return to Venice.	

Source: Based on the works of Ernest Hatch Wilkins listed in Bibliography, III, esp. Wilkins (1961), pp. 129–207.

TABLE 3

LATIN AUTHORS BEFORE A.D. 600

284–204 B.C.	Livius Andronicus	116–27 B.C.	Varro
270–201	Naevius	114–50	Hortensius
255–184	Plautus	109–32	Atticus
239–169	Ennius	106–43	Cicero
168	Caecilius Statius	102–44	Caesar
234–149	Cato	94–55	Lucretius
220–130	Pacuvius	86–34	Sallust
195–159	Terence	84–54	Catullus
180–102	Lucilius	82–47	Calvus
170–85	Accius	70–19	Virgil
150	Afranius	65–8	Horace

63 B.C.–A.D. 14	Augustus
59 B.C.–A.D. 17	Livy
55 B.C.–A.D. 40	Seneca Rhetor
50 B.C.–A.D. 16	Propertius
48 B.C.–A.D. 19	Tibullus
43 B.C.–A.D. 17	Ovid
	Vitruvius
19 B.C.–A.D. 35	Velleius Paterculus
	Manilius
	Valerius Maximus
	Celsus
	Quintus Curtius
	Pomponius Mela
15 B.C.–A.D. 50	Phaedrus
4 B.C.–A.D. 65	Seneca
	Columella
	Calpurnius Siculus

A.D.	23–79	Pliny the Elder
	26–101	Silius Italicus
	30–104	Frontinus
	34–62	Persius

37–95	Quintilian
39–65	Lucan
66	Petronius
40–104	Martial
45–96	Statius
50–127	Juvenal
92	Valerius Flaccus
55–116	Tacitus
61–113	Pliny the Younger
69–140	Suetonius
76–138	Hadrian
100–166	Fronto
123–165	Aulus Gellius
123–161	Apuleius
160–225	Tertullian
200–258	Cyprian
	Minucius Felix
	Arnobius
	Nemesianus
250–317	Lactantius
	Firmicus Maternus
	Juvencus
310–395	Ausonius
	Optatianus Porfyrianus
330–395	Ammianus Marcellinus
337–397	Ambrose
340–402	Symmachus
340–420	Jerome
348–405	Prudentius
408	Claudian
	Rutilius Namatianus
	Aurelius Victor
	Eutropius
353–451	Paulinus of Nola
	Sedulius
354–430	Augustine
	Orosius
	Macrobius
	Aelius Donatus
	Avianus
	Avienus
	Servius
	Tiberius Claudius Donatus
	Martianus Capella

431–482	Sidonius Apollinaris
	Merobaudes
	Ennodius
482	Salvianus
480–524	Boethius
480–575	Cassiodorus

Source: Hadas (1952), pp. 460–461.
Note: Many of these dates are doubtful, some merely an approximation.

TABLE 4

ROMAN EMPERORS, 27 B.C.–A.D. 476

27	B.C.	AUGUSTUS Gaius Julius Caesar Octavianus*
A.D.	14	TIBERIUS Tiberius Claudius Nero Caesar*
	37	GAIUS CALIGULA Gaius Claudius Nero Caesar Germanicus*
	41	CLAUDIUS Tiberius Claudius Nero Caesar Drusus*
	54	NERO Lucius Domitius Ahenobarbus Claudius Drusus*
	68	GALBA Servius Sulpicius Galba*
	69	OTHO Marcus Salvius Otho*; VITELLIUS Aulus Vitellius Germanicus VESPASIAN Titus Flavius Vespasianus*
	79	TITUS Titus Flavius Vespasianus*
	81	DOMITIAN Titus Flavius Domitianus*
	96	NERVA Marcus Cocceius Nerva*
	98	TRAJAN Marcus Ulpicius Nerva Traianus*
	117	HADRIAN Publius Aelius Traianus Hadrianus*
	138	ANTONINUS PIUS Titus Aurelius Fulvius Boionius Arrius Antoninus Pius*
	161	MARCUS AURELIUS Marcus Annius Aurelius Verus* LUCIUS VERUS Lucius Ceionius Commodus Verus to 169*
	180	COMMODUS Lucius Aelius Marcus Aurelius Antoninus Commodus*
	193	PERTINAX Publius Helvius Pertinax*; DIDIUS JULIAN Marcus Didius Salvius Julianus Severus SEPTIMIUS SEVERUS Lucius Septimius Severus*
	211	BASSIANUS CARACALLA Marcus Aurelius Antoninus Bassianus Caracallus* GETA Publius Septimius Geta 209–211
	217	MACRINUS Marcus Opellius Severus Macrinus*
	218	ELAGABALUS Marcus Barius Avitus Bassianus Aurelius Antoninus Heliogabalus*
	222	SEVERUS ALEXANDER Marcus Alexianus Bassianus Aurelius Severus Alexander*
	235	MAXIMIN Gaius Iulius Verus Maximinus Thrax*
	237	GORDIAN I Marcus Antonius Gordianus; and GORDIAN II, his son*
	238	PUPIENUS Marcus Clodius Pupienus Maximus; BALBINUS Decimus Caelius Balbinus; GORDIAN III Marcus Antonius Gordianus
	244	PHILIPP 'ARABS' Marcus Julius Philippus Arabs*
	249	DECIUS Gaius Messius Quintus Traianus Decius*
	251	GALLUS Gaius Vibius Trebonianus Gallus*

253   AEMILIAN   Marcus Iulius Aemilius Aemilianus
VALERIAN   Gaius Publius Licinius Valerianus to 260*; GALLIE-
   NUS   Publius Licinius Egnatius Gallienus to 268*

268   CLAUDIUS II   Marcus Aurelius Claudius Gothicus

270   AURELIAN   Lucius Domitius Aurelianus*

275   TACITUS   Marcus Claudius Tacitus

276   FLORIANUS   Marcus Annius Florianus;   PROBUS   Marcus Aurelius
   Probus*

282   CARUS   Marcus Aurelius Carus

283   NUMERIAN and CARINUS   Both named Marcus Aurelius like their father

284   DIOCLETIAN   Gaius Aurelius Valerius Diocles Iovius to 305*
MAXIMIAN   Marcus Aurelius Valerius Maximinianus Herculius 286–305

305   CONSTANTIUS   Flavius Valerius Constantius Chlorus to 306; GALER-
   IUS   Gaius Galerius Valerius Maximinianus to 311

306   SEVERUS   Flavius Valerius Severus to 307; MAXENTIUS   Marcus Aurelius
   Valerius Maxentius to 312

310   MAXIMINUS DAIA   Galerius Valerius Maximinus

311   LICINIUS   Gaius Flavius Valerius Licinianus Licinius*; CONSTANTINE THE
   GREAT   Flavius Valerius Constantinus*

337   CONSTANTINE II   Flavius Valerius Claudius Constantinus to 340; CON-
   STANTIUS II   Flavius Valerius Iulius Constantius to 361*; CONSTANS
   Flavius Valerius Iulius Constans to 350

361   JULIAN THE APOSTATE   Flavius Claudius Iulianus

363   JOVIAN   Flavius Iovinianus

East		*West*	
A.D. 364	VALENS	A.D. 364	VALENTINIAN Flavius Valentinianus*
		375	GRATIAN Flavius Gratianus Augustus*
			VALENTINIAN II Flavius Valentinianus*
379	THEODOSIUS THE GREAT Flavius Theodosius*	383	MAXIMUS Magnus Clemens Maximus to 388*
		393	THEODOSIUS THE GREAT (East and West)
			EUGENIUS 392–394
405	ARCADIUS	395	HONORIUS Flavius Honorius
408	THEODOSIUS II		
		425	VALENTINIAN III Flavius Placidius Valentinianus*

450	MARCIAN	455	PETRONIUS Flavius Ancius Petronius Maximus
			AVITUS Flavius Maecilius Eparchus Avitus to 457
457	LEO Leo Thrax Magnus	456	MAIORIAN Iulius Valerius Maiorianus
		461	SEVERUS Libius Severianus Severus
		467	ANTHEMIUS Procopius Anthemius
		472	OLYBRIUS Anicius Olybrius
		473	GLYCERIUS To 474
474	LEO II		IULIUS NEPOS To 475
	ZENO To 491	475	ROMULUS AUGUSTULUS Flavius Momyllus Romulus Augustus

---

Source: Based on Langer (1940), pp. 1145–1146.
*Indicates mention in the *DR.*

TABLE 5

HOLY ROMAN EMPERORS, 800–1378

800–814	Charlemagne
814–840	Louis I the Pious (crowned 816)
840–855	Lothar I
855–875	Louis II
875–877	Charles II the Bald (West Frankish)
877–887	Charles III the Fat (East Frankish; crowned 881)
887–891	vacancy during the war between Guido of Spoleto and Berengar of Friuli
891–901	Co-emperors Guido and Lambert; Arnulf crowned by the pope
901–905	Louis III of Provence
905–924	Berengar

German Line		*Italian Line*	
911–918	Conrad I (never crowned in Rome)	924–926	Rudolf of Burgundy
918–936	Henry I the Fowler (never crowned)	926–945	Hugh of Provence
936–973	Otto I the Great (crowned 962)	945–950	Lothar III
973–983	Otto II	952–962	Berengar
983–1002	Otto III (crowned 996)		
1002–1024	Henry II the Saint (crowned 1014)		
1024–1039	Conrad II the Salian (crowned 1027)		
1039–1056	Henry III the Black (crowned 1046)		
1056–1106	Henry IV (crowned 1084)		
	Rivals: Rudolf of Swabia, 1077–1080		
	Hermann of Luxemburg, 1081–1093		
	Conrad of Franconia, 1093–1101		
1106–1125	Henry V (crowned 1111)		
1125–1137	Lothar II (crowned 1133)		

1138–1152	Conrad III (never crowned)
1152–1190	Frederick I Barbarossa (crowned 1155)
1190–1197	Henry VI (crowned 1191)
1198–1212	Otto IV (crowned 1209)
	Rival: Philip II of Swabia, 1198–1208 (never crowned)
1212–1250	Frederick II (crowned 1220)
	Rivals, never crowned: Henry Raspe, 1246–1247
	William of Holland, 1247–1256
1250–1254	Conrad IV (never crowned)
1254–1273	*The Great Interregnum*
	Rivals, never crowned: Richard of Cornwall, 1257–1273
	Alfonso X of Castile, 1257–1272
1273–1291	Rudolf I Habsburg (never crowned; recognized by the pope 1274)
1292–1298	Adolf I of Nassau (never crowned)
1298–1308	Albert I Habsburg (never crowned)
1308–1313	Henry VII of Luxemburg (crowned 1312)
1314–1347	Louis IV, Bavaria (crowned 1328)
	Rival: Frederick of Habsburg, co-regent 1325–1330
1347–1378	Charles IV of Luxemburg (crowned 1355)
	Rival: Guenther of Schwarzburg, 1347–1349

Source: Based on Langer (1940), p. 1150.

MAP 1

Rome of Constantine A.D. 330

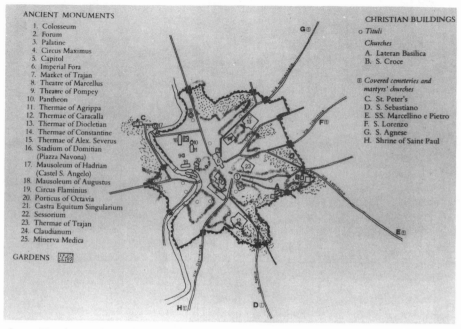

ANCIENT MONUMENTS

1. Colosseum
2. Forum
3. Palatine
4. Circus Maximus
5. Capitol
6. Imperial Fora
7. Market of Trajan
8. Theatre of Marcellus
9. Theatre of Pompey
10. Pantheon
11. Thermae of Agrippa
12. Thermae of Caracalla
13. Thermae of Diocletian
14. Thermae of Constantine
15. Thermae of Alex. Severus
16. Stadium of Domitian
    (Piazza Navona)
17. Mausoleum of Hadrian
    (Castel S. Angelo)
18. Mausoleum of Augustus
19. Circus Flaminius
20. Porticus of Octavia
21. Castra Equitum Singularium
22. Sessorium
23. Thermae of Trajan
24. Claudianum
25. Minerva Medica

GARDENS

CHRISTIAN BUILDINGS

o *Tituli*

Churches
A. Lateran Basilica
B. S. Croce

*Covered cemeteries and
martyrs' churches*
C. St. Peter's
D. S. Sebastiano
E. SS. Marcellino e Pietro
F. S. Lorenzo
G. S. Agnese
H. Shrine of Saint Paul

Source: Krautheimer (1980), fig. 1. With permission of Princeton University Press.

MAP 2
Forum Romanum

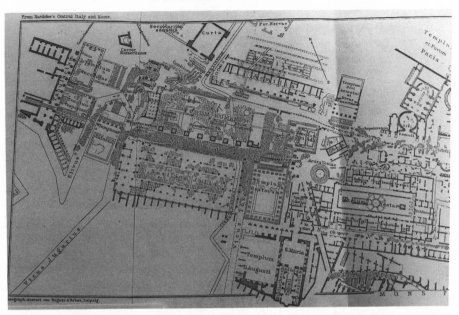

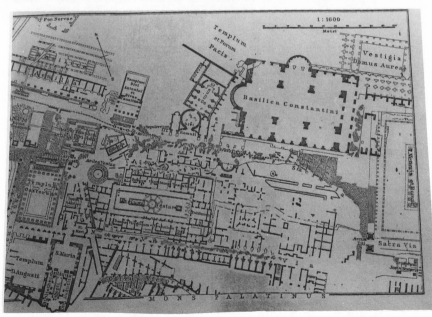

Source: After Sandys (1929), facing p. 46.

MAP 3
The World According to Eratosthenes

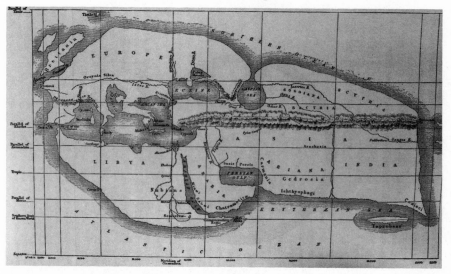

Source: Cohen and Drabkin (1948), p. 154. With permission of Harvard University Press.

MAP 4
The World of Persia and Classical Greece

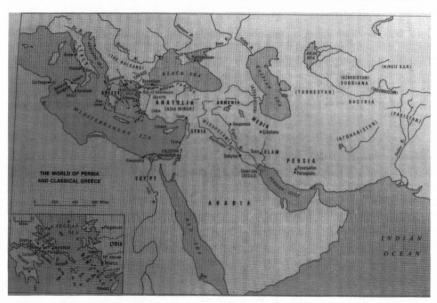

Source: Garraty (1972), p. 165. With permission of Harper & Row.

MAP 5
The Roman World

Source: Garraty (1972), p. 198. With permission of Harper & Row.

MAP 6
Europe in Mid-Fourteenth Century

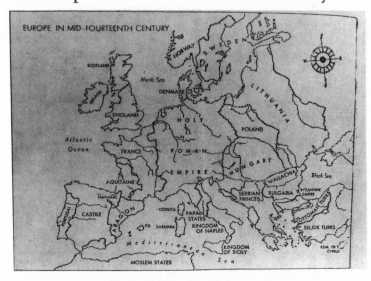

Source: Cantor (1963), p. 586. With permission of The Macmillan Company, New York; Collier-Macmillan Limited, London.

CONRAD H. RAWSKI is Professor Emeritus of Information and Library Science at Case Western Reserve University. He is the author of a number of Petrarchan studies, including *Petrarch: Four Dialogues for Scholars.*